BRAZIL'S
MODERN
ARCHITECTURE

D1757569

BRAZIL'S
MODERN
ARCHITECTURE

BRAZIL'S MODERN ARCHITECTURE

ELISABETTA ANDREOLI & ADRIAN FORTY

INTRODUCTION
ROUND TRIP: EUROPE TO BRAZIL & BACK
ADRIAN FORTY
& ELISABETTA
ANDREOLI

Claude Levi-Strauss, São João Avenue, São Paulo, 1935–37. During his time as professor of sociology at the University of São Paulo, Levi-Strauss made everyday photographic portraits of the city and carried out studies of aboriginal tribes that were to have a major influence in his future writings.

ROUND TRIP: EUROPE TO BRAZIL & BACK

Brazilian architecture is famous, but it is a fame that rests upon the work of a few architects – Oscar Niemeyer, Lucio Costa, Affonso Reidy and one or two others – built in the mid-twentieth century. Travelling to Brazil now, it is a surprise to discover any architecture built since the 1960s. If you read the standard histories of twentieth-century architecture, like William Curtis's *Modern Architecture since 1900* or Kenneth Frampton's *Modern Architecture: A Critical History*, after the building of Brasília there is no mention whatsoever of Brazil. Compared to the 1940s and 1950s, when European architectural magazines published every significant new Brazilian project, since the 1960s there has been only silence. A recent book entitled *Contemporary Latin American Architecture* (2000) contained not a single Brazilian building. It is as if Brazilian architecture had ceased to exist.

And yet, as this book shows, architecture in Brazil did not stop in 1964. The Brazilian architecture of the last quarter of the twentieth century has been no less interesting than what was produced in the third quarter. Why, then, is it not acknowledged; why do the history books not tell us about it? What has caused the silence about Brazil's recent architecture, a silence not only in the Western world, but even within Brazil itself?

We could say that the reason Brazilian architecture has been ignored on the world architectural scene is because it is no longer in the interests of the European and North American axes of political and cultural power to draw attention to Latin American architecture. Brazilian architecture's fame came about through *Brazil Builds*, the 1943 exhibition and book produced by the Museum of Modern Art in New York, yet the United States' interest in Brazil at this moment only occurred as part of its 'Good Neighbor' policy of cultivating relations with the Latin American nations so as to ensure their neutrality in World War II[1]. However, with the onset of the Cold War, Brazil and other Latin American countries became of minor importance in global strategy, and after the debt crisis of 1982 they all increasingly became, in effect, dependents of the developed world. Politically, Brazil ceased to count, and its culture could be ignored by the rest of the world.

But this explanation is less than half the answer to the neglect of Brazil's new architecture, for it is also within Brazil that there has been silence about it. Here we are faced with a more complex problem, a question of how Brazilians see their own past, and consider the present in relation to it. In short, it is a question of how history is made. There can be no new architecture unless what preceded it becomes historical. To make the new architecture visible is not simply a matter of reproducing pictures of it: one has also to change history, so that the new architecture neither eclipses the work that preceded it, nor appears as a mere appendix to it. This is the task to which the essays in this book aim to contribute: how to create a history of Brazilian architecture that allows the space for a new architecture to emerge. Nor is it likely that the new history will be singular; unlike the orthodox history of Brazilian architecture, which was created as propaganda for Brazil and for the International Style of modern architecture – and which, like all

Round Trip: Europe to Brazil & Back

Claude Levi-Strauss, São Paulo, 1935–37. The rapidly developing city already started encroaching on its rural surroundings in the first half of the twentieth century.

propaganda histories, reduced the story to a single version of events and excluded everything discordant or contradictory – any new history has to be open to the coexistence of discontinuities and differing points of view. Written by five young Brazilian architects and historians, the essays in *Brazil's Modern Architecture* present differing versions of the heroic period of Brazilian Modernism, in such a way as not to belittle or diminish its achievements and originality, but yet at the same time allow the inventiveness of new Brazilian architecture to be recognized.

Elsewhere, in Europe and North America, this process of giving modern architecture a history, and of creating the conditions for new architectures to succeed it, occurred during the 1960s through the writings of critics like Reyner Banham and Manfredo Tafuri, who showed successfully that modern architecture's claims to belong to an eternal present could not be sustained. But Brazil's modern architecture had never formed part of this discourse: Brazilian Modernism was celebrated precisely because it was seen to have diverged from the main current of Modernism, and so, while both indisputably authentic modern architecture, it was also evidence of that Modernism's ability to develop and rejuvenate itself. As a consequence, there was no need in Brazil for the debates about the succession to modern architecture that took place in other parts of the world, for Brazilian architecture had already been acknowledged to be different. It is one of the peculiarities of Brazil: to have produced neither any significant post-modern architecture, nor a critique of its own architectural Modernism.

Indeed, to develop a critique of its modern architecture was, in the Brazilian context, unthinkable, for from its very beginning, Brazilian Modernism was identified by the fact of its being a national architecture. As Reyner Banham had put it in 1962, Brazil was the first country to create 'a *national* style of modern architecture', and if this point of view was acknowledged worldwide, it was a fundamental article of faith within Brazil.[2] From the 1920s, the development of Modernism in all the arts in Brazil was connected to the pursuit of a national project, criticism of which could only be seen as a betrayal of the nation. Loyalties to Brazil have made it difficult for Brazilians to advance a critique of their own modern architecture; to do so could only be seen as damaging to the collective national enterprise. Part of the significance of the essays in this book is that they attempt to mark out this criticism, but in such a way as not to compromise Brazil's modernist heritage.

A further complication in developing a critical history of Brazilian architecture is that between 1964 and 1985 Brazil was governed by a military dictatorship. During these so-called 'Foul Times', – particularly up until the end of the 1970s, when the regime became less repressive – censorship and fear of persecution put an end to critical debate, and many architects aligned with the Left either went into exile (like Oscar Niemeyer), or were obliged to give up practice. Since the restoration of constitutional government in 1989, there has always been a problem about how to deal with the architecture built during the period of the dictatorship; many feel that it cannot rightly be included within the 'tradition' of Brazilian architecture, and simply ignore it. On the other hand, there were many projects of exceptional architectural quality built during this time, and they can neither be dismissed nor removed from their context in a pretence that they belong to another historical period. Such complications, and the fact that architectural criticism was frozen for twenty-five years, may explain why it can be rather easier to talk about the architecture of the mid-twentieth century than that of the late twentieth century.

In addition to these reasons why criticism of the modernist legacy within Brazil has been so largely absent, another is to do with newness, and its peculiar significance within the Brazilian context. The reflections of the French anthropologist Claude Lévi-Strauss on the features of São Paulo help make this clear.

In the cities of the New World it is not the absence of traces of the past which strikes me; this lack is an essential part of their significance [...] What struck me first when I visited New York or Chicago in 1941, and when I arrived in São Paulo in 1935, was not the newness of these places but their premature ageing. It did not surprise me to find that these towns lacked ten centuries of history, but I was staggered to discover that so many of their districts were already fifty years old and that they should display the signs of decrepitude with such a lack of shame, when the one adornment to which they could lay claim was that of youth, a quality as transitory for them as for living creatures.[3]

The particular feature of New World cities is, as he puts it, that they 'pass from freshness to decay without ever being simply old.'[4]

In Brazilian terms, the 'old' does not exist. Even allowing for the passage of half a century since Lévi-Strauss wrote these words, during which time a greater appreciation of 'heritage' might be said to have emerged worldwide, Brazil remains a country within which newness of things is valued, and 'oldness' is not easily distinguished from dilapidation. In this scheme of things, the works of Brazil's heroic period of modern architecture are condemned to everlasting newness: they can never become old, for were they to do so, they would instantly slide into decay. This might explain why the buildings designed by Oscar Niemeyer, Lucio Costa, Affonso Reidy and the other leading architects of their generation, seem often to be treated as belonging more to the present

Round Trip: Europe to Brazil & Back

than many buildings from the 1970s and 1980s. This sense of Brazil's period of heroic modern architecture as being of the present rather than past is compounded by the longevity of its best-known architect, Oscar Niemeyer, creating a living connection between the works of the 1940s and the present day. Although the architectural historian David Underwood has tried to periodize Niemeyer's work, and to draw distinctions between the various phases of his career, the attempt has been only partially successful, made difficult as it is by the architect's own tendency to describe his work in terms of universal architectural principles that underline the continuity between his late and his early work.[5]

Considered in this light, there can be no such thing as 'new Brazilian architecture', because all Brazilian architecture since 1936, provided it is modern, and not in the style of some historical revival, is 'new'. To single out works of the 1990s as 'new' risks precipitating the heroic era of the 1940s and 1950s into the abyss of 'oldness', and therefore worthless decrepitude. The task faced by the new generations of historians in Brazil is to find a way of describing contemporary work as 'new' without

threatening or overshadowing the undoubted originality of the work of the mid-century. Fear of compromising the architecture of the heroic period has made historians and critics reluctant to advertise recent work as 'new', or to talk about it independently of the work of the earlier period. In this book, the authors of the essays set out to position the work of the 1940s and 1950s as occupying a historical past, and as having an 'oldness' that would give a foothold from which it would then be possible to describe the 'newness' of current and future work.

How is this critique to develop? Where are the ideas, the theories, which are to inform it, to come from? Should they be drawn from other practices, from literature or from anthropology, or should they derive from architecture itself? Should they draw upon the international post-structuralist discourse, or should they reject ideas with a foreign origin, and take only from Brazil's own culture and traditions? These questions immediately draw us into disputed areas within Brazilian culture. Some argue that all the strengths of that culture follow from the recognition of its own traditions, and that just as the qualities of Brazilian architectural Modernism came from the adaptation of Portuguese colonial architecture, so

Claude Levi-Strauss, Anhangabaú Valley, São Paulo, 1935–37. View of the *Viaduto do Cha* (Tea Bridge) joining the historical centre and business district with this former tea-growing area. In the centre, the Matarazzo Building by the Italian architect Marcello Piacentini.

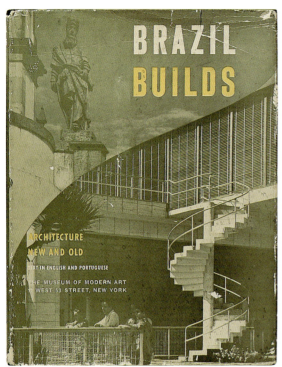
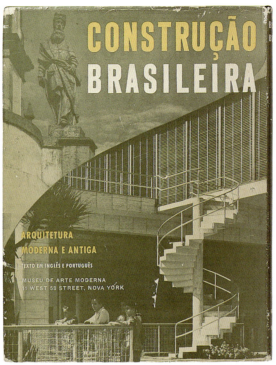

Philip L. Goodwin, *Brazil Builds: architecture new and old 1652–1942*, Museum of Modern Art, New York, 1943. The publication responsible for Brazilian architecture's first international prestige, it accompanied an exhibition at MoMA.

the critique of Brazilian Modernism should come from Brazil's own cultural heritage. Others say that the weakness of Brazilian culture is its inwardness, its self-absorption, its failure to engage with the wider critical scene, and that only by exposing itself to the post-Marxist and post-structuralist ideas developed elsewhere will it develop an effective critique. Both these points of view are represented in these essays. While Guilherme Wisnik makes use of arguments drawing on the legacies of Brazilian culture, other authors, Luiz Recamán and Pedro Fiori Arantes, emphasize the continuing relevance of Marxist critiques of urbanism.

The task facing Brazilian critics now has some similarities to the position of architects and critics in post-war Italy – of how to create a break with the past, without at the same time rejecting that past. But the parallel is only partial, for what clearly sets Brazil in the early twenty-first century apart from the situation of Italy, or any other European country, in the last century is that, as befits a former colony, Brazilian architecture is, and always has been, about a relationship with the developed world. Just as this introduction is itself a dialogue between Europe and Brazil, so every aspect of Brazilian architecture relates to, or has an implied relation to, the architecture of the developed world. The very history of architectural Modernism in Brazil – brought there by a European, Le Corbusier, cultivated by Costa and his associates in Rio de Janeiro, and then discovered and taken to North America by the two Americans, Philip Goodwin and G E Kidder Smith, who created the exhibition and book, *Brazil Builds* – is one of exchanges and transfers.

One trend in Brazilian criticism has been to downplay the country's dependency on imported architectural ideas. For example, the architect Carlos Eduardo Dias Comas has tried to lessen the connection between Niemeyer and Le Corbusier, and to argue that the originality of Niemeyer's work derives from his feeling for and sensitivity to Brazilian conditions, rather than from his understanding of Le Corbusier's practice.[6] None of the authors in this book choose to reject so completely the connection between Brazil and the developed world, but instead see their task as to understand it better, and to give a better account of the process of exchange.

Some of the most productive and fruitful new scholarship in architectural theory over the last decade has come from applying the concepts of post-colonial studies to architecture and urbanism. Terms such as 'hybridity', 'translation', 'transculturation' and 'symbiosis' have entered the discourse of architecture. What all these terms have in common is the attempt to escape from the presumption that cultural transfers involve a 'handing down' from a dominant culture to an inferior recipient. Instead, what these concepts aim to suggest is that out of the meeting between two cultures is created a wholly new product that is not a second-hand derivative of a foreign culture, but something unique in itself, and for which no definitive 'origin' can be identified. These ideas have been developed primarily within the study of literature – a more mobile art, and one that crosses boundaries, physical as well as social, more quickly than architecture – but one of the intellectual tasks of architectural theorists and critics in the last few years

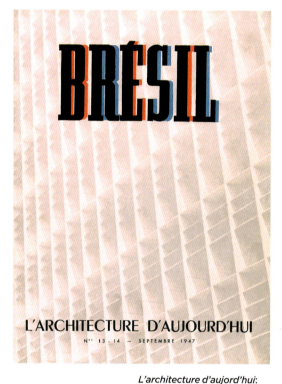

L'architecture d'aujord'hui: *spécial 'Architecture au Brésil'*, 13–14 (September 1947). During the 1940s and 1950s North American and European architectural magazines not only published every significant new Brazilian project but also dedicated special numbers to the country's architecture.

has been to explore their possibilities in the field of architecture.

'Hybridity' is a concept employed in particular by the Indian post-colonial literary theorist Homi Bhabha in order to shift attention away from the presumed identities of different cultures on to the very act of translation that occurs between them. In it, Bhabha sees all the processes of oppression, of discrimination, of domination and of resistance. 'It unsettles the mimetic or narcissistic demands of colonial power but reimplicates its identifications in strategies of subversion that turn the gaze of the discriminated back upon the eye of power.'[7] There have been some attempts to describe architecture in terms of hybridization, though all too often this has amounted to no more than the description of an aesthetic strategy, in which elements, forms and materials from different cultures are combined together. The result is treated as a resolution of different identities, rather than something with the permanently dynamic instability of Bhabha's concept.[8]

The Colombian architectural historian Felipe Hernández has argued that, in architecture, a more productive concept than 'hybridity' is 'transculturation', because it is less inclined to be reduced to an aesthetic formula. Coined by the Cuban anthropologist Fernando Ortiz, 'transculturation refers to a multidirectional and endless interactive process between various cultural systems that is in opposition to unidirectional and hierarchical structures determined by the principle of origin that is always associated with claims for cultural authority'.[9] Whereas acculturation

'implied the unidirectional imposition of one dominant culture upon another', and implies the loss of the culture of the subordinate group, in the manner of the modern Euro-American cultural and political homogenizing agendas, 'transculturation' offers a more dynamic model for such encounters, and one that acknowledges the survival of both parties. As opposed to acculturation, a once-and-for-all conquest, transculturation accepts that the process of interaction is permanent and continuing.

Generally in Latin America, the architectural and urban results of the processes of hybridization and transculturation have been looked down upon, as producing results that are impure and impoverished. Modernism in Brazil, as elsewhere, aimed to produce a homogeneous culture, and from this point of view, transculturation is its opposite, delighting in the disorderliness of multi-ethnic societies.

Post-colonial discourse has not been much favoured in Latin America, partly perhaps because it has been developed in countries that gained independence a century or more later than the Latin American states, and partly because of its tendency to treat all post-colonial societies as the same. Little discussed in Brazilian intellectual circles, it does not feature in any of the essays in this book. None the less, there is in Brazil a high degree of sensitivity towards cultural transfers, though Brazilians have their own preferred ways of talking about the process. One in particular uses the analogy of cannibalism. Sometime in the sixteenth century, members of the Tupinambà tribe ate a Catholic priest, causing horror and outrage in Europe when

Attilio Corrêa Lima, Seaplane
Station, Santos Dumont
Airport, Rio de Janeiro, 1940.
The concrete-frame building,
covered in yellow travertine
was located at the entrance
to the Bay of Guanabara
(above and opposite).

reports of the event arrived there. But, as was later pointed out, cannibals only eat those whom they respect and wish to gain strength from. This historical episode was taken up by the Brazilian writer Oswald de Andrade in the 1920s and used as the basis for his *Manifesto Antropofágico*, a manifesto of Brazilian Modernism. Devouring the priest became a metaphor for the process of creating a new identity by appropriating cultural elements from other contexts. And while violating the European moral code, it was, at the same time, an act of homage to European authority.[10] As a way of describing the process of cultural exchange between Brazil and Europe, this story has often been referred to, and it reappears in Guilherme Wisnik's essay in this book.

One of the lessons of post-colonial studies is that the exchanges between cultures are never simply one-way: however much they may resist and deny it, the colonizer is invariably as affected by the experience as much as the colonized. In the case of Brazil and its architecture, what has been the content of these exchanges? In terms of imports, the trade is clear: a new architectural language, developed in Europe in the 1920s and linked to new

technologies of construction. An architectural language that rejected the values of bourgeois culture, that discarded decoration, celebrated light and air, and that rationalized construction so as to take advantage of industrial processes. And yet, what did the bearers of European Modernism find when they arrived? A society without a fully-developed bourgeois culture to reject, a climate that was already over-sufficient in sunlight and air, and an economy lacking the industrial infrastructure that was the premise of European modern architecture. In the circumstances, the original European models of modern architecture could only undergo a deformation. From its beginnings, the principal client for modern architecture in Brazil was, throughout the heroic period and well into the 1960s, not private individuals but the state – a situation that only became normal in Europe after World War II. Rather than letting light and heat in, the main technical problem was to keep them out. And in construction the primary considerations were the cheapness of labour and the costliness of any of the 'new' materials – the inverse of the situation in Europe and North America. These paradoxes, and others, have become the distinguishing features of Brazilian architecture

and, far from expecting them ultimately to disappear, the reality is, as Roberto Conduru argues in his essay, that they are there to stay, and they make Brazilian architecture what it is.

What, then, did the European emissaries take back from this environment? In the case of Le Corbusier it was, as has often been pointed out, his exposure to Brazil, to its landscape and to its exoticism, that precipitated a change in his architecture and urbanism, from the rigidity of his work in the 1920s to the softening of forms and greater responsiveness to landscape evident in his work of the 1930s.[11] But if the significance of Brazil to Le Corbusier was curvilinear shapes and the validation of natural topography, these are not the only things that Europeans can take from Brazil's architecture. It is also the entire situation of Brazilian architecture, positioned as it is within a country so sharply divided by extremes of wealth and poverty as to be, in effect, two countries, that makes it significant.

One of the key features of modern architecture as it developed in Europe in the 1920s was that it was intended to be socially liberating. As the Viennese architect Otto Neurath, writing in the 1920s, put it, 'in former times they [architects] went to Popes, Queens, Princes and entrepreneurs, today they will serve those who are most powerful now, the workers; and together they will create a new kind of architecture'.[12] This new kind of architecture was expected to transform the lives of the previously oppressed and disadvantaged: the working class, women, the old, and the sick. But translated to a society like Brazil, where the revolution described by Neurath never happened, and which remained marked by extremes of wealth and poverty, this message could not be sustained. Although the ideology of 'development' – that, given sufficient investment, the economy could be transformed into a state of universal affluence – persisted into the 1960s, by the 1980s it was clear that the 'backwardness' of the Brazilian economy, and the extreme poverty of the majority of its inhabitants was not a temporary, but a permanent state of affairs. The ideals that underlay European Modernism were just about plausible in Europe, but not in Brazil. In these circumstances, what social agenda could there be for architecture?

None the less, some Brazilian architects, including Oscar Niemeyer, were firmly committed to the

Modernist ideal of a socially transformative architecture, but in order to maintain the ideal they had to translate this concept into terms that could carry some meaning in Brazil. In Niemeyer's case, he chose to stress the ritual aspect of architecture, its potential to enact the participation of the masses in social, educational or cultural programmes. As the clients for Niemeyer's buildings were principally the state and the political and social élite, there was something of a paradox in the way his architecture aspired to flatter the life of the masses; the paradox remained unresolved – one of many in Brazilian architecture.

In many ways it was the more politically engaged but less well-known 'Paulista' school from São Paulo, rather than the Carioca school from which Niemeyer came, that developed the more interesting answers to the political situation of architecture in Brazil. During the 1950s, the leading figure in São Paulo was Vilanova Artigas: a communist hostile to United States involvements in Latin America.[13] He was also a strong critic of the Carioca style promoted by *Brazil Builds*, precisely because this version of the country's architecture had been 'made' by the North Americans; likewise he was critical of the influence exercised by Le Corbusier upon the Carioca school, because of the dependent status in which it cast Brazilian architecture. Instead, Artigas held that Brazilian architecture could only develop by addressing Brazilian problems, above all the backwardness and poverty of the mass of its population. A building like Artigas' Faculty of Architecture and Urbanism is simultaneously crude and sophisticated: primitive

Lina Bo Bardi, São Paulo Art Museum, São Paulo, 1957–68. Bardi intended the severe lines of her architecture to be complemented by popular participation. In her own words: 'I would like people to go there to see open air exhibitions and discuss things, listen to music, see movies. Children, too, playing in the sun, from morning to evening. And brass band concerts.'

in its finish, reliant on a very low level of manual skill in its construction, but sophisticated in the engineering of its slender columns (see pp. 177–9). What we see here is a building that makes use of the one material that Latin America has in abundance, unskilled labour, and combining it with Latin America's other great resource, human invention, suggests a strategy for the endemic social and economic crises of Brazil. Unlike the Carioca school, who were more pragmatic in their approach to the techniques of construction, Artigas and his successors, the Arquitetura Nova school, who went on to search for strategies for mass housing (discussed by Arantes), emphasized the importance of the building process itself as part of the liberational aspect of architecture. How the building was built was as important as what it was for, in the development of a strategy for architecture's service to society.

Most successful of all amongst the Brazilian architects who set out to create a social programme for architecture in a society where this was superficially impossible, was Lina Bo Bardi. Although a building like the Museum of Art at São Paulo is, both in its origins and its contents, a monument to high culture and to the political élite, Bo Bardi managed none the less to create a building that gave space to the masses (see p. 82). By the disconcerting effect of removing the central floor of the building, between the galleries above and below, and giving it over to the street, the building suggested an appropriation by the populace of its main level. Even more striking in the confidence with which it creates a place for collective cultural activity is the SESC-Pompéia, funded and managed co-operatively. No more than

the conversion of a redundant factory, this remarkable project nevertheless succeeds in creating an extraordinary variety of rooms with some remarkable architectural experiences (see pp. 91-3). Little acknowledged within Brazilian architecture until the early 1990s, Lina Bo Bardi's work is evidence of Brazilian architecture's ability to develop a social agenda in a society where social opportunities remain permanently out of reach to the large majority of the population.[14]

Brazilian architects' experience of working in conditions of extreme division between rich and poor has up to now been regarded as a situation peculiar to 'third world' countries. Yet, as the countries of the Western world become more and more like third-world countries, as the divisions between rich and poor within them increase rather than diminish, and they become increasingly reliant upon an underclass of disenfranchised immigrants to maintain their economic competitiveness, assumptions about the scope of architecture start to be put under pressure, and to narrow. The long experience that Brazilian architects have had of finding ways to develop socially inclusive projects within a society that is so socially exclusive begins to look more and more interesting from a first-world perspective. It is ironical that in a country without any of the apparatus of social democracy it should have been possible to create some of the most optimistically radical social projects to be found anywhere in the world. There is a lesson of hope here for those who have abandoned modern architecture's social agenda as hollow and unrealizable.

CHAPTER ONE
DOOMED TO MODERNITY
BY GUILHERME WISNIK

Oscar Niemeyer, Planalto
Palace and National
Congress, 1960. A *candango*,
name given to the builders of
Brasília, shows the new
capital to his family. The city
was a *tabula rasa*, the place
where 'everything could start
anew', and from where the
Modern became Brazil's
'natural habitat'.

DOOMED TO MODERNITY

Brazil and histories of modern architecture

In the history of architecture, the early 1960s was an important moment of revision for the course of the Modern Movement, with frequent references to the 'exhaustion', 'escapism' and 'superficiality' of contemporary architecture. In this climate of uncertainty Siegfried Giedion, the celebrated historian and Congrès Internationaux d'Architecture Moderne (CIAM) General Secretary, wrote in an article entitled 'Architecture in the 1960's: Hopes and Fear',[1] that he was both afraid of, and yet confident about, the development of a 'new tradition'. In his opinion he was witnessing not the end of a period, but its formative years. Signs of reinvigoration came, according to Giedion, from the new impetus brought by regional contributions from 'faraway countries', such as Finland and Brazil, where there was architecture that went beyond mere utility and demonstrated characteristics of a new monumentality.[2] Hence, at the beginning of the 1960s, Giedion reaffirmed what he had noticed earlier in the 1940s, and rejoiced with some surprise at the fact that 'our civilisation' had been developing 'from more than one centre'.[3]

Another seminal figure within the debate on the future of modern architecture, Nikolaus Pevsner, expressed a similar uncertainty, but warned of the dangers of what he called 'the return of historicism'.[4] In a lecture at the Royal Institute of British Architects in London, Pevsner identified, amongst the new developments of the time, a tendency 'towards exteriors which are created not necessarily at the expense of function'.[5] For this tendency, Brazil was held directly responsible, for it was there, according to Pevsner, that it had first become apparent, with Oscar Niemeyer's work of 1942–3. 'His are the earliest buildings which are emphatically no longer of the so-called International Style, and they are buildings that have force, that have power, that have a great deal of originality, but they are, emphatically, anti-rational.'[6]

It is interesting to note how at this historic moment, the same year as the inauguration of Brasília, Brazilian architecture could be perceived both as a regional Modernism (a role in which it had been cast in the 1940s and 1950s, and that was by then running out of steam) and as a Postmodernism *avant la lettre*, an interpretative hypothesis that was to be short-lived.

Nevertheless, despite their differing opinions as to the role of Brazilian architecture on the international scene, both Giedion and Pevsner assumed that, as part of a widespread process of decentralization, cultural manifestations emerging from economically peripheral countries were altering the course of what was being produced within the developed centres. Pevsner acknowledged that: 'To me it is a fact that Pampulha and Ronchamp and the historicist neo-expressionists belong together quite organically, whether I like it or not.'[7] In fact, such was the destabilizing influence that Pevsner attributed to Brazilian architecture, that he actually blamed it for the change which occurred in the career of the master Le Corbusier: 'It is conceivable that the country had the effect on him of forcing into the open the irrational traits of his character and that he then passed on his impulsive enthusiasm to his young admirers'.[8]

Oscar Niemeyer, Church
of Saint Francis, Pampulha,
Belo Horizonte, 1940.
View of facade with mosaic
panel by Candido Portinari
(above) and view from lake
(left).

The English critic and historian Reyner Banham, in his overview of international modern architecture,[9] of the following year, while not endorsing Giedion, did not, as Pevsner had done, exclude Brazilian architecture from the Modern Movement. Of Brasília's buildings, Banham wrote, 'functional or not, they are still modern architecture as we have known it, clean, crisp, precise';[10] and added, 'from Lucio Costa's Ministry of Education in Rio, obviously Corb-inspired, to Oscar Niemeyer's government buildings in the all-new capital city of Brasília, this style has been the envy of the world'.[11]

Banham's perception is important because it represents a view of Brazilian architecture as a distinctive 'style' that had developed from nothing and refined itself in a mere quarter-century, from the Ministry of Education and Public Health in 1936 to the inauguration of Brasília in 1960. One could add that in the same period a considerable number of excellent architects, based predominantly in Rio de Janeiro, had achieved maturity, and their work had acquired recognizable characteristics. It was this context that allowed Banham to describe Brazilian architecture retrospectively as 'the first *national* style of modern architecture'. Banham thus reiterated Philip Goodwin's interpretation made two decades before, in 1943, at the exhibition 'Brazil Builds' at the Museum of Modern Art, New York.[12]

That exhibition, the event responsible for the launch of Brazilian architecture's international reputation, had proposed a direct relationship between the new work and the colonial buildings of the seventeenth and eighteenth centuries. In the exhibition, the link that was made between modern architecture and the colonial buildings built prior to the nineteenth-century obsession with the foreign and, more specifically, French styles,[13] had encouraged Brazilian architecture to be seen worldwide as a manifestation of a national identity, and it was this perception that informed many subsequent interpretations, both in Brazil and abroad.[14]

However, the view of a local creativity linking modernity with a pre-existing cultural heritage was not a North American invention, nor was it created by Philip Goodwin. Although disseminated from New York, this interpretation was in fact based upon Lucio Costa's own historical reading, first formulated in the text 'Razões da Nova Arquitetura' (Reasons of the New Architecture) of 1934 and further developed in his 1937 essay 'Documentação Necessária' (Necessary Documentation).[15] The latter text was adopted as the operational manual for the Office for National Historic and Artistic Heritage, founded that same year.

Costa's interpretation was, in turn, informed by the wider aesthetic environment of literary and artistic Modernism in Brazil, which had proposed that through a 'cannibalistic' process of 'devouring' elements of European culture locally, the backwardness of the country would be transformed into an advanced model of cultural action. In the same way that the European avant-garde privileged exotic art as part of the cult of the uncivilized, primitive instinct, the Brazilian modernists turned towards their own culture, creating from their 'pre-civilized' past a tradition to counteract the affectations of bourgeois academicism.

Lucio Costa and team, Ministry of Education and Health, Rio de Janeiro, 1936. The first example of 'curtain wall' to be built in Brazil, the glazed north facade was screened with concrete *brise-soleil* (left).

Oscar Niemeyer, Itamaraty Palace, Brasília, 1960. View of foyer on the occasion of the first visit of Queen Elizabeth II to the recently inaugurated capital (right).

In architectural terms, Costa proposed an analogy between the rigorous simplification of modern forms and the tranquil, unadorned sobriety of the old Brazilian rural constructions. This analogy, it should be stressed, ran counter to the teleological principle of the European avant-garde, with its insistence upon a radical rupture with history. Indeed the 'originality' attributed to Brazilian architecture arose from just such a presupposition of its spontaneous creation, placing it in the same tradition as international Modernism.[16] Costa's proposal associated avant-garde aesthetics, anti-traditionalist par excellence, with a popular Luso-Brazilian tradition, here considered as being pure and genuinely national.

Although Costa's analogy was clearly a piece of historical construction – and similar constructions are found elsewhere – it is fair to acknowledge that Brazil's new architecture presented certain specific characteristics that made it independent of, and distinct from, its European sources. Features such as the diverse ways of controlling the heat and strong light of the tropics (trellises and *brises-soleil*, verandas, patios), and formal treatment of floors and insulation (artisanal tiles, Venetian and Portuguese mosaics, tiled panels) were all distinctive to colonial construction. In each case, there is a conjunction between the functional dimension of the architecture – the ventilation of its spaces, the control of humidity – and its aesthetic dimension – the decorative interest, the movement of the facades. Furthermore, several of these features refer to even longer-running colonial traditions, such as *muxarabis*,[17] inherited by Portugal from

the Arabs, and some, such as tiles, inherited in turn by the Arabs from the Chinese.

The conventional account of what has become recognized as the 'Brazilian Style' is that it was a local adaptation of the International Style, an apparently miraculous and spontaneous deviation from the Functionalist norm. Flowering like a tropical plant amidst seemingly hostile conditions, Brazilian architecture expressed a 'utopian hedonism' and was seen internationally as 'the model for an entirely "other" way of life'.[18] It is this perception that explains why Giedion was unsure whether to be confused or to be dazzled, and was led to say 'there is something irrational' in this architecture.[19]

It is not by chance that there should be so many references to 'irrationality' in the attempts to make sense of Brazilian architecture, for it expresses the ambivalence that is at the core of the nation's process of modernization: on the one hand, miraculous and surprising, and on the other hand, illogical and paradoxical.

Giedion's celebration of the spontaneous creativity of Brazilian architecture is a good illustration of the former case, while Pevsner's reaction exemplifies the latter. His mention of 'irrationality' may be interpreted as the culmination of a critique initiated by the Swiss artist Max Bill, who, when he visited the 2nd São Paulo International Biennial in 1953, violently attacked the hitherto celebrated 'Brazilian example' as 'barbarism' and 'anti-social academicism'.[20] Bill's surprising and unprecedentedly outspoken attack had, it should be said, only limited relevance to the Brazilian context, having more to do with a defence of functionalism

Lucio Costa, Saavedra House, Petrópolis, Rio de Janeiro, 1942. This project combined elements from the Portuguese colonial tradition such as the wooden trellis (above) with a modern distribution of space and the use of *pilotis* .

Oscar Niemeyer, Itamaraty Palace, Brasília, 1960. A modern derivation of the wooden trellis used here as a device to control solar intake as well as decorative treatment of the facade (opposite).

Roberto Burle Marx, preparatory study for a mosaic panel in the school of the Pedregulho Housing Development (1950-2), drawing on card and gouache. Panels made of pastilles as well as mosaic tiles were used by modern artists and architects to emphasize the continuation of what was seen as a typical Brazilian tradition (above).

in post-war Europe. Nevertheless, the Swiss artist's criticisms would provide important ammunition for Bruno Zevi's[21] critique. Together with Giulio Carlo Argan, Zevi was the critic who established the most consistent objections to the development of Brazilian modern architecture.

Given Zevi's advocacy of 'organic architecture', it was unsurprising that he found no praise-worthy architectural work in Brazil. But his distance from both the Corbusian lineage and the Ulm orthodoxy allowed him to see how Brazilian architecture curiously was both condemned and approved by apostles of rationalism, such as Giedion and Bill.

The first, according to Zevi, found in Brazil a compensation for the failures of modern architecture. The second, one could add, tried to teach good manners to a primitive people. Neither Gideon nor Bill had approached Brazilian architecture with an open mind.

Zevi himself did not dwell on the inexplicable paradoxes of Brazil, nor did he have the *naïveté* to try to convert them to the path of social responsibility as if it were a question of formal education. Taking a broader view, he saw the 'figurative fluidity' of this architecture as a reflection of a 'state of uncertainty' that characterized the country's culture as a whole: a consequence of its territorial immensity and the absence of 'permanent values or economic stability'. That is to say, the figurative 'formalism' of this architecture was seen as a manifestation of a weak, fragile culture where formal standards had not yet been established as a productive expression of society.

Argan's essay on Brazilian architecture dates

from the same year, 1954, and, of all the European discussions of Brazil from this period, is the most perceptive.[22] With more discernment than Zevi, Argan portrayed the Brazilian architectural phenomenon as belonging within a complex frame of cultural circumstances. His focus was not on figurative formalism, which for someone educated in the study of iconology and the 'theory of pure visibility' was a secondary issue. Instead, for Argan, Brazilian architecture did not exhibit figuration explicitly since it 'was capable of avoiding the rhetoric of nature'. Neither was it the expression of a retarded culture. On the contrary, its vitality 'emerged from the positive and comforting expression of a society satisfied with the prosperity of its commerce'.

In his view the fundamental problem of this architecture was precisely its initial success: a self-indulgent and immature self-satisfaction obtained from the limited scale of individual buildings obscured a more profound analysis of the social reasons that had informed the creation of the modern canons in Europe.

As a consequence, Brazilian architectonic production had not spread into the field of urban planning, where the serious problems relating to housing and the cities' outskirts resided. Neither had it succeeded in breaching the barrier created by the 'top to bottom' structure of production dominated by a technical intelligentsia.

From these interpretations, and Argan's analysis, we may conclude that the Brazilian problem was not due to the passage to the modern, and to the difficulties encountered by the country 'becoming'

Affonso Eduardo Reidy,
Pedregulho Housing
Development, Rio de Janeiro,
1950–2. Site model showing
(clockwise from right) the
curvilinear main block, the
secondary habitation blocks,
the playground, the health
centre, and the school with
pool and changing rooms
(above).

modern. On the contrary, it was due to the ease of modernization: to the way Brazil became modern almost instantaneously and without any questioning of, or distancing from, the process. Modernity occurred, it could be said, without any accompanying cultural sedimentation.

Whether the features of Brazilian architecture are interpreted as 'figurative' or 'technical', there is always an underlying formalism to the debate. And, as a rule, this formalism is confused by the notions of, on the one hand, 'irrationality' and, on the other, 'regionalism'. In relation to the term 'regionalism' and the idea of a 'national style', the confusion derives from the fact that, in the various formulations of the argument, the concept of 'local tradition' is generally treated as if it were a constant, without recognition of the various changes in meaning that it has undergone over the years.

The 'local' quality initially valued by Lucio Costa within the Luso-Brazilian tradition lay in the austerity of its crude and simple construction, making it close to the formal restraint of modern architecture. The 'local' was therefore a factor giving proximity to international Functionalism, rather than distance from it. This was then the initial concept of 'local regionalism' adopted when modernism was first introduced in Brazil: the adaptation of modern precepts to tropical conditions through the use of elements borrowed from the local building tradition, such as trellises, tiled panels, water mirrors and tropical gardens. Such initial experimentation would further develop into the varied and creative transformation of Le Corbusier's *brise-soleil* blades,

making them fixed, mobile, vertical, horizontal, etc.

The vision of Brazilian modern architecture as being a slight deviation from the Functionalist norm coincided with the view taken by external commentators, such as Goodwin and Giedion. However, Costa's idea that it was the local elements that made Brazilian architecture 'modern' does not correspond to the second notion of Brazilian regionalism that will become predominant at a later stage, particularly following the construction of Brasília.

This second concept of local identity was based upon a tradition quite distinct from that chosen initially by Lucio Costa, and it was invoked in order to explain the proliferation of an architecture that was not restricted to regular prismatic shapes, and that made form the defining rationale of the whole construction.

In this new interpretation of regionalism the point of reference was no longer Brazil's anonymous and ordinary colonial constructions, but its religious Baroque buildings of the seventeenth and eighteenth centuries.[23] It is in the wake of this decidedly aesthetic tradition, one very distant from the avant-garde's formal restraint, that the problems of irrationality were posited so forcibly in the Brazilian context.

Compared to Max Bill's accusation that Brazilian architecture – more precisely, Niemeyer's free-form version of it – was 'irrational', Argan was more tolerant, observing that one should not expect Brazilian architecture to be exemplary, since it was representative of the country's own 'intrinsic efficiency'. Moreover, the search for the definitive

Affonso Eduardo Reidy,
Pedregulho Housing
Development, Rio de Janeiro,
1950–2. Access to the main
habitation block was from
two bridges (see cross-
section, below left) on to
the main corridor on the
'intermediary level' (see
partial elevation, below
and view of back facade,
opposite) on which the
social services were located.

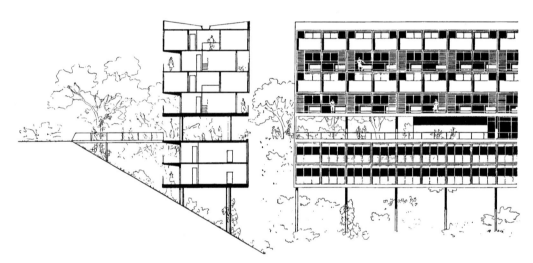

standards set by modern design was not appropriate to Brazil's reality. The capacity of Brazilian culture instantaneously to adopt all modern forms derived from Brazil's historical vocation as a new country rather than from the demands of technical and industrial standardization. According to Argan, it was from this condition that Brazilian architecture acquired its desire to 'merge the functional with the representational', or, in other words, 'the resort to the technical with the celebration of technique'.

As far as Bill's critique is concerned, it is fair to say that Brazilian architecture produced few works of social interest, an issue in any case beyond the scope of any individual architect. Nevertheless, it is necessary to understand what was behind the accusations of irrationality and formalism that were constantly made against Brazilian architecture. Were curved forms inherently irrational? Were the 'thick and thin pilotis' that Bill saw, 'placed all over' and 'lacking any sense of rhythm' really irrational?

What are obviously at stake here are moral issues, as the recurrent accusations of 'frivolity' and 'lack of decency' reveal. Beneath the idea of rationality, and its opposite, is the issue of individual expression, which is seen by Bill as reactionary and contrary to collective expression. The objection is not on technical grounds, that is on grounds of industrial reproducibility, for, as far as reinforced concrete is concerned, orthogonal and regular prisms are no more rational and reproducible than irregular and curved volumes.

Rather, the objection to Niemeyer's designs was that by emphasizing the individuality of each building, Niemeyer disregarded the Functionalist principle of the building as a series of generic cells reproduced many times over, and presented each building as a unique and indivisible whole. In this approach one may see an allusion to the Baroque heritage, beginning with the parabolic vaults of the Pampulha Church (1943) and developed further in subsequent housing projects such as the halls of residence at the Centre for Aeronautical Technology (CAT), the Copan (both in São Paulo in 1953) and the Niemeyer Building (1954) in Belo Horizonte.

With the CAT project, which comprises four different typologies, the architect used various reinterpretations of trellises and cobogós[24] from traditional Brazilian architecture. These in turn were not treated as juxtaposed 'elements', but merged

Doomed to Modernity

Oscar Niemeyer, Copan Building, São Paulo, 1951-3. The building's curvilinear plan closely followed the site's outline, which was in turn reflected by the glass and *brise-soleil* facade (opposite and above right).

Oscar Niemeyer, Niemeyer Building, Belo Horizonte, 1954. The glass and *brise-soleil* facade completely enveloped the building making it impossible to distinguish front and back faces (above left).

into continuous surfaces: plans pierced by double-height spaces, marking the horizontal but not the orthogonal extension of the volumes.

Both Copan and Le Corbusier's Unité d'Habitation in Marseilles (1947), are conceived as a multifunctional urban apparatus containing shops, a cinema, a hotel and housing units. However, unlike the French example, Copan is defined by its sinuous volume composed of horizontal *brises-soleil* that transform the building's north face into an entirely formal, continuous and autonomous volume. This approach was further developed in the Niemeyer Building, where all recollection of the prismatic forms of modern architecture is lost under the continuous amoeboid external shield, making it impossible to distinguish front, side and rear facades.

However, Niemeyer never employs the curve as a detail or adornment, but always as a means of constructing 'an architectonic form in its integrity',[25] since his line of thought already internalizes the mouldable and indivisible logic of reinforced concrete. In this manner, his work approaches Le Corbusier's sense of totality in terms of its 'telluric' freedom. There is, nevertheless, a fundamental difference between the two: in their means of organizing space.

As Sophia Telles has observed, Niemeyer's spatiality does not obey the classical rationalism of formal construction evident in Le Corbusier's work – whereby order is established through conventions of scale, proportion and rhythm, in other words in the ordering of the parts – nor does it follow the organicity of the structural tensioning.

She nevertheless ponders on the fact that the strangeness of Niemeyer's forms does not entail an estrangement from 'architecture's habitual vocabulary'. On the contrary, those forms appear as a consequence of their 'matter of factness', of the fact that they 'do not require justification'.[26] Within this line of thought, she observes that what makes Eero Saarinen's 'muscular forms' 'more acceptable compared to the sinuosity of Niemeyer's concrete' is the 'spatial character' of the Finnish architect's structures, which are more 'organic' and expansive. Alternatively, with Niemeyer the figure appears to emerge 'finished' and 'closed' like a flat profile, since the required structural effort in his works is 'sublimated'.

This is precisely the point at which Sophia Telles' analysis touches upon the alleged irrationality of Niemeyer's work: its voluntary suppression of the tectonic dimension of the building. Searching for an unexpected lightness, the architect does not load the material with any expressive charge. This is the grounds for his frequent resort to covering the concrete with tiles[27] and marble. In this respect his procedure is similar to the temporal suppression produced by *bossa nova*, where the fluid pulse acts by relativizing the opposition between the strong and weak tempos – which is a characteristic of jazz, rock and reggae for example – not allowing it to be incorporated, like other South American rhythms, into the better-known musical languages. As Lorenzo Mammì has observed, this indefinable pulse 'acts as if time (tempo) has not yet become solidified into a mechanical movement leaving space for individual variations'.[28] Determinant yet

Oscar Niemeyer, Alvorada Palace, Brasília, 1957–8. View of the colonnade and courtyard (above left and right).

Oscar Niemeyer, National Congress, Brasília, 1958. The main building housed the Chamber of Deputies (inverted dome) and the Senate (dome) on two levels, while the twin glazed blocks contained the Secretariat and services (right and opposite top right). Also part of the Plaza of the Three Powers, it affords a view of the standard Ministries flanking the city's main axis (opposite bottom left).

Oscar Niemeyer, Itamaraty Palace, Brasília, 1960. Based on a square plan and four identical facades and surrounded by water, it is accessed via footbridges (opposite top left).

Oscar Niemeyer, Brasília Cathedral , Brasília, 1958–67. Sixteen glazed concrete ribs cover the underground nave that can only be entered through an enclosed ramp (opposite bottom right) .

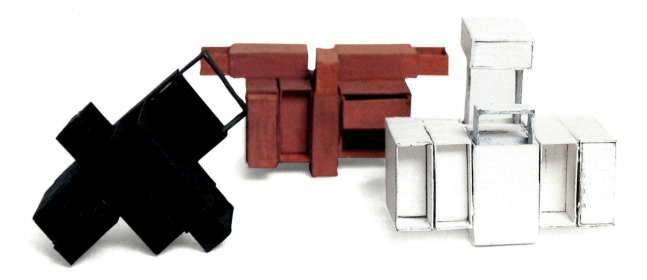

Lygia Clark, Matchbox Structures, 1964, painted and glued matchboxes, private collection. Thinking about architecture and space played a large part in Lygia Clark's work. Early experiments included her matchbox clusters in which the little drawers could be pushed out to modify the structure. Later, the body itself became the support for a 'biological and cellular architecture'.

invisible, Niemeyer's technical endeavour allows the materialisation of light, stable and surprisingly poised forms that are frequently described as surrealist.[29]

These various considerations do help to explain some of the formative processes of Brazilian architecture as well as its international reception, both up to the early 1960s and subsequently. For, after the early 1960s, Brazilian architecture virtually disappeared from the international debate as far as general publications on architectural history are concerned. While Finland, having produced long-lasting architectural solutions was lauded as an exemplar, Brazil, together with Japan and India, became known merely as an example of the 'Corbusean school in distant lands' and thus lost its own individual character.[30]

From the mid-1950s onwards, this appreciation of the regional contributions by 'distant countries' was gradually displaced by the revisions of the Modern Movement that took place in central countries such as England and France – through the 'New Brutalist' production of the English couple Alison and Peter Smithson, and the post-war work of Le Corbusier – and in the United States – with the work of Louis Kahn. In the mid-1960s such revisions were articulated through, on the one hand, megastructural speculations and, on the other, the publication in 1966 of the first anti-Modern manifestos: *L'Architettura della Città*, by Aldo Rossi, and *Complexity and Contradiction in Architecture*, by Robert Venturi.

Confronted by such an abrupt reconfiguration of the international scene, the so-called 'Brazilian

Style' seemed to lose its historical place as that of a contemporary production belonging to its time.[31] It thus fell into a historiographic limbo, whence it seems to have emerged only recently – albeit timidly, and certainly no longer exemplifying a 'national style'.

The apparent decline of Brazilian architecture, and its loss of novelty and innovation from the 1960s onwards, should also be considered as a reflection of changes in the way that Latin American countries came to be regarded within the global economy.

The consequences for Brazil of the relationship between capitalism's oscillations within the leading economic centres and its reconfigurations at the periphery have been described by the Brazilian philosopher Otília Arantes. Her work discusses the deadlock of modernist aesthetic theory and its postmodern simulacra, from Jürgen Habermas to Peter Eisenman.[32] Following her argument, it is possible to see how , to a certain extent, a temporary reversal of hierarchies had allowed the 'Brazilian Style' to become, at a particular historical moment, 'the envy of the world', to use Banham's expression. The stagnation of the European states during the inter-war period, and of the North American bourgeoisie during the years following the 1930s economic depression, gave Third World states a temporary 'authority', as Le Corbusier put it. But above all, this historical conjuncture had been sustained by a broader ideological convergence between modernism's goal of social utopia and capitalism's destined expansion through the increase of mass production and the growing integration of world markets. However, in the following decades

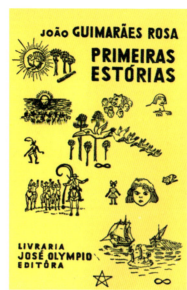

that model of ever-expanding markets throughout the world as the basis of capitalism's growth was replaced by one that gave greater value to uneven development, and to the protection of pools of cheap labour in certain parts of the world so as to perpetuate an international division of labour. In this new model, it was no longer advantageous for countries at the centre to pretend that countries at the periphery, the sources of cheap labour, any longer occupied positions of cultural authority.

If such argument provides a general understanding of the fluctuations in the roles ascribed to peripheral nations within the international scene, there still remain to be discussed the internal reasons that led Brazilian architectural culture voluntarily to distance itself from international discussions.

Interior modernity

Brasília is at the crux of any discussion about the trajectory of Brazilian architecture in the twentieth century. Brazil's understanding of its own architecture relates in large part to the ways in which the story of Brasília has been told – and inside Brazil there are several versions, each of which emphasizes a particular aspect. Constructed at one of the most lively moments of political and cultural activity in Brazil's history, Brasília was the ultimate expression of a new aesthetic standard in the country, a standard that could be said to be sophisticated without being elitist. Brasília is, in this sense, a phenomenon parallel to that of *bossa nova* in popular music, and the Concrete and Neo-Concrete avant-gardes in fine art and poetry.

It is not by chance that, in all three of these areas of artistic activity, the production of this time is the distillation of a slow process of aesthetic maturity that, resonating out from its original context, finds success on the international scene.[33] In fine art, the Concrete Art movement succeeded the didactic and nationalistic agenda of modernist[34] artists such as Candido Portinari and Tarsila do Amaral. Popular music incorporated the influences of jazz, adding a level of sophistication to the syncopated pulse of samba over the prosodic continuity of the spoken language. Likewise, when in architecture an entire city was constructed in the middle of the *cerrado*,[35] the eminently symbolic buildings superseded the original influences of Le Corbusier.

Among the commentators on Brasília, one of the first and most important was Mário Pedrosa, a militant communist since the 1920s. A major art critic from the following decade onwards, Pedrosa was the intellectual who formulated in newspaper articles[36] the basis for architectural criticism in Brazil. A polemical and precocious defender of abstract art in the country, he foresaw in Brasília the materialization of a wide-ranging cultural convergence that he described as a 'synthesis of the arts'.[37]

Brasília represented an important link between the constructivist aesthetic project, conceived alongside the ideal of the creation of a social utopia, and the doctrines of political and economic developmentalism[38] that dominated Brazilian politics during the 1950s and 1960s.[39] In cultural terms, the aesthetic abstraction of the 1950s and 1960s succeeded the *Modernismo*[40] of the 1920s in

João Gilberto, Chega de Saudades, 1959 (cover photography and design by Cesar Villela). This was the first record by João Gilberto and included songs such as 'Desafinado' and 'Girl from Ipanema' that epitomized the new musical sytle of *bossa nova* in Brazil and throughout the world (right).

João Guimarães Rosa, *Primeiras Estórias* (*First Stories*), Rio de Janeiro, 1962. Together with Clarice Lispector and the poet João Cabral de Melo Neto, Guimarães Rosa belongs to the so-called '1945 Generation', a third wave of modern Brazilian writers searching for a linguistic and aesthetic breakthrough in Brazilian literature. Guimarães Rosa's greatest originality lied in his use of language based on the oral culture of the *sertanejos* which he combined with archaisms, neologisms and syntactical inventions (left).

Lucio Costa, Master Plan, Brasília, 1957–60. The new capital was planned and built on virgin territory in a region known as the *Sertão* in the heart of the country. An aerial city as much as a city of roads, Brasília is the symbol of a modernization implanted amidst a 'deserted wilderness and exposed to a wide open sky, as if placed in the open sea'.

seeking to liberate the country from its historical, social and ethnic prejudices. Similarly, in the field of architecture, Brasília represented an immersion into the interior of the country, constituting an anchor point for a national production. It is the 'place' towards which the *Carioca*[41] architecture of the 1930s, 1940s and 1950s converged. It was also from there that the *Paulista*[42] production of the 1960s and 1970s departed. To a certain extent, such a trajectory continues to this day. When, from the 1960s, Brazil began to experience rapid urbanization, swelling and disorganizing its largest cities, the construction of Brasília, both a demagogic political gesture and a manifestation of a new spatial consciousness, marked this historical process, and in particular signalled an attempt to look inwards, towards the country's interior, its emptiness, in order to overcome cultural dependency and to broaden the national market.

A large part of that scarcely inhabited region of Brazil is generically called the *Sertão*. This region extends from the south-east and centre-west regions of the country, from the states of Minas Gerais and Goiás, to the north-east.[43] Occupied by small cities and wandering groups of people, in the Brazilian imaginary the region has always represented an 'otherness' to civilization. It is perceived as a violent, centrifugal, parallel world that is governed by its own rules of conduct, where power relations remain patriarchal in nature, and law is not enforced.[44]

The *Sertão* has been represented as both a physical and symbolic territory by Guimarães Rosa, a novelist and central figure in the third generation

of modernist writers in the country. Rosa's entire literary production culminates in *Grande Sertão: Veredas (The Vast Sertão: Paths)*,[45] and, from this book, one can understand something of the symbolic impact that the construction of Brasília had on the region. Mere description of the facts is less effective than fiction, which conveys better the force of the violation and destruction done to nature and those mythical landscapes.

Brasília emerges as an unnamed city in the two tales that begin and end the book *Primeiras Estórias (First Stories)*, published in 1962.[46] In both stories – where a boy is taken by his uncle to visit the construction site of a new city, with its artificial lake, engineers and machines – modernity's eruption is accompanied by a continuous feeling of death.[47] Since this nameless Brasília is not exactly a city, but rather the spectre of the modern yet to be accomplished, it represents a principle that, in spite of everything, was already present within the *Sertão*, and which it does not contradict. For that constructive and destructive power that takes possession of space, that is blind towards the vegetation that it wipes out, is still the *Sertão*, other and yet the same, its fold.[48]

As it transforms the *Sertão*, Rosa's Brasília re-establishes the violent and archaic elements of Brazilian modernization, elements already present in the *Sertão*. Brasília does not seem to evoke the passage from the arcane to the modern, so much as the persistence of one within the other. Such a perception is very close to the diagnosis of the Brazilian situation proposed by Mário Pedrosa with respect to Lucio Costa's project for Brasília's Master

Plan. According to Pedrosa, having emerged as a colony and without a strong native culture, Brazil had no cultural identity to be preserved. For this reason, precisely because they are not oppressed by their past, Brazilians are condemned to the modern.[49] In other words, being a *tabula rasa* where 'everything could start afresh', the country made of the modern its 'natural habitat' and, almost indiscriminately, continuously plugs into the most recent cultural fashions. In a way it is what Argan had referred to, when describing Brazil's ease in becoming modern.

Yet despite its vocation to the modern, Brazil did not achieve modernity as such – this is its fundamental dilemma. The ultra-modern capital failed to civilize the 'other' Brazil, where archaic residues survived and redeveloped to such an extent that at certain moments they ceased to be residues and revealed themselves actually to be primordial conditions. Such was the case, for example, with the brutality and violence that the workers building Brasília were subjected to on site: the violence of the lawless *Sertão* was renewed rather than subdued by the modern city. Moreover, the spatial segregation that resulted from the appearance of poverty-stricken satellite cities around the Master Plan replicates the spatial structures characteristic of the social hierarchy of the traditional large estates and the power structures imposed by the political barons.[50]

Yet to what extent do these contradictions result from Lucio Costa's plan? One might argue that they are implicit within it, questioned and yet unresolved, just as they remain in the contemporaneous insights of Mário Pedrosa and Guimarães Rosa. Although Brasília was the subject of much discussion at the time of its construction,[51] the interpretations that associate it with authoritarian and out-of-date models of urban design only emerged some years after its inauguration. Such is the case with Kenneth Frampton and Manfredo Tafuri,[52] both of whom considered the city's plan to be a simple application of historical models formulated during the early 1930s, as exemplified by the *Ville Radieuse* and the Soviet 'Superblocks'. At the time, however, Brasília was seen as a radical and innovative model: for example Peter Smithson, during a debate in 1958, supported Costa's plan because he considered it to be an essentially hybrid and non-hierarchical plan that encompassed 'a constellation of principles'.[53] That Smithson, one of the key architects in the development of alternatives to modernist zoned cities, acknowledged the qualities of Brasília is significant. And a remark made by another Englishman, Sir William Holford, a member of the competition jury for Brasília, also suggests it was seen as a departure from the conventional modernist city. Holford claimed that Costa's plan was distinct from the other competitors because it resembled a 'vertebrate animal'. In other words, it was a plan that was thought of in an integral manner as opposed to a simple 'multiplications of parts'.[54]

Observations like this suggest a wholly different interpretation of Brasília to those made later by critics like Tafuri and Frampton, and instead lay stress on Costa's going beyond the functional division of the city and the Corbusian emphasis on circulation systems, and proposing an ordering

of the cityscape based on scales of spatial usage.[55] Within this logic, each urban function creates its own identifiable morphological structure and a corresponding spatial scale: the 'collective-monumental' (the axis where all the public buildings and the seat of government are placed); the 'residential-quotidian' (with its *superquadras* habitation blocks and local services placed around the central axis of circulation); the 'gregarious- concentrated' (with its leisure spaces and meeting points around the crossing of the two main axis); and the 'bucolic' (isolated, and for recreation along the lakeside).

Mário Pedrosa saw Brazil's problem as the lack of an established cultural heritage, and later critics have regarded the works of architects such as Lucio Costa, Oscar Niemeyer and Paulo Mendes da Rocha as all, in one way or another, symptomatic of this same problem. According to Sophia Telles, in Brazil, modern rationalism did not spread onto the urban space but took a more intimate path, but in a way that she calls 'surface drawing'.[56] At the origin of this version of events stands the architect Lucio Costa, educated in a nineteenth-century culture and effectively associated with a lifestyle not yet entirely modern – from this follows his insistence on preserving that 'memory of the colony' in the face of the anonymity imposed by mass society. For Costa, the continuous presence of this 'memory' within the modern project preserved a sense of nature as an untouched entity. He attempted to reduce, as if that were possible, the violence perpetrated by modernity, by keeping design distant from nature, so as to make clear the

impossibility of ever transforming nature into culture. And so, in his work, pre-modern Brazil remained, so to speak, in a state of hibernation.

For Telles, the plan of Brasília rejects a crucial aspect of modern design: the opening of the interior towards the exterior, and the construction of 'the space of sociability based on the equivalence of both terms'. Costa's deliberate separation of interior from exterior – or, one might add, of intimate from monumental – seems to suggest a desire to restrain the tradition of Brazilian sociability, where 'public' and 'private' domains are not clearly demarcated. Telles concludes that Costa's design suggests a transformation of the modern quality of endless space, 'into the image of a continuous surface, one which is prior to any construction, to any differentiation', and which acts as a support for Niemeyer's architecture of flat and exteriorized forms. In other words, the modern city in Brazil is dependent upon its being no-city-at-all: nature remains but it is disenchanted.

What subliminally emerges from then onwards is not the *Sertão*-world, with its uncontrollable raw force and its all-encompassing dimension, but a world of wide and undifferentiated spaces that embrace the city as if replicating the metaphorical image of the modern public space inside them. That is why this 'aerial and road' city, constructed in the middle of the *Sertão*, rather than representing, as Costa claimed, the 'victory of civilization', a 'sign of progress in a new country', emphasizes the isolation of such a modernization, implanted amidst a 'deserted wilderness and exposed to a wide open sky, as if placed in the open sea'.[57]

Lucio Costa, Master Plan, Brasília, 1957. The design concept was based on the crossing of two axes, 'the primary gesture of one who takes possession…the sign of the Cross' (below) which was then adapted to the local topography (bottom). First marks on site (above left) and final competition drawing resembling a 'vertebrate animal' (opposite).

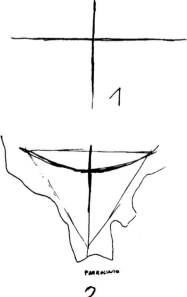

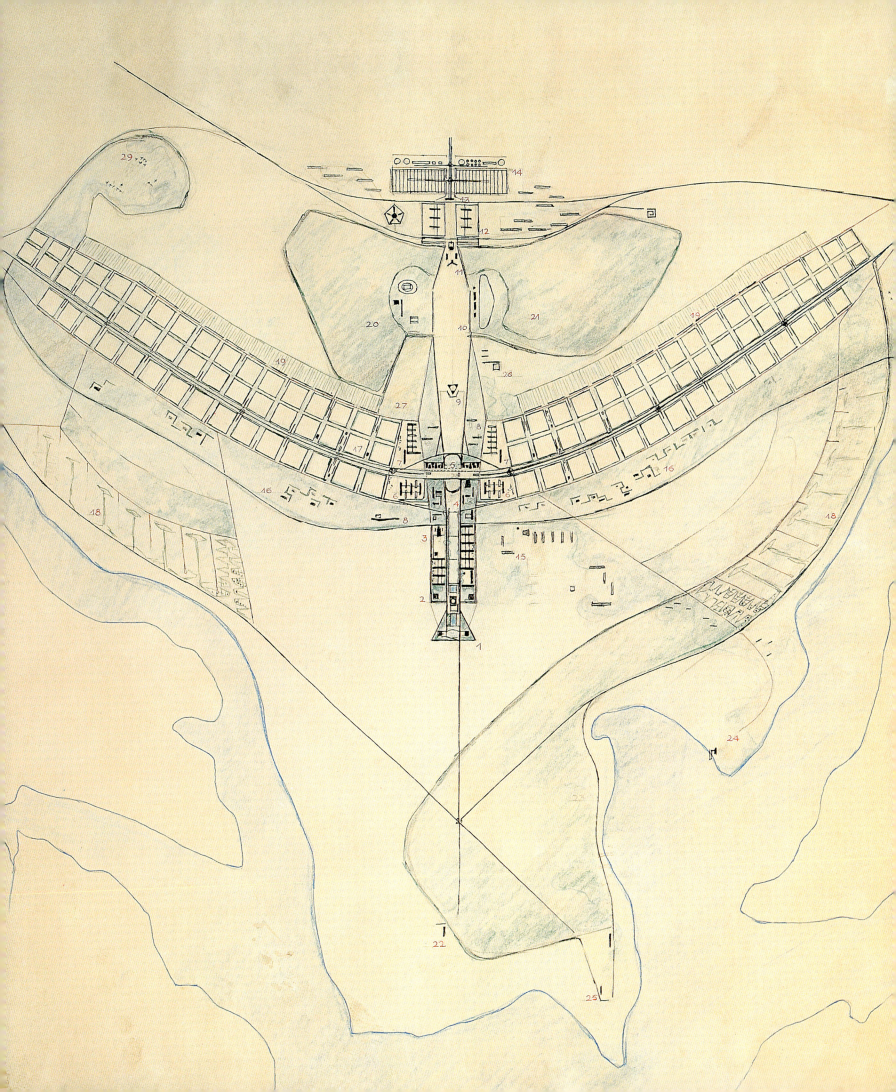

Lucio Costa, Master Plan, Brasília, 1957. Perspective sketch of the Plaza of the Three Powers from the competition presentation (top) and aerial view of the monumental axis (above) showing the Plaza of the Three Powers in construction in the foreground, the Ministries' blocks and the crossing of the residential axis in the background.

Equally, Niemeyer's buildings are figures of a 'suspended technique' over the image of a territory that resists occupation, except that is, for the inclusion of closed forms that clearly define their separation from the landscape at the level of the horizon. What results is an architecture with little urban character, demostrated most obviously by Brasília.

We see imprinted in Brasília the problematic of Brazilian modernization: the persistence of the archaic within the modern, without this archaic 'other' ever becoming the opposite of the modern, as happens in Mexico or in Peru, for example.

In Brazil, old-fashioned patriarchy and the modern avant-garde are not opposed to one another, but instead mingle with each other. Brasília is the ultimate expression of this paradox: its aesthetic refinement has come about not through a resolution of these antagonistic interests, but rather through the superimposition of the one upon the other. In other words, the Brazilian architectural avant-garde emerged outside politics and the formation of citizenship. The fact of being state sponsored does not contradict such a unique circumstance, but on the contrary, it explains it.

Interior territory

From the 1960s, the radically distinctive architecture of São Paulo began to treat the relationship between construction and territory in a novel way.[58] We see 'brutalist' architectural forms with blind facades – for example, the changing rooms at the São Paulo Football Club, and the Faculty of Architecture and Urbanism of the University of São Paulo, both of 1961 – as well as roof coverings supported directly by the building's foundations, such as the boat shelter at the Santa Paula Yacht Club of 1961, and the Brazilian Pavilion at the Osaka World Fair (1969–70).

Developed after Brasília, this *Paulista* 'Brutalism' brought to the insides of buildings attributes of the external environment – water, gardens and sunlight – thus internalizing a sense of the country's natural landscape. While taking into account the various uses expected of the buildings, they seemed to incorporate, by the fluidity of ramps, that continuous surface upon which Brasília was built.[59]

São Paulo's architectural production can be seen as a framing of a new historical moment in the country. If, up until 1960, one could say that Brazilian architecture experimented with various solutions to

Doomed to Modernity

Lucio Costa, Master Plan, Brasília, 1957. Sketch from the competition presentation of the residential sector showing the combination of habitation *superquadra* blocks, local services and vegetation which was planned to form a *vizinhança* or neighbourhood (right) and aerial view of residential sector in the 1960s (above).

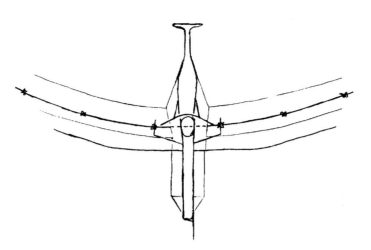

Lucio Costa, Master Plan, Brasília, 1957. South axis with view of the monumental axis in the background (far right). Sketch (top) and aerial view (above) of the crossing of the two axis and bus terminal in the 1960s.
Sketch of the circulation scheme (right) and recent aerial view of the bus terminal with transmission tower in the background (opposite). Recent aerial views of *superquadras* habitation blocks (see p. 46) and the monumental axis (see p. 47).

João Batista Vilanova Artigas, Santa Paula Yacht Club Boat House, São Paulo, 1961. The simple layout of this project included an approach for boats and a single roof-covering for the boat house, offices and a restaurant (top, above right and middle left). The structure was supported on the stone embankment by means of steel and neoprene articulations (above left).

the problem of constituting a modern nation, from then onwards the concerns would be quite different.

Emerging in a city that had grown in an unregulated fashion, it was an introverted architecture. The chaotic and opportunistic context meant that there were few attempts to establish direct and transparent relationships between construction and urban fabric, of the kind that had been so characteristic of the Modern Movement and of *Carioca* production.

We can see this particularly in the comparison of *Paulista* Brutalism and the megastructural experiments in other parts of the world. Whereas, generally, megastructures sought to incorporate all the various aspects of the city within a single building, in São Paulo the attempt was to make the building incorporate the social and physical landscape of Brazil, to make an 'internal geography'.[60]

In São Paulo the idea was to treat any building as if it was a piece of infrastructure, and it is this that connected the city to the international debate on megastructures, as well as giving a political dimension to the phenomenological understanding of the country's territory. Placing his faith in the architectural project as an instrument of political

emancipation and social transformation, Vilanova Artigas proposed a radical change in the status of buildings: even a house would be thought of in the same terms as large public buildings such as viaducts, airports, bus terminals and hydroelectric power stations. In this way, concrete box slabs and girders in pre-stressed reinforced concrete, spanning great lengths, appear as models for industrial production on a national scale.

This opposition to styles and specific solutions was not only manifested in formal terms. Artigas took issue with the other modern architects in São Paulo, such as Oswaldo Bratke, Rino Levi and Miguel Forte, on political grounds, seeing these architects as liberals who were preoccupied with elegant technical solutions to the requirements of a bourgeois project.[61] In changing the status of the built object, the operation undertaken by Artigas was implicitly proposing a wide-ranging project of national development, in which the architect's inventive 'drawing'[62] would mediate between the creative and humanistic intention of the artist and the productive capacity of industrial society.

Having its origins in engineering rather than the fine arts, the architectural profession in São Paulo

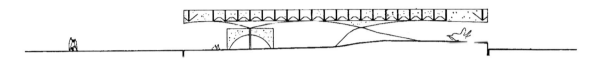

Paulo Mendes da Rocha,
Brazilian Pavillion for
Expo 70, Osaka, Japan, 1969.
A reinforced pre-tensioned
concrete and glass deck is
supported on three points
(top) offered by the sloping
terrain which was modified
to accomodate the pavilion
(above).

demonstrated more technical subtlety than the architects of Rio de Janeiro. Working in this tradition, Artigas made built form expressive of structural behaviour. In this sense, by concerning himself with the building's tectonics he was working in a way entirely opposite to Niemeyer. In Artigas' words, the role of the architect was to exhibit the ideological contradictions implied within the form of his works 'instead of resolving them through a harmonious and smooth fusion'.[63]

Thus his constructional principle was to attempt to indicate clearly the productive process within the finished work. This is apparent in both the brutal treatment of the visible surface of the concrete and in the explicit nature of the mechanics of construction, such as the loads and stresses that determine the design of columns, evident in projects such as his 1961 project for the Anhembí Tennis Club in São Paulo (see p. 78). If one can see in this practice an interpretation of the key principles of international architecture, such as Wright's 'truth to materials' and the 'ethic of construction' of English Brutalism, there is also present the outline of a very individual point of view: the affirmation of national sovereignty based upon the use of one's own technology and ability to express the local conditions of production and labour. In other words, it represents a conscious recourse to an economy of means similar in attitude to *Arte Povera*. It is nevertheless put in place through a Third World lens, which has its parallel in Glauber Rocha's notion of an 'aesthetic of hunger', employed within *Cinema Novo* (see p. 180, n. 8).

However, while the political radicalism of Artigas' approach would lead towards the critical and built work of Sérgio Ferro, Flávio Império and Rodrigo Lefèvre, a closer approximation with popular culture occurs in the works of Lina Bo Bardi. Artigas himself systematically avoided references to popular culture, firmly maintaining his conviction that for a work to be transformative it should arise from the 'drawing' produced by a technical expertise capable of defining the directives of Brazil's development. This was an attitude that was backed by the Brazilian Communist Party, with its aim of 'constructing a country' through the development of its productive forces.[64]

The *Paulista* version of Brazilian architecture thus grew radically introverted as it became preoccupied with issues that, to foreign eyes, no longer had any relation whatsoever to the pursuit of a 'national style'. Isolating itself from the international debate, this architecture inaugurated a new phase where, in the words of Sérgio Ferro, 'vanity led us to believe we already had our own route. Therefore our interest lay in developing this route further rather than searching for new sources and contacts outside.'[65]

With the military coup of 1964, and the hardening of the regime in 1968, architectural culture became increasingly xenophobic. As this happened, the ties with foreign critical debate were gradually cut, both by the dogmatic exclusion of all non-Brazilian issues and by the smothering of internal debate through the persecution of university lecturers, the imprisonment and exile of key architects and the closure of specialized journals.

Although the economy was to benefit from this centralized and authoritarian regime, it was achieved at the cost of an increase of social inequality and a heightening of the discrepancy between the country's modernity and its backwardness – developments that, while they increased the country's capital, failed to distribute the benefits of industrialization more widely.

Thus, while architecture aspired to a level of intervention compatible with the scale of economic development led by the state, its actions were not effective.[66] In particular, this model of development was incapable of confronting the increasing problems of large cities and their emergent peripheries, which started to become central questions during the 1970s.

It must be admitted that the avant-gardist architecture of São Paulo had a limited presence not only in other large Brazilian cities, but even within the state-capital São Paulo itself – a situation that was partly the result of the military government's repression, and partly due to the character of the architecture itself. Physically distancing itself from the urban surroundings, but metonymically reconstituting them within its buildings, *Paulista* Brutalism embodied a fundamental negativity while attempting to create laboratories for a new sociability.

Its most effective action could be said to have been the attempt to urbanize, in the private sphere, bourgeois domestic life and, in the public sphere, universities and secondary schools. However, given its negativity and its un-cosmopolitan nature, *Paulista* Brutalism was a long way from representing, as Niemeyer's architecture did, a public and urban domain.

But was it not exactly this dilemma, as to whether to represent an ideal of public social life or whether to refuse it, that was elaborated over and over again in Brazilian architecture's experience of modernity? Let us return, therefore, to Argan's acute remarks, presenting this process as a fluctuation between the necessary attempt to create universal standards and the voluntary affirmation of individual exceptions, or, in his words, a 'mixture between the functional and the representative'. Returning to this idea, one can see Brazilian architecture's tendency towards the formalization of technique as the tradition that best expresses its dialectical aspiration. This same formalization of the technical was synthesized by Artigas in the serial structural porticos he used in many of his works, such as the Mário Taques Bitencourt House (see p. 162) and the Itanhaém High

João Batista Vilanova Artigas, Itanhaém High School, Itanhaém, 1959. One porticoed stucture accommodates three different areas (classrooms, administration and services) and open air grounds.

(both of 1959 in São Paulo). We see here a tradition of construction that had its origins in Rio de Janeiro, extended and prolonged.

In the treatment of the portico, a structural element that contained both the constructional and aesthetic aspect of a building, the intrinsic character of concrete was transformed into a continuous malleable mass. This symbolic condensation that made, out of the structural flexibility of the construction, a powerful aesthetic unity was one of the most noticeable achievements of the more rigorous projects by Niemeyer and Reidy, culminating in 1953 in the building of the Museum of Modern Art (MAM) in Rio de Janeiro (see p. 64). In this case, such was the clarity of its aesthetic and construction that the work became at the same time self-referential, owing to the clear exhibition of its own procedures, and modular, due to its serial, generic and prototypical nature.

It is interesting to note how the aesthetic unity of Reidy's work was achieved through the process of the design rather than through a preconceived ideal. Such a route becomes obvious when the MAM is compared with the Brazil-Paraguay Experimental School (1952–65), started the previous year in Asunción, Paraguay. There, in the main building, Reidy made use of the portico structure in a way very similar to that of the museum. However, it was still essentially a Functionalist design, in which the north and south facades were treated differently according to the exposure to sunlight: the south face consisted of a glass-wall supported by a conventional beam-column structure, whereas the north face, which needed to be screened from the

sun, was protected by the protruding portico, which acted both as eaves and generous structural *brise-soleil*, leading to the building's asymmetry.

By contrast, at the MAM such a distinction was abandoned in favour of an organizing structural principle for the building as a whole, giving it an identical treatment on both facades, thus stressing technique rather than function.

Today one can say that an exaggerated structural formalism is still a strong characteristic of contemporary Brazilian architecture. It re-emerges in the most recent work of various architects and, above all, in that of Paulo Mendes da Rocha. Da Rocha is the most important representative of a generation that emerged from Brutalism and continued to develop its legacy. The structural portico is employed in his work both in a direct and affirmative manner, which is the case of the Avaré Forum (1962) and the Boulevard des Sports project (2000) for the Paris 2008 Olympic Games, and in a more subtle and almost disfunctionalized manner, with two columns and a beam enclosing a subterranean construction, in the Brazilian Museum of Sculpture, 1988. In both cases, his work creates a tension with the contradictions of Brazilian architecture: the fact that it is isolated as well as overdeveloped. Mendes da Rocha, seemingly immune to the criticism of Brazilian modernism, especially during the 1980s, refined an architectural language in which structural formalism ceases to be didactic since it no longer conveys a morality of construction.

The 'heroic years' of Brazil's modern architecture are left behind, but its capacity for debate is renewed, allowing for a critical assessment of the modern

Affonso Eduardo Reidy, Brazil-Paraguay Experimental School, Asunción, Paraguay, 1952-65. Perspective showing the classroom block, auditorium and gymnasium (below). Access ramp to the second floor (bottom right) and detail of brise-soleil (bottom left). North (opposite middle) and south facade (opposite top), and section of auditorium and gymnasium with view of south facade (opposite bottom).

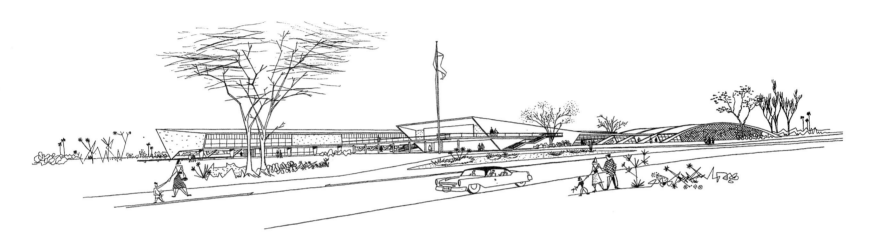

Doomed to Modernity

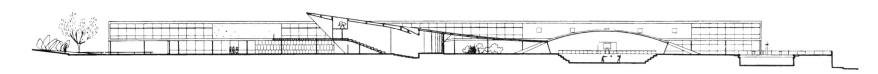

O museu da escultura e da ecologia será visto como um jardim, com uma sombra, e um teatro ao ar livre, rebaixado no recinto...

Paulo Mendes da Rocha, Brazilian Museum of Sculpture, São Paulo, 1985–95. Conceptual sketch (opposite below left) showing the museum as 'a garden with shade...a sunken open-air theatre'. A pre-stressed concrete portico frames the site, circumscribing the esplanade (above and opposite below right), courtyard (opposite top), and entrance and exhibition space (above right).

legacy. However, unlike North American Deconstructivism, it does not challenge the codes of architecture, nor does it resort to a topical or typological contextualism, as in the case of European Historicism. Viewing the city more as built landscape than as historical sedimentation, Mendes da Rocha aims to open a dialogue with nature in his projects. It is not an inactive nature, to be contemplated as in a still life, but an ever transforming 'nature-project', that retains the traces of human activity.[67] The construction of an artificial landscape, in projects such as the Brazilian Pavilion for the Osaka World Fair or the Museum of Sculpture, always bears the expressive signs of human presence. A pillar formed by two arches placed between artificial mounds, in the first case, forming a canopy that marks the building's 'presence-absence'; in the second case, emphasizing the public nature of the museum. Thus, his architecture has the ability to 'make us see' new spatial configurations by relational scale devices marked on the site. That appears to be the most obvious explanation for the horizontal slab at the Museum of Sculpture. Running parallel to the street, it traverses the whole site and, like a measurement

tool, demarcates the building with a recognizable, almost tactile, dimension: the domestic scale of the space under this concrete canopy. Here is an architecture that would rather be opportune than functional.

Brazilian architecture's highest achievement has been to make a theme out of its own paradox, that is the inconsistency between a highly developed engineering and construction industry – predominantly that of concrete – and an oligarchic society that has systematically resisted mass production and a widespread distribution of durable goods. Given the inadequate infrastructure for serial production, the most rigorous strand of Functionalism never found its ground in the country. Brazil's modern architecture conceptualizes this shift: its technical climax, formal liberty and structural formalism critically reflect this lack of ground – simultaneously expressing but also sublimating it; and in the best projects, turning it into its creative catalyst.

CHAPTER TWO
TROPICAL TECTONICS
BY ROBERTO CONDURU

Oscar Niemeyer, Museum
of Contemporary Art, Niterói,
1991–6. Situated 15 km
south of Rio de Janeiro,
the museum's sculptural
shape was inspired by the
architect's appreciation
of the surrounding natural
landscape.

TROPICAL TECTONICS

By the time the first works of modern architecture were being built in Brazil in the late 1920s, it was clear that there was a discrepancy between the ideas about construction articulated by Modern Movement architects and apologists, and the actual conditions of production available in the country. This discrepancy was to be a persistent feature of Brazilian architecture in the twentieth century and, despite the hope and expectation that it would disappear, it has stubbornly remained. Rather than presenting this gap between ideal and reality as an obstacle to be removed, as has so often been the case in the past, it might be more useful to accept it as a permanent feature: one that will never and, indeed, should never disappear. Instead of seeing it as a shortcoming, for which excuses have to be made, a more positive account of Brazilian architecture would acknowledge the discrepancy between constructional ideals and the reality of building as a normal and permanent state of affairs. Consequently, one could reconsider some of the more common twentieth-century assumptions about the processes of development and modernization in non-Western societies, and see that Brazil might offer an important but hitherto under-appreciated legacy to other parts of the world.

During the 1940s, foreign critics praised the Brazilian experience for the skill architects showed in adapting European and North American principles to the climatic, social and technical peculiarities of the country. In making these adaptations, Brazilian architects demonstrated a sophisticated understanding of the elements of modern architecture, causing their work to be recognized abroad and generating some surprise there. In particular, Brazilian architecture was marked both by an understanding of the modernist premise that new work should contain a critique of previous work, and the tendency, just emerging in countries like Finland in the late 1930s, of resistance to the idea of a single, universal model of an International Style for modern architecture. Foreign acclaim for the new Brazilian architecture was due in part to the expectation held in Europe and North America, and internalized within some sections of Brazilian culture, that, when the rational principles of Modernism were applied under local conditions, the result would be a variant of the original model, rather than wholly new forms. Although the work of some architects in Brazil conformed to this pattern, there were others who developed distinctively new forms that could not be seen as having evolved from the international model. Brazil's modern architecture, therefore, included designs that accepted the prevailing International Style, as well as those that were explicitly critical of its methods: it embraced a wide range of work with a variety of technological approaches and structural configurations, and with widely different attitudes towards the conditions of production and the reception of architecture.

Part of the story of Brazilian architecture is, therefore, an account of the way building technologies developed elsewhere were accepted, modified, or rejected outright when introduced into Brazil; and, in one respect, Brazilian architecture is about the hopes, the expectations and the disappointments that have accompanied these processes.

Gregori Warchavchik, House in Santa Cruz Street, São Paulo, 1929–30. The first house to be built in the new Modernist style, its clean, white facade (above left and top) hid the use of vernacular materials, such as the tiles on the back veranda (above right).

Fictions of mass production

Although during the early twentieth century Brazil produced few technical, artistic or social breakthroughs, the initial works by the pioneers of modern architecture in the country adopted the universal language of European architectural Modernism. This design vocabulary was thought to best express the logic of serial mass production, the aesthetic parameters of the artistic avant-gardes and the requirements of mass culture.

In order to establish, in a partially modernized society, an architecture of industrial, abstract and international appearance, the rationalist premises of this original European model were often reduced to mere images of a foreign way of thinking. The fascination with the latest technical and artistic achievements, combined with an eagerness to appear 'modern' and a complacency about the issue of social inequalities, produced buildings that, while appearing to be the result of industrial methods, betrayed their handicraft origins all too readily. Such buildings were just as much artificial socio-technical creations as those in the eclectic style to which they were opposed. In an effort to dissociate themselves completely from the

Beaux Arts tradition that still dominated Brazilian culture, the modernists did not pursue those late nineteenth-century architectural developments that had exploited new systems of construction. Earlier experiments with iron, such as the various projects by Adolfo Morales de Los Rios for public markets (1891–1919), or with reinforced concrete, such as the Mairinque Railway Station (1905-08) in São Paulo, designed by Victor Dubugras, were not followed up by Brazil's pioneer modernists.

The first indication of an awareness of the aesthetic possibilities of new materials occurs in one of the manifestos of the new architecture. Gregori Warchavchik in 1925 repeated the slogans of the time, proposing a new style of monumentality and praising 'the machines for living':

Just as the skeleton of such a building could be a characteristic monument of modern architecture, the same could be said of reinforced concrete bridges and other purely constructive works in the same material. And these buildings, once finished, would really be the monuments of the art of our age were it not for the work of the construction engineer being subsequently replaced by that of

Tropical Tectonics

Álvaro Vital Brazil, Esther building, São Paulo, 1935–8. Including residental units as wells as shops and offices, this was one of the first projects where the distinction between load-bearing and space delimitating elements was made. In this view, the Esther building stands to the left of the Arthur building, also by the same architect (above).

the architect decorator. It is at this point where in the name of ART, art begins to be sacrificed.[1]

However, Warchavchik's early buildings do not exhibit this new sensibility to the tectonic possibilities of bare structure, and his own house is evidence of some of the difficulties encountered in the process of implementing the new architecture in Brazil. Here, he adapted technical and formal ideals from rationalist architecture to the local climatic and construction conditions: the flat concrete slab, symbolizing the technical progress of modernity, was supplanted on the side and back verandas by a ceramic tile roof, a symptom of local backwardness that was, however, hidden by the main facade, which made the building appear as if symmetrical and composed of smooth flat planes.

Constructional principles, although present in what architects said and wrote, were rarely transcribed into the building's aesthetics. Reinforced concrete was used to produce designs whose combination of pure volumes was derived from both the Beaux-Arts tradition and the machine-age aesthetic, rather than out of a direct application of the principles of mass manufacture.

This was an architecture whose apparent rationality was grounded not in the logic of industrial production but on aesthetic principles.

At first, the visible emphasis on structural components had been approached cautiously, and it was exceptional for load-bearing elements to be given prominence. According to Paulo Santos, the beginning of the second phase of modernist architecture in Brazil came in 1935 and was marked by the 'implementation of the *independent structure* and Le Corbusier's *brise-soleil*.[2] From this date a sequence of buildings revealed an understanding of the distinction between load-bearing and space-defining elements, among them the Esther Building (1935) by Álvaro Vital Brazil and Adhemar Marinho, the headquarters of the Brazilian Press Association (1936) by Marcelo and Milton Roberto, the Ministry of Education and Health (1936) by Lucio Costa and team, and the Seaplane Terminal (1937) by Attilio Corrêa Lima. The configuration of these buildings, however, continued to rely on the functionalist analogy between building and machine; the junctions between the parts were made to appear as if they resulted from a process of industrial

assembly. Connecting elements, for example, disappeared behind unifying planes, and these, in turn, were subsumed into regular prisms, generating abstract volumes and taking machine aesthetics to an urban scale. Architects focused on forms rather than the means of construction, and only from the 1950s onwards was there a return to a greater emphasis upon the tectonic.

In this way, most designs either ignored or concealed the inherent contradictions of modern architecture in Brazil. The features giving rise to these contradictions were as follows: the almost exclusive identification of architects with the élite and the state apparatus; the dependency on imported construction materials, building components and equipment; the simulated machine-made appearance of buildings constructed by handicraft methods and their consequent high cost; and the employment of poorly educated, or illiterate, people in the production of apparent technical sophistication.

However, although these buildings with their pretensions of universality suggested a wish to become more fully a part of Western culture, they could also be critical of this aspiration. The idea that architecture alone would transform social relations and improve the local standard of life could never be more than a hope, but architects, by making use of and collaborating in the development of new construction technologies, particularly that of concrete, were able to participate in the process of modernization. Architecture thus became the symbolic framework

for the changes undertaken by Brazilian society, and the masterpieces of the Modern Movement in the country serve as signifiers of Brazilian progress.

The persistence of strictly rationalist architecture throughout the twentieth century in Brazil also implied the refusal to provide the exotic image expected of a South American country, or to play the part of 'other' to the West. Yet this determination to affirm themselves as part of Western civilization often led designers on to the fetishistic use of forms, materials and techniques of construction, giving rise to an architecture whose mimetic tendencies betrayed it as provincial. It is possible, however, to point to other, albeit less common, architectural approaches that were more pragmatic, or more critical of technology.

A unique example, modelled after the ideals of social transformation through new forms and methods of production, was developed by Luiz Nunes, together with the government of the state of Pernambuco, between 1934 and 1937. This was an exceptional, almost revolutionary, occurrence, where a public administration turned towards collective interests. A team of architects, engineers, technicians and artists constructed a series of public buildings (including those for health and education, supply stations and police headquarters) through the adaptation of rationalist principles to tropical conditions, developing existing techniques, enhancing local construction methods and rationalizing the process of construction. Within an architecture of multiple contemporaneous references (to Le Corbusier, Oud and Gropius amongst others), the tectonic character of these

Luiz Nunes, projects for the state of Pernambuco: Water Tower, 1937 (above) and Alberto Torres Rural School, 1935 (opposite below). These varied works already show an initial understanding of the distinction between load-bearing and space-defining elements.

Affonso Eduardo Reidy, Brazil-Paraguay Experimental School, Asunción, Paraguay, 1952–65. Commissioned by the Brazilan government as a gift to the people of Paraguay, it was built on an elevated site overlooking the countryside. The side facade of the main block under construction (opposite above) clearly shows how the structure determined the assymetrical outline of the building.

Tropical Tectonics

buildings was emphasized both as the means of political changes and as the sign for those changes. However, this process sometimes led to excesses, where the image exceeded the actual social benefits offered by the project. The honest expression of the supporting elements at the Military Hospital (1935) and the Water Tower in Olinda slides into grandiloquence at the Alberto Torres Rural School (1935), where the access ramp's supporting arches were exaggerated in relation to the scale of the building.

Affonso Eduardo Reidy widened the limits of rationalism through the architecture that he developed between 1930 and 1960, primarily for the municipality of Rio de Janeiro. Although he never had the opportunity to deal with the urban problem as a whole, Reidy explored the formal possibilities of contemporary construction systems, and continually searched for a balance between functional requirements and the social implications of each programme. During the mid-1930s, he began to emphasize the dialectical relationship between load-bearing systems and space-defining elements, following the example established by Le Corbusier. For the school and gymnasium of the Pedregulho Housing Complex (1950–2) Reidy produced expansive volumes by juxtaposing flat, curved and oblique planes with *pilotis*, arches and vaults. Here, as well as in other works, such as the Carmen Portinho House (1950) in Rio de Janeiro (see p. 151), the supporting elements were hidden inside, creating external planes and volumes that encroached upon their surroundings in centrifugal configurations. Such a spatial architecture reaches its peak at the classroom block of the Brazil-

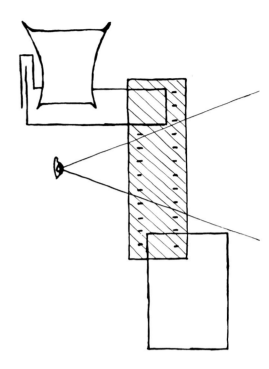

Affonso Eduardo Reidy, Museum of Modern Art, Rio de Janeiro, 1953. This 1960s aerial view (above left) of Flamengo Park designed by Roberto Burle Marx and built on reclaimed land, shows the museum's remarkable natural surroundings. In order to visually integrate his project with the surrounding landscape and the gardens designed by Burle Marx (top and opposite), Reidy raised the main block on *pilotis* (see plan, above right), making the structural system its main visual component, as this view of the interior in construction shows (right).

Paraguay Experimental School (see p. 52) built in 1952 in Paraguay, where the exposed concrete gives the building an autonomous formal quality, expressing its constructional character, while the relationship between the structural and the space-defining elements is articulated in true modernist manner. On the facade facing the interior of the complex, the load-bearing elements retreat from the plane of the elevation while, on the opposite facade, the asymmetric V-shaped pillar connects to the rooftop beam delineating the profile of the volume.

Soon afterwards, continuing the same approach of combining genuinely innovative constructional technology with modernist formal devices, Reidy designed the Museum of Modern Art (1953) in Rio de Janeiro. Situated in public gardens designed by Roberto Burle Marx, next to the old town and against the background of lush vegetation, this project took into account the changes in the concept of the museum taking place at the time, as well as the specific demands of the city's cultural and artistic milieu. The primary visual component of the museum's main block was its structural system, which was shifted from the interior to the exterior of the building. Here, and at Reidy's own Week-End House (1959) in Itaipava, the space-defining elements were withdrawn from the exterior, becoming contained within the load-bearing framework, which is what dominated the outline of the building. In these projects the volumes were concentrated internally, emphasizing their centripetal character. This inward movement implied a reference to Mies van der Rohe's approach

and represents the architect's appreciation of the limits of modernist form in creating an optimistic and expansive social architecture.

Therefore, what we see in Brazilian architecture is a continuous vacillation between the expression of industrialized production and, in compensation for the absence of that industrialization, the pursuit of formal originality. Such concerns were not unknown in Europe and North America, though there were more realistic expectations there than in Brazil of fully industrialized building production eventually being realized.

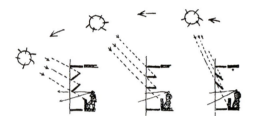

Rationalism adapted

In the Brazilian architecture of the mid-1930s there soon appeared a critical awareness of the need to adapt the principles of the Modern Movement both to the climatic variety within such a vast country and to its technical, artistic and social inadequacies.

As a response to the climate and as a reaction to the monotony of rationalist architecture, Le Corbusier's *brise-soleil* seemed to be the perfect solution: it allowed the control of sunlight within while animating the surfaces without, even though it was contradictory and costly to glaze an entire facade, only to cover it with light-controlling elements. The Roberto brothers explored the possibilities of sun-breakers, using grilles that were set apart from the planes of the facade to filter the air, optimize luminosity and create a dynamic composition from the building's planes and volumes. However, from the 1950s onwards further experimentation along this line was curtailed by the house-building industry, whose attempt to

simplify construction and cut costs led to the use of other, mechanical means of controlling temperature and light.

The facades of Lucio Costa's three residential buildings at Guinle Park (1948–54) in Rio de Janeiro represent a specific interpretation of the concept of *brise-soleil* (see p. 122). As a version of the modern grille rendered in the style of Brazilian colonial architecture, they were the architect's way of circumventing industrial inadequacies and answering criticisms regarding the rootlessness of modern architecture. For Costa, there was an essential affinity between traditional Brazilian and rationalist architecture, on account of the similarities between the wattle-and-daub and reinforced-concrete systems, especially since both technologies distinguish between load-bearing and space-defining elements. This, according to Costa, justified the development of modern architecture in the country and allowed for the reconciliation of modernizing and conservative projects, then in conflict within Brazilian society.

Adapting the rationalism developed in Europe during the 1920s – and more specifically through his appreciation of the vernacular traditions within Le Corbusier's works, such as the Villa de Mandrot – Lucio Costa developed, during the mid-1930s, a proposal for the reconciliation of tradition and modernity that would resolve these technical-social contradictions both culturally and symbolically. Appropriating artisanal materials and techniques such as ceramics and mud-hut construction, as well as colonial architectural elements such as inclined roofs and *muxarabis*,[3]

Lucio Costa and team, Ministry of Education and Health, Rio de Janeiro, 1936-45. Following a suggestion by Le Corbusier, movable sun-breakers were developed for the north facade. With this mechanism (above left) the amount and quality of light entering the building could be controlled (above).

Lucio Costa, Guinle Park residential buildings, Rio de Janeiro, 1948 (Nova Cintra), 1950 (Bristol), 1954 (Caledônia). View of the west facade of the Bristol and Caledônia buildings, protected by a combination of sun-breakers and hollow bricks (opposite).

Tropical Tectonics

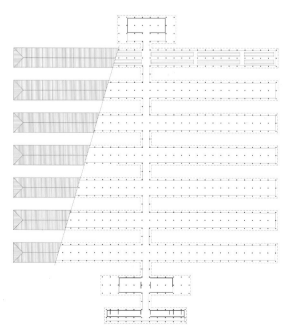

Álvaro Vital Brazil,
Shelters for SEMTA
(Workers' Transport System),
North East region, 1943.
Due to the German naval
blockade during Word War II,
the transport of workers
between regions had to rely
on a terrestrial network for
which these posts were
designed. The shelters
(opposite and above left)
were built using local
materials and construction
techniques, following a
modular logic (right).

Francisco Bologna,
Hildebrando Accioly House,
Rio de Janeiro, 1949–50.
Two views showing the
combination of a wooden
structural system with stone
and concrete (above right
and top right).

he outlined a style that responded to the demands
for the creation of a national modern art and
architecture – one that was obviously Brazilian in
conception, production and use.

With a series of works with traditional elements
such as the Hungria Machado (1943) and Paes
de Carvalho (1944) Houses (see pp. 146-7), Costa
opened up a wide-ranging experiment to which
various architects contributed. This experiment was
developed, above all, in residential projects realized
with sophisticated craftsmanship, but also showed
itself capable of application to other programmes
with different technical and financial conditions.
Projects such as the Park Hotel São Clemente (1944)
by Costa, and the Accioly House (1949-1950) by
Francisco Bologna explored the picturesque charm
of the wooden structural system. At the Grande Hotel
(1940) in Ouro Preto by Oscar Niemeyer, the Holiday
Complex of the Insurance Institute of Brazil (1943) by
the Roberto brothers, and the Guinle Park buildings,
characteristics reminiscent of old Brazilian
architecture were combined with structural systems
in reinforced concrete. Francisco Bologna at the
Paquetá Residential Complex (1947) and Carlos Leão
at houses in Samambaia (1940s) emphasized how

Carlos Leão, Weekend house for a fisherman, Cabo Frio, 1943. Using adobe bricks, artisanal tiles and other commonplace materials, as he had done in his houses in Samambaia, Leão portrayed in this project images of Brazil's colonial architecture (above).

Carlos Leão, Homero Souza e Silva House, Cabo Frio, 1961. Plan, elevation and section for the housekeeper's house and garage (right).

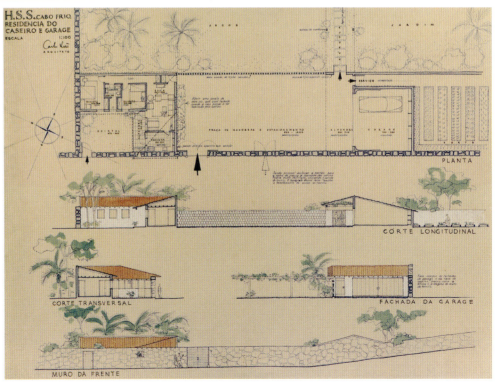

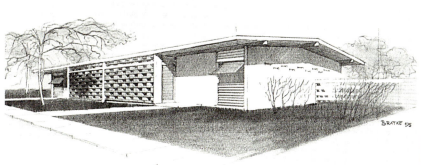

the past could be evoked through ordinary and cheap materials in, respectively, an abstract or a figurative manner.[4]

There were, however, other ways of adapting rationalism, through the use of material and methods of construction. More pragmatic approaches to the prevailing construction methods – themselves not yet fully industrialized – that, at the same time, rejected references to the past, resulted in a body of work which, however, had less obvious visual appeal and received less attention from the media and critics. During World War II, Vital Brazil designed shelters for the Workers' Transport Service in the Amazon region (1943), where the sharp contrast between the rigorously modulated orthogonal form and local conditions (labour, materials[5] and construction techniques) was evident.

In the designs for the Levi (1944), Guper (1951) and Hesse (1952) Houses in São Paulo, Rino Levi made use of ordinary materials (masonry bricks, fibrous cement tiles and hollow clay blocks) in simple and introverted configurations that were a domestication of Brazilian nature. He structured these projects around internal courtyards, creating

a close link between the sheltered spaces and the gardens, the result of his research into the varied natural habitats of Brazil. With small openings, and forms that were not obviously modern, his houses had an unassuming presence in the city. This focus on the interior, however, was not anti-urban: in these projects for a city that was already growing and deteriorating, Rino Levi intended to integrate its inhabitants with nature (see p. 156).

At the Serra do Navio (1955-1960) and Amazonas (1955-1960) villages of Amapá, in the equatorial region of Amazonas, Oswaldo Bratke took the local climatic and cultural conditions, into account, in both design and construction, without compromising the constructivist rigour of his previous works.

During the 1950s, when developmentalist (see p. 37) concepts were being propagated in Brazil, universal internationalism was more suited to the prevailing political ideology, and the regionalist trend was partially eclipsed not to resurface until the 1960s, when it spread with increasing force throughout the country for the rest of the century.

Illustrative of this tendency is the use of timber in the work of São Paulo architects Carlos Milan and Joaquim Guedes during the 1960s, although their

Oswaldo Bratke, Serra do Navio Village, Amapá, 1955–60. This urban settlement was located in the heart of the Amazon forest and accommodated the workers of a newly opened mine (top). The design of the housing units took into account climatic conditions, adapting modern ideals to the availabe materials and construction techniques (above and above left).

Severiano Mario Porto, Manaus Free Trade Zone, Manaus, Amazonas, 1980–9. The use of reinforced concrete was adapted to shelter the building's users from the climate. Large truncated pyramids allowed hot air to escape naturally through the roof.

Tropical Tectonics

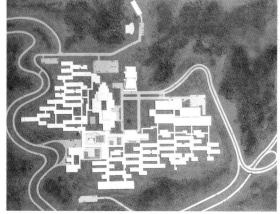

Severiano Mario Porto, University of Amazonas, Manaus, Amazonas, 1973–86. Located near the forest, the design of the campus was adapted to the sloping terrain and the hot and humid climatic conditions of the equatorial region. Each building was insulated by a double-deck roof (above) and in turn strategically placed in relation to the other units to provide sheltered open-air spaces and enhance ventilation, as shown in this site model (above right).

choice came more as a response to each project's construction possibilities and requirements than from any longing for the past.

In Pernambuco, Gil Borsoi coordinated an experiment in 1963 with mud-hut prefabrication as a way of improving housing conditions and making use of the local community's knowledge and participation. This project, however, was interrupted following the military coup of 1964.

Although an evocation of the past still persisted in works by Leão and Bologna in Rio de Janeiro, their dominant factor was the construction process itself, a debt to Brutalism and its emphasis on structural expression. During the following decades, originating in Rio de Janeiro, two figures in particular would stand out for this tendency to develop construction with traditional materials: José Zanine Caldas and Severiano Mário Porto.

Zanine's main contribution was his use of Brazilian wood. Although there had been research on its possible applications, and it had briefly been developed for the prefabrication of furniture and for social housing, indigenous timber was primarily used as a luxury material in the construction of houses for the élite. Zanine himself was committed

to high-quality craftsmanship, and to exploring the construction potential and sensory qualities of the material. He made use of geometric and unusual details in creating highly appealing graphic patterns, spaces and volumes that were influential for subsequent residential architecture.

Porto is known for his use of untreated timber, but is mainly notable for his respect for the full range of the Amazon region's bio-climatic factors, and for his use of a variety of materials and techniques (not only timber) in response to specifically local conditions. The wooden roofs in many of his projects, the reinforced ceramic vaults at the Activities Centre of the Industrial Social Service (1977) in Fortaleza and the reinforced concrete dome at the headquarters of the Manaus Free Trade Zone (1980–9) revealed the use of different construction systems that could be combined, as was the case in the campus of the University of Amazonas (1973-1986). He gave this special attention to roof forms in order to generate areas of ventilated shade. The overall emphasis was at times tectonic-pragmatic and at other times formal-symbolic: while his project for telephony stations (1984) in the Amazon prioritized bio-

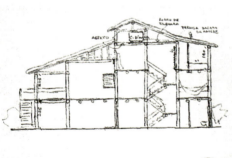

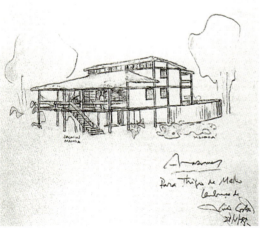

climatic issues, the available materials and the possibilities of construction, projects such as the hotel at Silves Island (1979-83) and the Balbina Environmental Centre (1983-8) display a formal fluency and, at the same time, a backward-looking reference both to *ocas* (indigenous structures) in the first case and to Niemeyer's curves in the latter.

A taste for the alternative and the rustic has spread across Brazil in the last few decades. This was stimulated by environmental preservation campaigns, by a reaction against the widespread use of reinforced-concrete building systems and by the re-emergence of the regionalist ideal on the international scene. From the Atlantic to the Amazon forests, from Curitiba to the Parnaíba Delta, in a more or less experimental way, whether figurative or not, the development of a regional, artisanal and ecological architecture has taken place. It has developed in different ways, taking greater or lesser account of local peculiarities, following a path opened by Costa, Bologna, Zanine and Porto, whose works were taken by subsequent architects as sources of principles or forms.[6]

In the Amazon, this tendency was developed both by its initiator Costa, who explored the possibilities of the wooden load-bearing system in the houses he designed for Thiago de Mello (1978), and by a younger generation that expanded this formal repertoire through the reinterpretation of the rooftop as a key element of the building. José Castro Filho, Octacílio Teixeira, Milton Monte and Paulo Sérgio Nascimento responded to the climatic conditions of the region in a more or less abstract manner, always emphasizing rustic craftsmanship.

In the south-west, the main emphasis was on structural elements and their prefabrication. Sérgio Rodrigues minimized the hand-made look of his buildings by using low-tech standard elements, which reduced costs, speeded up construction and made possible a variety of forms reminiscent of Constructivism as well as Western and Oriental vernacular precedents. From the 1980s onwards, Marcos Acayaba explored with greater dynamism the formal possibilities of timber as a construction system. Taking into account issues of cost and practicality, he designed sophisticated spaces and volumes derived from patterns created by the supporting elements.

Despite recent increased use, the challenge posed by the architectural employment of timber

Lucio Costa, Thiago de Mello House, Barreirinha, 1978. A timber structure framed a modern layout of uninterrupted spaces, both vertically and horizontally, as the section and perspective drawings show (opposite below). Partition walls were built in brick and openings were covered with fabric.

Marcos Acayaba, Hélio Olga House, São Paulo, 1987–90. General view of the building showing its adaptation to the surrounding terrain (opposite above) and details of the interface between timber, concrete and steel (left).

Tropical Tectonics

Oscar Niemeyer, Mondadori Headquarters, Milan, Italy, 1968. The long facades, treated with a pattern of arches following an irregular rhythm, support the roof slab from where the five office floors are suspended.

still remains. Abundant in Brazilian forests, wood continues to be applied as a sign of distinction in the houses of the élite, as an auxiliary and finishing material in reinforced-concrete buildings, or as basic building material for huts in the *favelas* (shanty towns) where it is replaced as quickly as possible by reinforced concrete and bricks. Although important, none of the few research projects on the potential of timber as a construction material has had much impact on the industrialization of building, nor managed to infiltrate the social-housing sector.

From critique through form, to critique through production

In 1944, with the four projects he designed in Pampulha (see p. 118), Oscar Niemeyer introduced the new architecture that he had been searching for since the end of the 1930s. Distancing himself from the strict rationalism of his initial projects, such as the Rio de Janeiro Crèche of 1937, and from the reconciliation of modernity and tradition present in some of his works, such as the Grande Hotel in Ouro Preto, at Pampulha Niemeyer made clear the possibilities of formal invention through contemporary construction techniques. In the terms of the link Costa had established between old and new construction systems, Niemeyer associated wattle-and-daub with steel construction, which only allowed for 'simple, rigid and cold' solutions. Instead, he felt that the inherent freedom of reinforced-concrete better conveyed the Z*eitgeist*.[7] By exploring the formal potential of reinforced concrete – one could even say making

the case for it – and by playing with Corbusian and Miesian references, Niemeyer devoted himself to creating unusual, daring and even totally new forms that challenged structural mathematics, and surprised the world.

In a 1958 self-critique, which was also a response to foreign criticisms of Brazil's modern architecture, Niemeyer suggested that he had been searching for 'a simplification of the aesthetic form and its balance between issues of function and construction', as well as an appropriate expression for buildings with 'their own structure, adequately integrated within the original formal concept'.[8] The majority of his projects began to take advantage of structural elements (columns, arcades, porticos, beams, slabs, vaults and domes) based on the technical challenges and the formal possibilities of reinforced concrete. However, their final configuration always resulted from a formal arbitrariness originating in Niemeyer's own imagination.

At the Pampulha Ballroom (1942) the distribution of columns was free and arbitrary. At the Alvorada Palace (1957-8), the arcade was arbitrarily interrupted, and at the headquarters of the Mondadori Publishing Company (1968) in Milan there was a variation in the width of the arches. These buildings were characterized by a manipulation of structural elements that resembled musical notes composing new chords, rhythms and melodies. Although he acknowledged how little modern architecture was concerned with the country's basic economic and social problems, Niemeyer did not substantially alter his production, satisfied with the creation of designs that were

merely symbolic of a more just society. In his understanding of architecture as an art, and of art as a limitless exercise of creativity, Niemeyer placed technique at the service of new forms, and as such he achieved the most powerfully original aesthetic work in twentieth-century Brazilian culture.

Like Niemeyer, Vilanova Artigas thought of architecture as a means of social transformation, and championed reinforced concrete as a preferred construction system. Nevertheless, instead of aestheticizing it, he politicized its form by adopting exposed concrete as a sign of truth and restraint that indicated an alternative construction ethic, one directed towards the collective interest. In his understanding of design as a 'human project' he concentrated on the structural system as an expressive element, and transformed columns into the new symbols of art or 'brothers of the new techniques'.[9] At the Anhembi Tennis Club (1961) in São Paulo, there is a poetic justification for the fact that the columns also incorporate the rainwater drainage channels: 'With this I attempted to make the most of the rain providing an almost bucolic effect with the sound of falling water.'[10] At the Berquó House (1967), which was constructed

during a time when the military regime was particularly intransigent, he placed the concrete slab on tree trunks (see p. 186) in order to say 'that all this reinforced concrete technique, which produced the magnificent architecture that we know, was nothing but irremediable foolishness in the face of the political conditions that we lived under at that moment.'[11]

At the Bus Terminal (1973) in Jaú – where the pillars started on the lower level, climbed through the intermediary floors, and became divided, arching over to connect with the roof slab and, in the process expose the material to light – it was obvious that the central issue within such a poetic of opposites is one of space rather than form.

While Niemeyer conceived images to surprise and enchant people, Artigas constructed spaces to congregate and to educate the masses. Although 'structure' in his oeuvre refers to the load-bearing system in the normal architectural sense, his work also opened up the possibility of the term's anthropological use: as 'an intellectual frame through which things become intelligible'.[12] As such he articulated columns, beams and slabs in order to create shelters of exposed concrete,

Tropical Tectonics

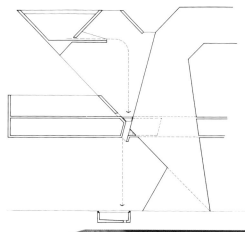

João Batista Vilanova Artigas, Anhembí Tennis Club, São Paulo, 1961. The load-bearing elements were in the shape of pyramidal columns (right), which gave the impression of wedges inserted in a solid mass. This highlighted the the contrast between the free-flowing internal spaces and the containment provided by the structural portico (opposite). Rain gutters were fitted in these columns to enhance the atmospheric sound of falling water (above left and right).

João Batista Vilanova Artigas, Jau Bus Terminal, 1973. A single perforated slab supported on eighteen columns (opposite top) sheltered the different levels of circulation. On the ground floor a dedicated access for buses (opposite bottom) was linked via a series of ramps to the pedestrian access on the upper level (above and top).

Lina Bo Bardi, São Paulo Art
Museum, São Paulo, 1957–68.
Situated on the intersection of
two main traffic routes
(opposite above), the building
was designed to allow for the
uninterrupted views from the
Trianon Park on to the rest of
the city. Its main structure, a
portico spanning 70 metres
long, holds the permanent
exhibition galleries and by
freeing the ground floor also
frames the vistas of the Vale
do Anhangabaú. The
suspended volume offers
protection to the belvedere
whose use as a public arena
was already indicated in early
studies for the project (above
left). A partially underground
block (above right) houses
the temporary galleries,
restaurant, library, servicing
area and civic hall (opposite
below).

preferably lit from above, which would act as
continuous and dynamic spaces capable of
bringing the public together.

In Artigas' work, architecture was reduced to
a minimum: load-bearing elements and spaces.
While Aldo Van Eyck and Herman Herzberger's
Structuralism was based on the combination of
small identifiable units,[13] Artigas privileged large
spatial structures of varied configurations, capable
of sheltering different programmes: houses, clubs,
schools, stations and laboratories. Later, Paulo
Mendes da Rocha and Fábio Penteado were to
extend this system to encompass, amongst other
building types, a chapel, bus terminal, shop,
maternity ward and even a cathedral, all using the
same architectural language, which thus proved
to be aesthetically prolific.

In this same line, Lina Bo Bardi opened the
ground floor at the São Paulo Art Museum
(1957–68) in its entirety, in one stroke transforming
it into pavement, museum entrance hall, public
square and belvedere creating a kind of public
space rarely seen in Brazil: one whose 'public'
nature had less to do with its potential multiple
uses than to its effective appropriation by the city's
inhabitants. At the Community Cultural Centre
(1967) in Campinas, the roofs of Penteado's
administrative buildings were like terraces around
the central square on to which they faced, which
thus effectively became a public arena. Similarly,
Marcello Fragelli interpreted Reidy's hollow portico
as a bridge, suspending it at the Armênia Metro
Station (1968) in São Paulo. The potential of such
spatial structures had been clearly indicated by

Reidy's Brazil-Paraguay Experimental School
and the Museum of Modern Art in Rio de Janeiro,
where a sense of space was achieved by the serial
repetition of porticos. By comparison, in Niemeyer's
work, with projects such as the Duchen factory
(1950) in São Paulo, the portico was taken more as
the element generating the final form than as a
spatial device.

In this respect, Reidy became an important
reference for both of the Brutalist trends that
developed in Brazil: analytical Brutalism in Rio
de Janeiro and synthetic Brutalism in São Paulo.
In the first case, projects were centred around the
expression of construction, in accordance with the
didactic ideal of rationalist architecture, at times
running the risk of reducing architecture to the
level of composition and refined tectonic
arrangements. In the second strand, technical
ingenuity and formal expression represented the
building's programme as both aesthetic and
ideological, following the revolutionary ideas of the
Modern Movement, though they were sometimes
compromised when spatial structures became mere
symbols that could just as well serve conservative
as progressive intentions.[14]

It did not, therefore, take long for the use of
materials, construction systems and structural
elements to become 'acritical', and as a result
gradually lose their expressive vitality and symbolic
relevance. An excess of exposed concrete,
exaggerated load-bearing elements and a gratuitous,
almost limitless, formalism became the architectural
emblems of Brazil during the military dictatorship
between 1964 and 1989; there was little critique

Fabio Penteado, Campinas
Cultural Centre, São Paulo,
1967. Aerial photograph
showing the Centre and the
surrounding area (opposite).

of this fetishism, and only infrequent discussion about the conditions of the country's architectural production.

Notable exceptions were the São Paulo architects Sérgio Ferro, Flávio Império and Rodrigo Lefévre, whose work was critical of architecture's complicity with the developmentalist politics of Brazil at the time. Ferro and Lefévre held a position based upon the 'poetics of economy', already suggested in Imperio's earlier projects: the aesthetic use of simple and cheap materials as a sign of the construction process, amounting to an asceticism of construction that was not far from the dominant brutalist ideals. In their building forms, they developed Artigas' spatial structure through the use of vaults, but for technical-economic rather than aesthetic reasons. Ferro had drawn attention to how under the dictatorship, the country's social development slowed down and alienated architecture from its public duty,[15] but his own work was almost exclusively restricted to residential projects for a small circle of friends. He also tried to demystify the drawing process, which was sometimes seen as an alienating factor on building sites, proposing, with great ingenuousness, its replacement by a new process, not directed *towards* production but *of* production, capable of incorporating its tensions, discontinuities and improvisations.[16] Ferro, Império and Lefévre's theoretical output was not always matched by the quality of their built work, which remained limited to the experimental, providing material for subsequent developments. (see p. 183).

By comparison, the São Paulo-based architect Paulo Mendes da Rocha took architectural

experimentation a step further. Thinking of architecture as based on nature's potential and on human inventiveness, and at the same time being critical of the historical process of land occupation and the current social situation, he suggested that: 'It is a question of establishing reconfigured territories so that the high ideals of humanity can be achieved.' Within this reconfiguration, technique is not simply a means, since it is inherent to the actual concept: 'One must reason with the available skill, one does not think with forms that are autonomous or independent of a manufactured vision of those very forms.' Technique is not an end in itself, since the intention is to 'approach the technical issue from an architect's point of view, as someone who bridges the apparently inexorable distance between humanism and technique, between philosophy and mathematics, between reason and imagination'.[17]

In this way, he both privileges construction systems within his radical interpretation of spatial functions, programmes and configurations, and also places them in relation to other concerns. Without being nostalgic about past techniques or dazzled by present advances, Mendes da Rocha uses contemporary technology in order to test its limits. He resorts to sophisticated solutions, but also makes use of very simple resources. At the Brazilian Museum of Sculpture (1985–95) in São Paulo, he used both pre-stressed concrete and simple welding techniques (see p. 54). 'The idea behind the latest technology and science is the intelligence of where and when to apply it .'[18] Inventiveness (*engenho*[19]) is what is important to Mendes da

Rocha – moreover, it is necessary 'to bestow beauty with inventiveness of a technical-scientific character'. The complex relationships between the site, the building's programme and its construction system were resolved with the use of simple geometrical forms, 'the minimum amount of design possible that resolves that problem', yet complexity returned within the spaces created. Rocha's forms approach the initial purism of the Modern Movement, but, rather than referring to the neo-Modernism of North America and Europe in the 1980s and 1990s, in Brazil they represent the persistence of the idea of obtaining maximum productivity with a minimum of effort.

Hybrid construction

In the 1951 project for her own house, Lina Bo Bardi used slender-sectioned steel to suspend a glass box over the surrounding forest, thus boldly announcing the arrival of metal structural systems in Brazil (see p. 152). While at the headquarters of the Institute of Social Security of the State of Guanabara (1957), Reidy covered the framework with a sober version of the 'Brazilian style', at the Avenida Central building (1957–61) Henrique Mindlin incorporated the Miesian style of steel and glass skyscrapers. In Rino Levi's projects, the programmes allowed him to give a greater emphasis to the framework: at the América multistorey car park (1952-8) the *brise-soleil* elements that had been intended for the facade were not built and its metal columns remained exposed; while the supply warehouse at the Parahyba Weaving Company (1953) was precisely

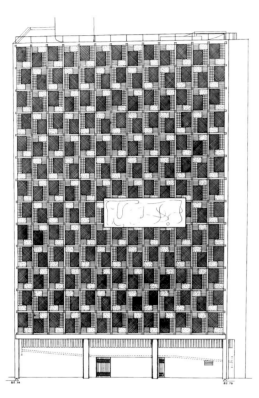

Henrique Mindlin, Avenida Central Building, Rio de Janeiro, 1958–61. The steel-structured building rising thirty-four storeys high in the city's skyline became a symbol of the International Style during the 1960s (opposite).

Rino Levi, America Multi Storey Car-Park, São Paulo, 1952–8. Drawing illustrating an idea for the back facade comprising an elaborate *brise-soleil* structure that was never realized (above left and centre). View of the front facade (above right).

Rino Levi, Supply Warehouse for the Paraíba Weaving Company, São Paulo, 1953. View of the structure comprising two paraboloid arches supported by three lines of columns and beams (right).

characterized by a structural system of parabolic arches supported by three series of pillars. But it was Sérgio Bernardes who profited most from the formal possibilities of steel, exploring expansive, graphic patterns in projects such as the Soares House (1953), the National Steel Company Pavilion for the Fourth Centenary of the São Paulo Exhibition (1953), and the Brazilian Pavilion for the Brussels International Exhibition (1958).

Despite these varied and creative precedents, steel only began to be used extensively in Brazil during the 1980s. This was encouraged by critiques – aesthetic, ideological and economic – of the prevalence of concrete, and by the systematic campaigns by producers of steel to promote the material via the specialized press, similar to an earlier campaign by the cement industry. However, to this day, steel has not been used in large-scale social projects, nor has it ever become a popular material to rival reinforced concrete, which remains the preferred choice amongst the most deprived and under-educated sectors of the population.

The effective use of steel coincided with the influence of the postmodernist vogue and the critical revision of the Modern Movement in Brazil, but it generated little significant creative experimentation. Instead, formal variations of volumes exposing structural systems were more common, and they ranged from the banal to the sensational. Although there were other paths that at times were explored, this was done in a very superficial manner. At the Portuguese Association of Brasília (1984), João Filgueiras Lima (aka 'Lelé') adapted Miesian prototypes to the openness

demanded by the local climate. Walter and Odiléa Toscano, at the Largo 13 de Maio Station (1985–6) in São Paulo, used steel to achieve suspended volumes and spaces configured by porticos with repeated columns, giving a hollowed-out feel to the spatial structure developed by Reidy and Artigas. At the Cachoeira Primary School (1984–5) in Minas Gerais, Éolo Maia composed nostalgic and caricature-like figures and at the Arame Opera (1992) in Curitiba, Domingos Bongestabs abstractly revised the iron architecture of the nineteenth century. Finally, at the passenger station of Santo André (1999) in São Paulo, Marcelo Ferraz and Franscisco Fanucci explored the contrast between the coldness of the material and the dynamics of the organic forms that could be achieved with it.

Rather than a full-scale use of steel, during the 1980s, Brazilian architectural production displayed an extremely varied employment of construction systems, but still dominated by concrete. This diversity had some precedents: within his few, but instructive projects, Costa had already illustrated through the use of stone (Museum of the Missions, 1937), steel (Brazilian Pavilion, New York, 1939), timber (Park Hotel São Clemente) and concrete (Guinle Park) how formal modernist principles were independent of materials and construction systems. The Roberto brothers had extended their experimentation to involve construction systems other than concrete: at the Sotreq Sales Stand (1953) they mixed concrete and timber, and at the Lowndes Pavilion (1953), timber and stone.

However, the most notable work during this initial moment of experimentation was that of

Lucio Costa and Oscar Niemeyer, Brazilian Pavilion, New York, USA, 1939. Representing Brazil in the 1939 World Fair, the Pavilion displayed a sample of the country's flora and fauna, as well as typical Brazilian products. The steel structure could be seen on the east facade across the garden designed by Roberto Burle Marx (above right). A ramp on the main facade gave access to the mezzanine and partially covered auditorium (above left).

Lucio Costa, Park Hotel, Nova Friburgo, Rio de Janeiro, 1944. Located on a sloping site, the wooden structure framed ten rooms, the reception, a restaurant and servicing areas. The facade showed the combination of local materials – timber and stone – and modern design (opposite above).

Lucio Costa, Museum of the Missions, Rio Grande do Sul, 1937. Referring back to the traditional plan of the Jesuit missions, the project combined archeological materials found on site with the modern use of glass in order to achieve the desired transparency for the exhibition rooms (opposite below).

Tropical Tectonics

Walter and Odilea Toscano, Largo 13 de Maio Station, São Paulo, 1985–6. Suspended from metallic porticos, the station was built next to a motorway with an elevated pathway for pedestrian access (opposite above).

Marcelo Ferraz and Francisco Fanucci, Santo André Passenger Station, São Paulo, 1999. Based on a suspended pathway covered by a metallic structure connecting a local bus terminal, a train station and a long-distance bus terminal this project aimed to reorganize the urban configuration (opposite below).

Lina Bo Bardi, SESC-Pompéia Factory, São Paulo, 1977–86. General view of the complex with the new concrete towers in the foreground and the recycled factory building in the background (above left). Bo Bardi's designs especially took into account people's appropriation of spaces, as is shown in this preparatory drawing of the bar in the sports block (above right).

Sérgio Bernardes. At the Soares House (1953), he combined metallic load-bearing elements, stone and ceramic-brick masonry, and thatch-covered aluminium rooftops. His Exhibition Pavilion project in Rio de Janeiro implied the articulation of reinforced concrete, masonry bricks, steel cables and plastic. His special inventiveness led him to create construction systems that, in the late 1950s, actually became industrialized and commercialized. However, more than an interest in mixing materials or in prefabrication, what distinguished Bernardes' work was his approach to technology, which generated an architecture with innovative programmes, sophisticated structural elements and simple forms that were connected to the contemporary international trend towards megastructures. Inspired by the constructivist ideal of social transformation through new forms and techniques, his intention was to use technology to enable a renewed and free contact amongst people, and between them and nature. Making radically creative use of technology, Bernardes was often extravagant. He transcended the field of his original discipline with a series of provocatively radical proposals: revisions of ordinary human utensils, such as his new designs for a bicycle, aeroplane and cargo-ship; geographical changes, such as his proposal for the unification of Rio de Janeiro's bays by a navigable canal; the occupation of extreme regions of the planet, such as in his projects for the Amazon and Alaska; geo-political restructuring, such as his idea for the administrative reorganization of Brazil based upon its river network; and even historical-political revolutions, such as his proposal

for the extinction of property rights on Earth.

Lina Bo Bardi also forged her own path of free experimentation and cultural action through architecture. From her education in Italian Rationalism during the 1930s and 1940s, she developed a preference for ample and synthetic forms with great plasticity and symbolic power, while Brutalism gave her architecture an emphasis on load-bearing elements and on unrefined materials. In the north-east of Brazil, where she witnessed not only the survival of handicrafts but also of a way of using and making things that she described as 'disseminated domestic proto-craftwork', she lived an 'experience of simplification' that led her to the idea of a 'Poor Architecture'.

When introducing the SESC-Pompéia Factory (1977–86), she stressed that it was: '"Poor architecture", not in the sense of extreme destitution but relating to a craftsmanship that expresses to a maximum degree its Communicative power and Dignity through the smallest and most humble means.'[20] The act of making is 'poor yet it is rich in fantasy and inventions. It is a premise for a free and modern future that, together with the achievements of the most advanced scientific practice, will retain at the beginning of a new civilization the values of a history full of hardships and poetry.'[21]

This project, from its general layout down to its details, showed how Bo Bardi treated a variety of influences – constructional and formal; architectural and artistic; archaic and modern; European, Oriental, North American and Brazilian; cultured and popular, in ways that ranged between the creative, the anti-

Lina Bo Bardi, SESC-Pompéia Factory, São Paulo, 1977–86. These concrete buildings stand as a bold landmark and integral part of the urban landscape of this semi-industrial district. Regular fenestration was replaced by *buracos* (holes) on the three facades of the sports block (opposite above right). These large irregular openings cut into the concrete wall provide dramatic views of the city from the west face (below right). The sports block accommodates a swimming pool and four sports courts and can only be accessesed through the circulation ramps that link it to the servicing tower (above and opposite above and below right). The converted warehouses have been adapted for a variety of functions, including a library, theatre, exhibition spaces, restaurant and workshops (opposite below left).

Paulo Mendes da Rocha, FIESP Cultural Centre, São Paulo, 1998. The exhibition galleries were housed in a new steel and glass structure that was attached to the existing concrete building (above and right).

nostalgic, and the irreverent as well as the self-controlled. Rather than comprising a landscape, her buildings for workshops, sports, arts and recreation, the rivers (interior water features) and *cachoeira* (open-air collective shower) configured a microcosm that refers back to Bardi's urban ideas: a raw and poetic city whose built heritage is enhanced by contemporary, albeit historically pregnant additions, and by social democratic practices; a playful and inclusive city; a place for the imagination and free existence.

Without romanticizing or mystifying popular culture, Bo Bardi confronted the contemporaneous 'Foul Times '[22] through the use of a variety of construction systems, materials and modes, as well as by creatively incorporating common building practices developed by construction workers, often migrants from Brazil's poor Northern regions, lacking specialized knowledge.

Bo Bardi's critical and innovative attitude towards the alienation of work, and architectural deficiencies in Brazil, gave her a clear sense of the potential for transformation: 'Our experience is not one of a "folkloric elite" but a test of vitality, one that has in mind the possibility of a housing production

within the economic reach of the people, achieved with the active collaboration of these same people.'[23] Such a process was never developed on a large scale, but ultimately depended upon her own personality and talent. Despite a group of faithful collaborators, Bo Bardi's imaginative and intransigent architecture did not spread. Characterized by its simplicity, grandeur and rigorous details it remained one of the most encouraging proposals for escaping the intrinsic difficulties of the Brazilian situation.

At the same time, in parallel with the random creative examples of non-professional construction that grew up around the peripheries of Brazilian cities, some architects adopted the most diverse means of construction imaginable, whether based on industrial processes or craftsmanship, according to the specific conditions of each building (the needs of users, programme, materials, techniques and available resources) and its design.

Even architects usually associated with concrete accomplished significant experiments with other construction systems. Mendes da Rocha, for example, explored the dialectic of heavy and light in combinations of concrete and steel.

Paulo Mendes da Rocha, Club Atletico Paulistano Sports Hall, São Paulo, 1957–8. The main area was covered by a ribbed reinforced-concrete structure from which the metal roof was suspended on steel cables (above).

Tropical Tectonics

Paulo Mendes da Rocha, Forma Shop, São Paulo, 1987. The glazed exhibition room was supported by two hollow columns at either end, which accomodated the servicing areas (left). Retractable stairs provide access from the ground. Interior view (right) showing access between and across different levels.

This was the case with his gymnasium project for the Clube Atlético Paulistano (1957–8), the bus terminal in Goiânia (1985) and the Forma shop (1987–94) in São Paulo. Recently he arrived at the 'idea of a structure that is a parasite of another'[24] – which is how he described the association between metallic elements added to an existing concrete system at the FIESP Cultural Centre (1996), where he made use of the additional loadings possible on the existing supporting system of the headquarters of FIESP-CIESP-SESI. The idea of taking advantage of the unexplored potential of the great concrete load-bearing systems in Brazil is one that could have been developed further, generating rich technical, aesthetic and social experiences.

Within this synthetic tendency that often retreats into a fetishism of materials, the CHESF Headquarters Building (1977–80) in Salvador by Franscisco Assis Reis was a highlight. It stands as a true tectonic *vatapá* (an Afro-Brazilian dish composed of rice-flour, dendê-oil, chillies, sea food, etc.) with its masonry bricks, concrete and steel, creating textures and varied spatial situations with different scales and climates that allude to the local landscape of Salvador.

These structural hybrids, some of the most poetic features of Brazilian architecture, serve to draw attention to the extremes of the Brazilian condition, and at the same time turn to advantage the shortages of labour skills. However, it has to be said that as a solution to Brazil's problems they are sometimes pessimistic, accepting of the status quo – and even celebrating it.

Prefabrication and assembly

Despite the attempts at modernization, technical backwardness has left constant traces in Brazilian architecture during the twentieth century. Not only did it characterize the pioneering adaptations of Modern Movement principles, but it has persisted even in the recent work of widely acclaimed architects. Among the modernist pioneers, Enéas Silva and his team, who designed a series of state schools during the 1930s in Rio de Janeiro, found themselves unable to satisfactorily adapt modernist formal principles to the climatic requirements and local construction possibilities, and ended up producing unsuccessful buildings that became easy targets for rivals from the Beaux Arts tradition. Latterly, Niemeyer's Museum of

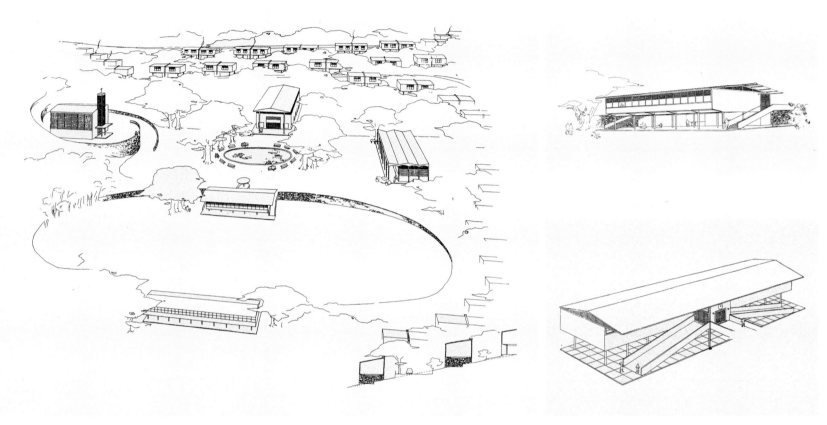

Lucio Costa, Monlevade Village, Minas Gerais, 1934. A project for a competition organized by a mining company, the design of this urban settlement (above left) shows a careful combination of modern elements, such as ramps and *pilotis* (see the perspective drawing of the school, above right) and vernacular materials, such as tiled roofs and brick walls (see the perspective drawing of the club, top right).

Contemporary Art (1991–6) in Niterói, suffered from errors in calculations and construction that resulted in the modification of the original concept, and at Mendes da Rocha's Plaza of the Patriarch (1992–2002), construction errors also compromised the final result.

Attempts to circumvent backwardness of construction resulted in more pragmatic approaches such as can been seen in Costa's project for the Monlevade Village (1934), Carlos Frederico Ferreira's Realengo Residential Complex (1940–2), Levi's Sedes Sapientiae Institute (1940–2), and Vital Brazil's state schools in Niterói (1941). The employment within these projects of roofs made of ceramic tiles rather than flat concrete slabs – an icon of Modernism, costly to produce and of doubtful performance in tropical weather – indicated a more realistic, freer and anti-formalist way of adapting rationalist principles to the climatic necessities and to the constructional and economic possibilities of the country. Marginal and unrecognized, such pragmatism gained some attention in the 1950s with the brutalist vogue, when although the display of materials derived merely from formal intentions, it nevertheless often also reflected a greater level of

Rino Levi, Sedes Sapientiae Institute, São Paulo, 1940–2. The various buildings of this complex were placed around a central courtyard where circulation routes were covered by a curvilinear concrete canopy (right). The design of the classroom block included one of the first glass facades built in Brazil, here set in a concrete grille (above).

Luiz Paolo Conde, Alfabarra
Housing Development,
Rio de Janeiro, 1980.
The urban planning included
the design of twelve main
residential tower blocks,
positioned among several
other minor residential
towers, some shops, schools,
pedestrian pathways and
a church (above).

attention to the realities of local construction.

Influenced by this pragmatism, Luiz Paulo Conde revealed his preoccupation with the improvement of construction in works such as the Alfabarra Housing Complex (1980) in Rio de Janeiro by using materials and elements of proven quality and easy maintenance that were readily available within the construction market. Although commercial property developers were accustomed to this approach, in Conde's case it derived from an engagement with the existing built environment, from an emphasis upon the urban context rather than the 'building-event', and from his critique of the over-valuation of daring techniques and clever detailing in much Brazilian contemporary architecture.

Joaquim Guedes is also a noteworthy case. The decision from the start to operate only within the limits of available building practices is evident at his Landi (1965), Guedes (1968), Beer (1975) and Mariani (1977) Houses in São Paulo. Even in a large-scale project such as the one for Caraíba (1976), a new city for 15,000 inhabitants, Guedes responded to the local climate, incorporated the current construction practices of the region and

arrived at solutions that, by combining learned and popular references, became open to cultural appropriation. Aware of Alvar Aalto's work, Guedes, with his use of materials and techniques suited to the conditions of each project, followed a method that has produced a diversity of creative works. With a technological approach that was at the same time pragmatic, critical and inventive, he created a variety of forms that were not gratuitous and exaggerated, and which did not make users radically change their behaviour. Such simplicity longs for wider dissemination:

The choice of material requires an attentive and sensitive architect in order to make the most of its usefulness, producing expression and meanings. The association of material and intelligence builds architectures, places, cities and maintains the intense relationship with everyday life, the economy and the organisation of societies, culture and human happiness.[25]

Against this pragmatic approach there have been Brazilian architectural projects whose scale has genuinely required the standardization and

Tropical Tectonics

serialization of elements, and the forward planning of their construction. Among them are the campus of the University of Brazil (1949–62) by Jorge Machado Moreira and team, and the Serra do Navio and Amazonas villages by Bratke and team.

On the whole, however, the increasing tectonic emphasis in Brazilian architecture from the 1950s onwards should be seen more as the result of technological advances in reinforced concrete than of effective industrialization of construction or of the adaptation to social ends of constructional technology in Brazil.

The 'anti-example' of Brasília, the paradigmatic case of precedence of form over construction in Brazil's modern architecture, encouraged a great concern with prefabrication during the 1960s, but neither the construction industry nor politicians gave it any significant backing. The Zezinho Magalhães Prado Housing Complex (1967) is the best example of these 'failures': the largest work of its kind (12,000 units) up to that date, it was a radical project with high initial expectations and subsequent frustration. Artigas, Penteado, Mendes da Rocha and their team designed all the construction components, standardizing

the infrastructure, load-bearing and partition elements, and even certain domestic appliances, in order to manufacture them in factories that were to be installed on the construction site, and thus promote prefabrication. However, only a small number of units was built, and that by conventional methods, because of the developers' and the government's lack of interest – for all their public declarations of support for the industrialization of civil construction (see p. 187).

The most remarkable attempt to industrialize architecture and solve the impasse demonstrated by Brasília has been developed by Lelé who, having worked there as an engineer and experienced the chaotic erection of an entire city from nothing, later preoccupied himself with the rationalization of future projects, the serialized production of construction elements and the planning of construction and its adaptation to local conditions.

Recognizing the advances in building, and especially in concrete technology, over the last three decades, but also the continuing neglect of the problems of the poorest sectors of the population, Lelé attempted to adopt 'an independent and disassociated position in

Joaquim Guedes, Francisco Landi House, São Paulo, 1965. The exposed concrete frame of varying height determined the outline of the north facade (above).

relation to the consecrated technical orthodoxy'.[26] Aiming for a rationalization of construction, and an adaptation to Brazilian bio-climatic and economic conditions, he established some general principles: the flexibility and extendability of spaces, construction and installations; the standardization of construction elements; environmental comfort, through the use of natural ventilation; and the creation of green spaces. Lelé concentrated on the production of pre-cast reinforced concrete, and managed to establish a number of temporary factories for architectural components, supplying infrastructure elements, equipment and street furniture to projects within a variety of programmes (administrative, transport, education, social-security, police), predominantly in poor and run-down areas.

At the Sarah Kubitschek Network, in Salvador (1989), capital of the northern region of Bahia, Lelé created a plant for the construction of hospitals specializing in human motor disorders, in which all the building components were designed and serially produced: from load-bearing elements and partitions to furniture, hospital equipment and vehicles. Easy to transport and handle, these

pre-cast units could be effortlessly assembled in a variety of forms and combined with lighter metallic elements, reducing both building costs and construction times whilst providing functional, pleasant and playful environments. In addition to rationalizing the building process, Lelé's designs took advantage of Brazil's climate and light. To avoid the use of costly mechanical air-conditioning systems, he devised a natural cooling alternative in which fresh air was circulated through an underground network of galleries into the rooms from where, once warmed, it left the building through ducts formed by curved openings in the roof. These same openings, together with the glass walls facing tropical gardens in the patients' wings, improved the intake of natural light as part of the general energy-saving strategy. Access for movement-impaired patients to the gardens as well as to other therapeutic facilities was enhanced by the specially designed mobile beds, also produced in Lele's Sarah Kubitschek Network Technology Centre in Salvador.

The villages of indigenous tribes of the Alto Xingu were the inspiration for this technological approach. Lelé had visited these settlements, and

Tropical Tectonics

Jorge Machado Moreira, University of Brazil, Rio de Janeiro, 1949–62. The Master Plan (opposite above left) aimed to centralize all the buildings of the university on an artifical island in the Bay of Guanabara (opposite middle). Surrounded by gardens designed by Roberto Burle Marx, the Pediatrics Institute (1949–53) (opposite above right) was organized as three parallel blocks on three storeys to accomodate the different levels of the site. The south block, where the entrance hall is located, was raised on *pilotis* (above left) while the playground on the north block was built on the lower level (below right). The main hall in the Faculty of Achitecture (1957) (above right) was located under the main classroom block, also on *pilotis*.

João Filgueiras Lima, Regional Electoral Tribunal, Bahia, 1997. The building was designed with the view of creating maximum flexibility for the occupation of internal spaces. The main block is constituted of parallel wings separated by internal gardens covered with large undulated roofs with the openings facing south to avoid excessive exposure to the sun. The offices are on the upper level while services and the plenary council are in the lower level. The independent circular block of offices for notaries was planned on two levels with a central garden protected by a translucent polycarbonate roof (opposite).

considered them 'a very intelligent creation that used nature's resources with great ingenuity [...] a very correct architecture which is adequate to their way of life'.[27] However, the formal patterns are different: specifically influenced by the works of Mies van der Rohe and Niemeyer, he highlighted the tectonic elements of projects, oscillating between discrete, pragmatic, orthogonal designs, and curved or angled ones which he has only recently started to integrate. The building of the Administrative Centre Secretariat (1973–4) in Bahia combined the expression of the state's programme and the rationalization of construction through the formal exuberance characteristic of Brazilian architecture during the military dictatorship. His schools in Rio de Janeiro, built between 1984 and 1986, relied on the emphasis of discrete forms, as a result of their assembly with prefabricated elements. At the Bom Juá Crèche (1987) there was evidence of an attempt to add a greater formal appeal to the rules of construction, which has gained greater eloquence in recent works such as the hospital of the Sarah Kubitschek Network in Fortaleza (1991) and the Regional Electoral Tribunal of Bahia (1997).

However, as is the case with so many of the other works discussed here, Lelé's production is an exception rather than the rule. Despite the slightly more varied range of products offered by the construction market, an industrial infrastructure capable of supplying good quality components at low cost still does not exist in the country (see p. 214).

The deficiencies of Brazilian society have grown rather than diminished with the passing of time, and this has encouraged some research on both industrial and alternative construction systems, particularly for large-scale housing programmes. The work of Joan Villá at the Housing Laboratory of the University of Campinas (1980s), stands out, as does the Clean House-ECO 92 project (1992) of Siegbert Zanettini. Despite the high architectural quality of some of these experiments, this research is hardly sufficient to the needs of the country, and is out of touch with current studies abroad. To develop new approaches to large-scale construction in a society with limited industrial infrastructure and a largely unskilled labour force remains one of the great challenges in Brazilian culture.

Looking at the situation today, the vast majority of new buildings in Brazil neither respect local bio-climatic conditions, nor take adequate advantage

of natural and human potential, nor tackle the country's social misfortunes. Architecture in Brazil remains an art of exception, dealing with the individual, the special, but never the ordinary, the normal or the everyday – but perhaps this is an unavoidable condition. Different, divergent, and even conflicting, but with many common characteristics, these exceptions together constitute a cultural heritage, a heritage of which full advantage has not yet been taken. We are left with the image of an irregular, incomplete, yet beautiful scaffolding that remains in pieces on the ground, waiting to be assembled.

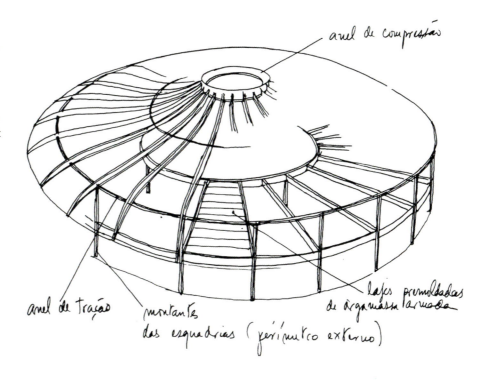

CHAPTER THREE
HIGH-SPEED URBANISATION
BY LUIZ RECAMÁN

Anhangabaú Valley,
São Paulo, 1995. Aerial view
showing the historic centre
and business district of
São Paulo. The aerial towers
on Avenida Paulista can be
seen in the background,
an aerea where many
companies and banks moved
to in the 1970s.

HIGH-SPEED
URBANISATION

Almost the whole of Brazil's existing built environment was created in the twentieth century, during a period of one of the fastest rates of industrial development ever to have occurred on the planet. Such accelerated development nevertheless took place a century too late, if compared to Western Europe and the United States. There are two immediate consequences of this rapid and untimely urbanization.

Firstly, the transition from a colonial-agrarian society to an urban industrial one occurred without the country ever going through a classic 'bourgeois revolution'. Brazilians never built the ideological representations of bourgeois civilization, nor the corresponding productive infrastructure that had characterized nineteenth-century Europe and defined its main cities. This peculiarity still leaves its mark today in the heterodox nature of Brazilian social relations. Secondly, in the tremendous suddenness of its modernization, Brazil bypassed the phase of great urban reforms that had accompanied European and North American industrial capitalism in the second half of the nineteenth-century, at the founding moment of the modern metropolis.

Juxtaposed, these two consequences result in a single urban phenomenon: that the great expansion of Brazil's main cities occurred directly on top of a rudimentary colonial base. Although modest interventions following nineteenth-century methods of urban improvements were implemented here and there – in the old federal capital, Rio de Janeiro; in São Paulo, with the exploitation of coffee cultivation; and in Santos, the port for São Paulo's

coffee production – the fact remains that, as far as urbanization is concerned, everything in Brazil is extremely new.

As distinct products of such a particular development model, the country's large and medium-sized cities are a direct spatial expression of the social upheaval perpetrated by Brazilian modernization. In this sense, as the historian Sérgio Buarque de Holanda has suggested, Brazil's colonial heritage is different from that of the parts of Latin America colonized by the Spanish. Whereas the Spanish opted for regular, orthogonal lines, creating for their cities in the New World a pattern that could subsequently be extended and built upon, the Portuguese were solely concerned with the protection of their territory, and only constructed small fortified trading posts. Efficient in commercial terms, they did nothing to encourage the consolidation of a civilization in the New World. Born out of improvisations around existing trade routes and patterns, Brazilian cities had as their final objective the efficient accumulation of wealth, without the concurrent additional aim of developing a classical concept of the city as a cultural and civilizing event.[1]

It is as if the spontaneity of the Portuguese colonial occupation, which Sérgio Buarque de Holanda contrasted with the planned regularity of Hispanic America, had been prolonged – for the purpose of maximum profits – into Brazil's rapid twentieth-century industrialization. The culmination of this process, ocurring now within the current phase of global capitalism, is embodied by the São Paulo megalopolis – itself a highly efficient

Map of the City of São Paulo, 1887. Portuguese colonial cities in America were not the result of a clear strategy of territorial occupation. They tended to imitate their metropolitan models – Porto and Lisbon – often resulting in irregular grids adapted to the local topography (opposite above).

Map of the city of Buenos Aires, Argentina, 1708. The cities founded by the Spaniards in the New Continent were based on a regular grid around a central plaza. Following laws and regulations set out to organize the colonization of the new territories, they reflected many ideals of the time, such as the Roman tradition of military planning and Renaissance theories of perspective (opposite below).

'ruin-construction' as far as the accumulation of capital is concerned. Brazil's modern architectural culture emerged in apparent opposition to this spontaneous and deregulated process of city production, a form of resistance to the growing social imbalance created by post-colonial laissez-faire policies at all levels. The contradictions of such an ideology within the cultural centres that had given rise to it have been widely discussed. In Brazil, however, these contradictions are of another order and they still sustain the myths that give shape to its architectural culture and its response to the chaos of its cities.

The politics of Brazilian Modernism
The new Brazilian Republic of 1889 was established in a country dominated by regional oligarchies, economically sustained exclusively by coffee cultivation. During the First Republic, vigorous monetary policies of fiscal control and of economic liberalization were carried out under the guidance of British capital. This model entered a period of crisis in the 1920s, with the fluctuations of capitalism worldwide in the inter-war period, provoking in Brazil great economic hardships and social pressures. These culminated in the 1930 Revolution, led by Getúlio Vargas, whose government was centralist and interventionist. The subsequent strengthening of the economy was expected to transcend the twin scourges of the high profits of the coffee proprietors and London's financial speculators. In 1937, in the prevailing conservative and authoritarian climate, President Vargas established a dictatorial government, known as

Estado Novo, the 'New State' which lasted until 1945.[2]

This centralizing economic model was able to consolidate its power because of the difficulties created for international trade by World War II. It maintained its relatively long-lasting hegemony even during the military government established in 1964 following the democratic interlude from 1945 until 1964.

Both developmentalist and conservative, the Brazilian modernizing project, which had begun during the 1930s, lasted until the close of the 1970s with the end of the military regime. It favoured high rates of economic development through large investments of capital in productive infrastructure, accompanied by varying degrees of repressive and exclusionary social policies.

At the core of this industrial advancement, the national state had also to be constructed – both politically and ideologically – and Brazilian modern architecture was, without doubt, one of its most effective emblems. It was brought into play at exactly the same moment as the Vargas dictatorship (1937), itself an authoritarian but nevertheless modernizing project. In a country that went from a slave-owning and archaic society to a modern, centralized and authoritarian state in a few decades, modern architecture fulfilled a key ideological function.

Modernity in Brazil, however, did not correspond to the concrete, productive reality of the nation, but instead, preceded it. In this way, it helped create the ideological conditions for the emergence of 'the nation', through a centralizing state synchronized with the anti-liberal environment of the inter-war period.[3]

High-Speed Urbanisation

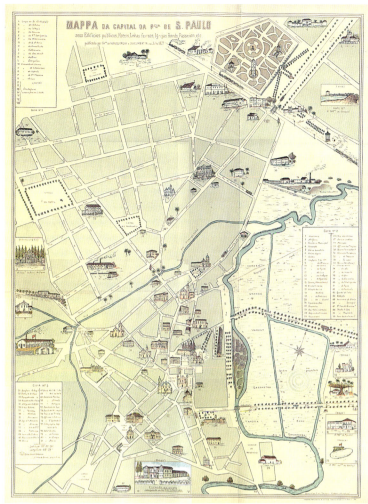

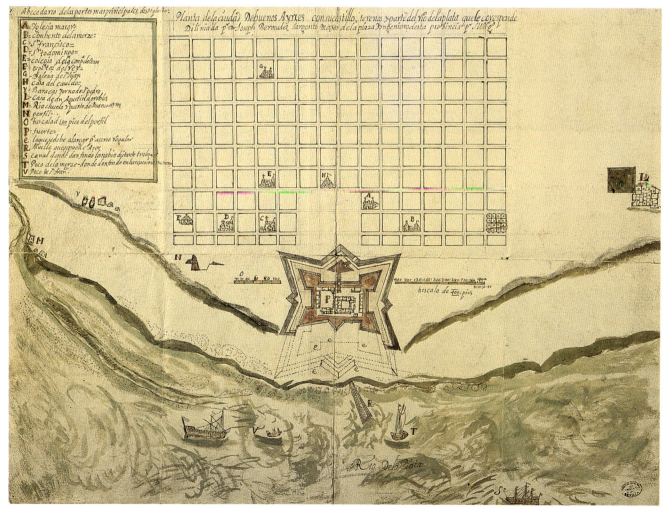

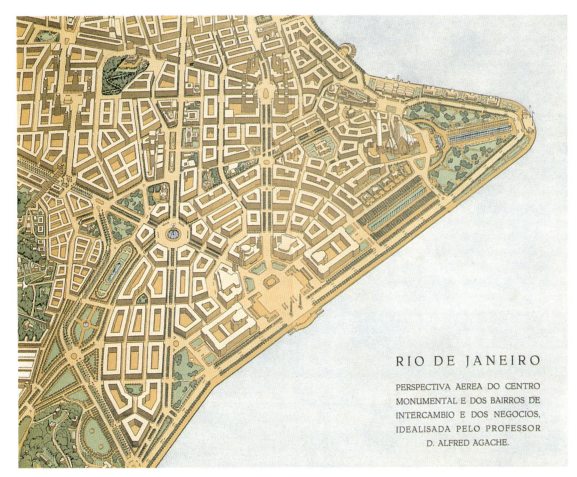

RIO DE JANEIRO

PERSPECTIVA AEREA DO CENTRO
MONUMENTAL E DOS BAIRROS DE
INTERCAMBIO E DOS NEGOCIOS,
IDEALISADA PELO PROFESSOR
D. ALFRED AGACHE.

The artificiality with which modern architecture was introduced in Brazil, therefore, should not alarm those who look for a link between the productive base and its reflections on the cultural domain. If we take the analysis of modern architecture made by the Italian historian Manfredo Tafuri in his book *Architecture and Utopia*, Brazilian architecture does not conform to his account, missing out, as it does, on several of the historical stages he identifies. Central to Tafuri's analysis is how, from its origins in the eighteenth century, modern architecture combined ideology – that is to say, the 'mythology' by which the bourgeoisie made tolerable the disjunctions and contradictions of urban life – with planning, by which he means the actual strategies for physically changing the urban environment towards socially orientated goals. According to Tafuri, from the 1930s onwards, the work of physically reconfiguring cities was taken over by state agencies and became part of the strategy of national economic planning. As a result, the ideological aspect of architecture was deprived of any prospect of realization, reducing architecture to an empty game of formal experimentation in which it is condemned, as he puts it, to 'sublime uselessness'.

In Brazil, there had never been the bourgeois revolution, which had elsewhere created the ideology of modernity and, in this respect, the country lacked one of the fundamental preconditions of modernity. Furthermore, in Brazil the historical occasion when modern architecture combined ideology with planning also never occurred: modern architecture arrived in the country directly at the stage of purely formal experimentation without ever having been

through the previous phases. The fact that Brazil knew only this final stage, described by Tafuri as 'form without utopia', and had missed out on the earlier stages – when architecture had been linked with liberal, social and urban reforms – gave Brazilian Modernism its single most important characteristic: from its very origins it was defined by its formalism.

In Brazil, this lack of a social foundation for modern architecture relieved it from its original utopian endeavour, allowing it to fulfil its programme with no constraints. In turn, this revealed the ideological and formalist nature of the Modern Movement itself, and emphasized the fragility of the link that reformist ideologies had made between social advancement and industrial capitalism.

Moreover, from 1935 this intrinsic formalism was summoned to participate in the construction of the image of the nation; from the first studies for the construction of the headquarters of the Ministry of Education and Health in Rio de Janeiro, until its apotheosis with the federal capital in the country's central plateau from 1957. This essay aims to deal with the subject from which the precarious historiography of Brazilian modern architecture has always distanced itself: the chaos of its cities and the proposals for apparently overcoming this.

City and Plan

The initial dilemma of modern architecture in Brazil lay in the confrontation between the social and utopian potential of modern architecture in general and its communicational dimension, its language.

Alfred Agache, *Cidade do Rio de Janeiro* (*City of Rio de Janeiro*), Paris, 1930. Commissioned by the Municipality of Rio de Janeiro, and published in Paris, Agache's Plan for the city's 'extension, reorganization and embelishment' provided for major changes to the city's topography, including levelling hills and claiming land from the sea, as shown in this map of the Castelo district where the new headquarters of the Ministry of Education and Helath were later built.

Lucio Costa and team, Ministry of Education and Health, 1936. The final scheme resulted from a negotiation between Le Corbusier and the local team led by Lucio Costa. The sketches show the evolution of the project (opposite from top) starting with the initial project proposed by the Brazilian architects, the first proposal by Le Corbusier for the site on the Bay of Guanabara, his second proposal for the site on the Castelo district and the final scheme adapting Le Corbusier's solution to Agache's urban plan.

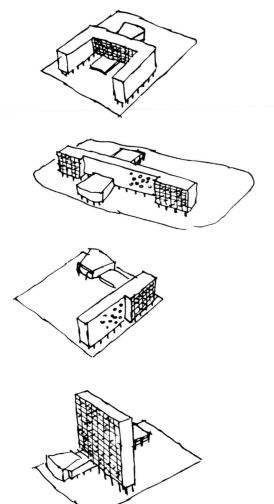

Drawing from the work of Le Corbusier, abstraction and standardization was taken as evidence of modernity. Gregori Warchavchik's first houses in São Paulo, built during the 1920s, and the Ministry of Education and Health building of 1936 in Rio de Janeiro, made use of craftwork to imitate the appearance of technologically advanced construction. Similarly, Le Corbusier's first villas, with their pure, white, geometrical volumes, had been made to look as if they were products of industrialized building techniques, when in fact they were executed with handicraft methods. It can be seen, therefore, that Brazilian architects did not invent modern formalism by corrupting concepts from elsewhere; but did, however, take great advantage of characteristics already present in the first modernist works.

The Ministry of Education and Health building is the origin of Brazil's modern architecture. It is a direct translation of Corbusian concepts, receiving its seal of approval from the actual presence of the master himself, during his famous visit to South America in 1936. In its final form, it nevertheless showed, in every particular, a revision of the original model. This did not relate in any way to the climate or to the local materials – issues that had always been foreseen by Le Corbusier – but rather to a flexibility towards each one of Le Corbusier's 'five points for a new architecture' .

At this inaugural moment for Brazil's modern architecture, the autonomy of form – its reference to exclusively architectural values – seemed to be in conflict with social functionality, a conflict that underlies the communicative dimension of modern architecture and that was at the very basis of this project's absolute modernity. This modernity had nothing to do with the regional characteristics attributed to Brazilian modern architecture by the British critic Kenneth Frampton. The divergence between form and functionality should be understood within the dialectics of Modernism, rather than as a local reaction against its universalism.

The Ministry of Education and Health building embodied all the possibilities that would be present within Brazilian modern architecture from then onwards, whether in other buildings or in urban interventions. As an experimental laboratory of ideology and form, the Ministry project is of interest here for two crucial aspects: firstly, the relation that it established with the urban context ; and secondly, the conflict between the allegory of modernization and its social function.

Corbusian buildings during the inter-war period invariably referred to the ultimate object of intervention for the architect: the urban plan. Despite the heated arguments over the Ministry building, an initial observation would suggest that the scheme drastically restricted this urban character while maintaining the Corbusian 'five points'. It developed a complex arrangement between the new building and its immediate location, a site that had greatly displeased Le Corbusier himself. According to him, this modern palace should have been part of the great intervention that had been sketched in his beautiful perspectives of the new city of Rio de Janeiro. This is why he insisted on the site in front of the Guanabara Bay, which had

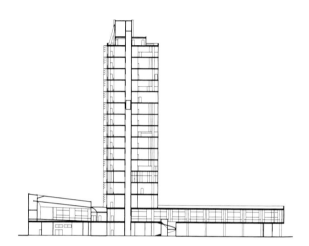

become unviable due to bureaucratic obstacles. The final site, within the traditional street pattern set by Alfred Agache in his project for the Castelo area, altogether lacked any Corbusian character. It was nevertheless there that the young Brazilian team meticulously produced one of the most complex and contradictory pieces of modern architecture ever built.[4]

In both of Le Corbusier's studies – the one for the ideal site in front of the Guanabara Bay, and the one for the final site, which was quickly revised by Le Corbusier on the eve of his return to Europe – the relationship between the building and the site had defined the arrangement of volumes. Following Le Corbusier's departure, the Rio team returned to his studies but by altering the horizontal and vertical dimensions of the volumes changed the building's relation to the site and to Le Corbusier's ideal urban plan. In the final study, the one that was actually built, there was a close relationship to the existing geometry and the hierarchy of surrounding streets, which went against the whole Corbusian logic of planning for an ideal site. Yet this characteristic, established by the team against Le Corbusier's will, gave the building its own monumentality, one which has successfully resisted the incursion of the new skyscrapers that now surround it.

In the same manner, the use of the Corbusian 'five points' went through a subtle process of alteration in the design of the Ministry building. The *pilotis* became elongated and lost their vertical, modular logic. Placed without relation to the load above – they did not actually support the building in the direction of the exhibition room on the ground level – they created an Expressionist rhythm, which is unheard of in Le Corbusier's oeuvre. *The brise-soleil* and the *pan-verre* became absolute entities, giving the block an abstract purity far more radical than that seen in the previous studies. There are various other examples of this flexibility, suggesting a discontinuity between the architectural devices and the concepts from which they were initially derived.

Part of the building's success is due to the paradox that the use of the 'five points of the new architecture' are used here in a way that contradicts the reforming and planning ideals with which they had been originally conceived. It was not a case of betraying these principles, so much as giving in to their inherent formalism. Thus 'misplaced', they were able to function fully in new configurations, allowing for the liberation of form and its functionalist and urban associations to the ideal Plan. In Brazil, it was a question of overcoming that error, common to almost all modern architecture, that had tied – with no means of mediation – the social dimension of architecture to its autonomous form.[5]

From this equation, a new relationship between modern architecture and social modernization was established. No longer associated with those issues at the origin of modernity in Europe – that is, the liberal or 'machine-age' ideology – it became connected with the reality of the Plan. In other words, it was an architecture that became associated with an interventionist and essentially authoritarian state, of a kind that had become a characteristic of the 1930s around the world.[6]

Lucio Costa and team, Ministry of Education and Health, Rio de Janeiro, 1936. The first ocurrence of a glass curtain wall (opposite), this seminal project for Brazil's Modernism represented an original adaptation of Le Corbusier's 'five points for a new architecture', as shown in the section (left).

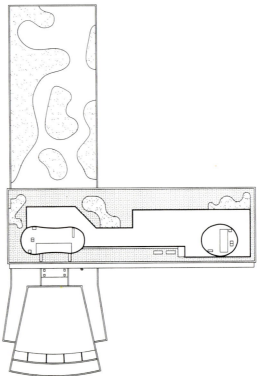

Lucio Costa and team, Ministry of Education and Health, Rio de Janeiro, 1936. The *brise soleil*, another of Le Corbusier's suggestions, was used for the first time on such a large scale on the north facade (above left). Roberto Burle Marx designed the gardens, including those on the exhibition galleries (left, above right and top). Mosaic tiles were applied throughout the building, a token gesture to Brazilian decorative traditions, as seen on the auditorium (far left) and on the panel designed by Candido Portinari on the entrance plaza (opposite below left), who also painted the mural in the children's playroom (opposite below right).

High-Speed Urbanisation

Oscar Niemeyer, Casino (later Museum of Modern Art), Pampulha, Belo Horizonte, 1940. The Casino was the first project to be built as part of of a new quarter by the artificial lake of Pampulha. With a glass facade that reflects the landscape (opposite), the elaborate circulation routes employing ramps, stairs and spiral staircases recall Le Corbusier's idea of *promenade architecturale* (above).

At the core of this strategy of a planned economy, architecture was undoubtedly one of the most decisive emblems of a new, modern and original nation that would emerge out of the great crisis of the 1930s, with a new role for itself within the international economic order.

It was this pressure at its origin that made subsequent Brazilian modern architecture viable, leading to the construction of Brasília where the authoritarianism of the country's modernizing process supervened over any tendencies towards democratization. Moreover, these original circumstances also gave Brazilian modern architecture the anti-social and anti-urban tendencies that are characteristic of its most renowned examples.

Pampulha

The institution of the Ministry of Education and Health was responsible among others for the standardization of education, the curricula of schools, the teaching of language, etc. This process occurred in a country that was such a mixture of races and nationalities as to be described as 'without character'. The Ministry building's architectural

features were further consolidated by the construction of a project on the outskirts of Belo Horizonte, initiated by Juscelino Kubitschek in the early 1940s – the climactic moment of the Vargas dictatorship – as a suburb and leisure area for the middle and upper classes.

Around an artificial lake in Pampulha were set small architectural masterpieces designed by Oscar Niemeyer. It comes as no surprise that the complex was never used as had been intended. The church was not consecrated until years later, because the religious authorities objected to its unconventional form. The ballroom, in effect the sole building with any popular appeal, was never used as such. Its distance from the city centre, and the absence of public transport, made it unusable by the urban populace. The famous casino was not even inaugurated, since gambling had been prohibited in Brazil. Nor did the yacht club function as it had been intended, as a water-sports centre, on account of the high level of pollution in the lake, caused by inadequate sewage infrastructure for the surrounding new upper-class neighbourhood.

As far as city planning is concerned, nothing could be more introverted than this display of

Oscar Niemeyer, Church of St. Francis, Pampulha, Belo Horizonte, 1940. The presence of load-bearing concrete vaults as well as Candido Portinari's mosaic panel reflects the different influences Niemeyer had started to combine in his architecture, ranging from Le Corbusier and Mies van der Rohe to Brazilian Baroque churches.

Oscar Niemeyer, Ballroom, Pampulha, Belo Horizonte, 1940. The sinuous shape of the concrete canopy follows the site's outline and represents Niemeyer's attempt to relate landscape and architecture (above right).

Oscar Niemeyer, Yacht Club, Pampulha, 1940. The inclined roof slabs were intended as an adaptation of the canonical horizontal slab to the tropical conditions of Brazil.

exotic, yet useless, architectural novelties around a lake. In no way were they reminiscent of the heroic Modernist projects for housing and new cities. Instead, they portrayed a scenario for the *dolce vita* of a bourgeoisie anticipating its meteoric entry into the world of consumption, and turning its back on the existing city, while fostering the expansive powers of the property market. The paradox was complete when this architecture was integrated into the aggressive mechanisms of city-building during Brazil's own industrial revolution.

Its cities with no past and its Plan without a future, Brazilian modern architecture concluded its process of ideological collapse with the construction of Brasília, itself a metaphor for the collapse of democratic possibilities in the face of Brazilian conservative developmentalism. Both past and future became formal abstractions within the regionalist argument, which celebrated the absorption of the country's colonial Baroque heritage into the sophisticated, curved forms of Oscar Niemeyer and other important architects of the period.

The conservative modernizing formula that made possible the 'quantum leap' of Brazil's industrialization was expressed in the combination of rudimentary technique (the careful, yet alienated, craftwork on the 'virtuous', wooden curved forms produced by armies of 'proto-proletarians') with the sophistication of the autonomous, avant-garde forms. 'The restitution of backwardness' formalized by this architecture, to use Otília Arantes' pertinent expression in her critique of the work of Lucio Costa,[7] corresponds to the perpetuation of aspects of a slave-owning society within the new industrial order, from the time of the New Republic (1930) until the present. Brazil's backward social relations and its conservatism, which had originated during centuries of slavery, are updated and re-enacted in modern Brazil, facilitating rapid industrialization. The 'modern' and the 'backward' Brazils do not clash, they are simply juxtaposed and, in so doing, make exploitation viable at the periphery of capitalism.[8] Such symbiosis, which was at the core of the developmentalism of the 1940s and 1950s, can be extended to Brazil's modern architecture, which can thus be seen as one of its privileged formalizations.

Notions of the city and its social function were, and still are, foreign concepts to Brazilian modern architecture, dominated as it is by considerations of form. While urban and social thinking have

Lucio Costa, Guinle Park
Housing Development,
Rio de Janeiro, 1948
(Nova Cintra), 1950 (Bristol),
1954 (Caledônia). Out of
the originally planned six
buildings (above) only three
were built. Following the
layout of Guinle Park,
Costa placed two of these
unfavourably facing west,
necessitating his ingenious
use of *brise-soleil* and hollow
bricks screening the facades
from excessive exposure to
the sun (opposite right).

appeared as fragments and traces in the work of various modern architects, they have, however, been gradually displaced by each step taken towards the creation of unique, 'a-functional' objects.

Pedregulho

The period prior to 1936 was characterized by projects and private houses for an enlightened élite curious about European modernity. From the mid-1930s, with the new political order, the construction of administrative public buildings in the then federal capital, Rio de Janeiro, timidly began appropriating the experiments in Functionalist architecture recently arrived in the country.

The contradiction between ideology and the reality of the city is most apparent in Brazil's modern social housing projects. Generally, public buildings in the country were intended to adopt the formal language of Brazil's dominant modernist trend. But such formal language becomes problematic when dealing with the issues of costs and standardization raised by the social-housing question, especially in a country with a growing deficit of housing for its large low-income population. This problem, in turn, is overshadowed

by the need for an urban strategy of some kind.

While the Ministry building may be taken as the historical starting point of modern architecture in Brazil, the mass housing issue, whether private or social, remained untouched for a further decade. Its neglect cannot be accounted for by any lack of market demand or political pressure, since this was a period of intense urban growth, when the peripheries of São Paulo and Rio de Janeiro started to expand rapidly. Even more curious is the fact that this attention to mass housing should appear first in the Guinle Park residential complex, designed by Lucio Costa between 1948 and 1952 in Rio de Janeiro.

According to Lucio Costa, the Guinle Park project was 'the first experience of a residential complex of flats for the high bourgeoisie, and the first one where, after so many frustrated attempts to leave the ground floor space empty, Le Corbusier's pilotis – which were to become commonly used in the city – were applied'.[9]

Yet, at the same time, Costa did not miss the opportunity to deepen the connection between this new architecture and the colonial past. At Guinle Park there are a number of exceptional features. The investment was private and aimed at the upper class (the surface area of the flats was between 286 and

604 sq m). It is set in the magnificent garden of one of Rio de Janeiro's most sophisticated palaces, in a central area of the city. It is an urban 'island', which differs totally from the chaotic fabric that surrounds it. As at Pampulha, these buildings are set around a free space – but where at Pampulha this space was a lake, here, it was a park.

While Niemeyer was the first to articulate Brazil's modern architectural vocabulary with his Pampulha complex, parading free forms devoid of function, Costa's Guinle Park suggested new possibilities; but because Costa relinquished the stage to Niemeyer, whose work became the definitive 'Brazilian modern architecture', these possibilities were never realized. Why Costa should have stood down at this moment is one of the key enigmas in the formation of Brazilian Modernism.

While housing was not at the centre of research interest for the new architecture in Brazil, it could not simply be ignored. Contemporary polemics about the social function of architecture demanded some kind of action from the profession, especially from its main protagonists, nearly all of whom were associated with the Communist Party. The early 1950s witnessed a surge of industrial activity in the country, generated by investment in its infra-structure and heavy industries, and a consequent growth in the urban population, which called for a coherent housing policy. Whereas the management of social-housing programmes in the 1920s had been a formative experience for the new architecture in Germany, Austria and Holland, nothing of the kind happened in Brazil. Even allowing for the experiments of a few well-known architects , such production was never more than a secondary activity. The rupture of this original connection between modern architecture and social housing led to a housing production made up, on the one hand, of unsuccesful single buildings, and, on the other, of vast projects with thousands of units placed in 'urban deserts' around the large cities.[10]

The distortion of modern architecture in Brazil should be understood from the perspective of the original conditions of Brazilian Modernism, rather than in relation to its audacious formal proposals or its ties with conservative policies. The precariousness of the housing projects that were built emphasizes the paradoxical nature of Brazilian architecture's modern agenda

Affonso Eduardo Reidy's renowned Pedregulho

High-Speed Urbanisation

Affonso Eduardo Reidy, Pedregulho Housing Development, Rio de Janeiro, 1950–2. This project aimed to provide affordable housing to 570 working-class families in the district of São Cristóvão. It included (aerial view, clockwise from top) one main habitation block, two secondary habitation blocks, health centre, laundry, community centre, school, gymnasium, pool and changing rooms. The main habitation block was situated on the highest point of the site and contained 272 flats on four floors organized in two levels (below).

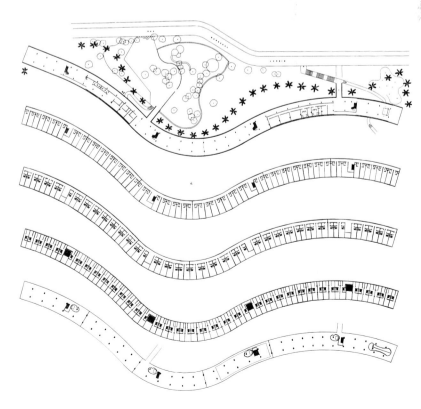

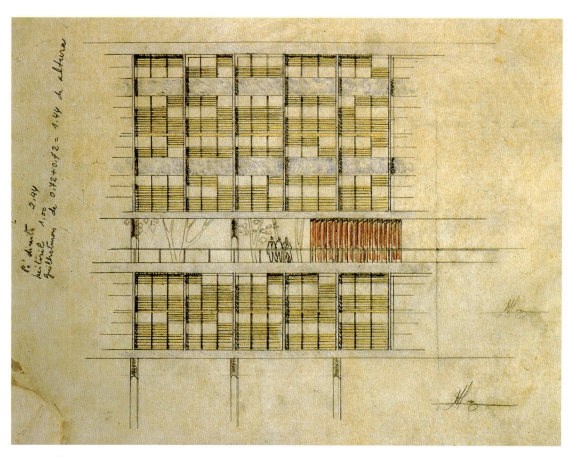

Affonso Eduardo Reidy, Pedregulho Housing Development, Rio de Janeiro, 1950–2. Profiting from the sloping site and raised on *pilotis* (opposite above), the main habitation block was accessed via two footbridges which gave on to an open plan corridor equally distant from the upper and lower levels (above) affording panoramic views of the Bay of Guanabara (opposite below).

complex illustrates this. Reidy was an architect who had participated in the crucial events of the early 1930s. He had been a student at the National Fine Arts School during Lucio Costa's reforms. There, he had assisted the new professor, Gregori Warchavchik, and also participated in the competition for the new headquarters of the Ministry of Education and Public Health, subsequently joining Costa's architectural team on the project.

Reidy's career was, from an early stage, associated with public administration. Even before becoming a municipal public servant in 1932, Reidy had already been working as an intern for the French town planner, Alfred Agache, since 1929 – on the development of a General Plan for the city of Rio de Janeiro. In 1938, Reidy was responsible for the implementation of Agache's proposals, but after his contact with Le Corbusier, he saw Agache's plans in a new, critical light. A protagonist of the new architecture in Brazil, Reidy developed an urban and social 'vocation', connecting what was being developed in the national context during those decades with the large-scale urban plans being promoted by the Congrès Internationaux

d'Architecture Moderne (CIAM) groups in Europe. His strong ties to Le Corbusier's urbanism were at the root of various conflicts with public administrators: over the Urbanization Plan for the Esplanada de Santo Antonio, for example, or the Glória-Flamengo landfill proposal during the 1940s and 1950s, as a result of which he eventually resigned from the board of directors of the town planning division of the General Secretariat for Road Works and Construction.[11]

As head architect for Rio de Janeiro's Department for Popular Housing, a position he occupied in 1947 during the 're-democratization' period following the Vargas dictatorship, Reidy immediately began some of the most audacious social-housing projects in the country. The Pedregulho complex (1947–52) and the contemporaneous, but only partially completed, Marquês de São Vicente complex (also 1947–52) are exceptional examples of social-housing projects from the high point of Brazilian modern architecture.

Such a return to the social lineage of modern architecture occurred at the same time that Brazilian architecture was becoming the target of severe criticism from abroad, culminating in the attacks

by the Swiss artist and designer Max Bill during the São Paulo International Biennial in 1953. These demands for greater social engagement seemed to be met in Reidy's work, which became an international reference for the social possibilities of modern architecture, not only in Brazil, but also world-wide. Meanwhile, the formalism of Niemeyer's architecture came under attack. His Canoas House near Rio de Janeiro, which had been inaugurated that year, displeased a considerable number of international critics. The debate, however, was not as clear-cut as might be supposed. The unusual Pedregulho complex maintained, after all, a noticeable connection to the work of Niemeyer: in the typology of its buildings, its curved and trapezoid forms and in its general organization; and references to Lucio Costa's work, particularly the contemporaneous Guinle Park residential buildings, were also evident. It is as if, amongst the formal and aesthetic solutions reached by Brazilian modern architecture, all that had been missing was the social content, and that this had been entirely accomplished by the engaged experience of Pedregulho.

This was a project that installed a fragment of utopia – now with a social emphasis – at the core of the city's peripheral development zone, yet it presented no continuity with the city. Its extraordinary typology did not accept the status quo, but nor did it propose its alteration. Amidst the surrounding chaos, it seemed like an island of tranquillity, with its infrastructure and extensive social amenities serving the poorer communities of the area. But even these did not alter the formal and self-sufficient nature of the complex, disengaged as it was from the ruthless social process that the city had been consolidating during those years. The discreet interruption of its serpentine blade is a blunt representation of this. Despite its meticulous planning, the implementation of the complex did not engage with the socio-spatial process of the city's growth. There is nothing more uncomfortable than the extroverted forms and the urban 'imprisonment' of this complex – in feel, like a permeable, enlightened and unrestrained fortification. Neither its rarefied surroundings during the 1950s nor the administrative disaster that brought about the collapse of the enterprise, altered or justified its formal ambiguity. Treated today as a 'historic monument', it equals any other peripheral development in terms of social degradation (violence,

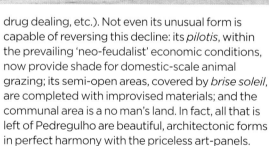

Affonso Eduardo Reidy, Pedregulho Housing Development, Rio de Janeiro, 1950-2. The school was designed as a square box on stilts that, together with the swimming pool, changing rooms and gymnasium (above left and top; see cross-section, opposite top) constituted the centre of social activities. View of front facade of secondary habitation block with staircase tower (above right). View of the laundry and community centre, with horizontal sun-breakers and pivoting doors (opposite bottom and middle).

drug dealing, etc.). Not even its unusual form is capable of reversing this decline: its *pilotis*, within the prevailing 'neo-feudalist' economic conditions, now provide shade for domestic-scale animal grazing; its semi-open areas, covered by *brise soleil*, are completed with improvised materials; and the communal area is a no man's land. In fact, all that is left of Pedregulho are beautiful, architectonic forms in perfect harmony with the priceless art-panels.

In effect, the deterioration of Pedregulho makes it similar to most of Brazil's other large-scale popular housing projects, whose day-to-day management has proved impossible. As far as public action is concerned, they have become inaccessible areas, and fortified domains for organized groups operating outside the power of the state. As segregated spaces, they are placed in opposition to the city. This is the case both for the areas occupied illegally, such as the *favelas* (shanty towns) and for those spaces managed by urban programmes.

The Pedregulho complex seemed the most audacious example of an association between Brazilian modern architecture and a wide-ranging programme of social housing. Yet the result suggests that its form was actually more the consequence of

a disregard for such an agenda. Oscar Niemeyer's refusal to consider his own Copan Building of 1951 in São Paulo as a possible alternative model was for similar reasons, because of urban restrictions that placed the building beyond the architect's control (property speculation, publicity boards, the unpredictable dynamic of occupation). Niemeyer always insisted upon the surrounding emptiness as an indispensable condition of his architecture. Similarly, he refused all social housing projects and private developments, which, in a society divided and without controls, tended to corrupt the architecture and its beauty. From the 1960s onwards, government-sponsored housing projects attempted to deal with the rapid increase in the demand for urban housing. The large housing complexes built in Brazil following the military coup of 1964 were like vast tumours inserted into the outskirts of the major cities. They were consequences of the perverse association between the military government's action, private property speculation and the self-interest of large construction companies. Such complexes were, and still are, the only solution that has been found in Brazil for large-scale housing problems. Constructed in remote areas, with no

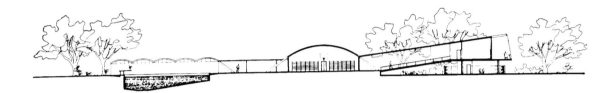

infrastructure, they became social and urban deserts. The Itaquera I and II, Carapicuíba and Teotônio Vilela complexes, amongst others, all constructed during the 1970s by the Metropolitan Housing Company of São Paulo (COHAB-SP) – the company responsible for the development of housing projects for the São Paulo city administration – are the most eloquent witnesses to this disastrous policy on the production of urban social spaces.

The inability of the architectural trend predominant since the 1940s to implement a social agenda provoked a schism in the profession. The housing issue was discussed in terms of cost-tables, investments and profitability, rather than in the terms of an architectural project. Attempts by this kind of architecture to intervene in the issue, almost all of them unfortunate – if the dimension of the problem over the last few decades is taken into account – only confirmed the ideological misunderstanding over the process. With the exception of Oscar Niemeyer who, as the practitioner with the highest prestige and output, was exempt from the controversy, this schism has weighed upon Brazilian architectural consciences,

giving rise to interminable debates, ambiguous political projects and disastrous collaborations.

Contemporary literature on Brazilian architecture perpetuates this controversy. This is the case with the recent outburst of historiography that attempts to put forward alternative architectural masters – who have all, in one way or another, been eclipsed by Niemeyer's presence – and with attempts to resume the most radical formal experiments, which can, in the context of the present discussion, be understood as profoundly anti-urban and anti-social. The country's sporadic experiments with social housing – whether official projects, such as Pedregulho, or the more 'popular' examples of joint efforts, such as self-build co-operatives – remain a reference for the more engaged of recent critics, who have resumed debates that were initiated by the political dissidents of the 1970s (see p. 177). For these critics, architectural Modernism, with its diverse local nuances, still remains a viable prospect.

Brasília
The city of Brasília represents the culmination of Brazil's particular brand of modern architecture. Brasília's urban conception was a direct conse-

High-Speed Urbanisation

Lucio Costa, Master Plan, Brasília, 1957. Night view of the monumental axis leading to the Plaza of the Three Powers (opposite).

quence of the political action that determined it, as well as its architectural solutions and their monumental spaces, all of which distance the city from the country's social and urban reality. The unusual character of the project, reinforced by the complete isolation of its location and the absence of an existing local economy, allowed for the establishment of a simulacrum of a city, an effect further heightened by the city's rapid development process. The sense of it as a simulacrum was not the result of the artificiality of Brasília's exclusively administrative purpose, but was also due to its architecture and urban planning. The total control exerted by its urban form excluded any recognizable human grouping from the social dynamic, and so, although to a great extent independent of each other, Lucio Costa's plan and Oscar Niemeyer's buildings both followed the same essentially anti-urban assumptions. They gave a definitive form to what is, after all, a multi-faceted and dynamic process.

The entire city was conceived as a total composition, in which all the components were geared towards its monumentality: the Master Plan's highly centralizing cruciform layout, the monumental axis, the skilful succession of scales, and the individual buildings (see pp. 40-7). The form of the buildings made use of previous experience, drawn mainly from Pampulha's architecture, but now each building was subject to the general composition. The coherence that, in other modernist plans, was difficult to achieve because of the random forms of individual buildings and the variety of site conditions, became possible at Brasília because of the overall plan and the way in which it

controlled the emptiness of the city's location. All buildings, whether original or subsequent, are subject to the compositional dictates of the initial mega-complex. Despite its congested underground pathway system, with its tunnels and links, the rigorous isolation and independence of each building is still maintained according to its original conception.

Brasília was an appropriate operation for a country that underwent modernization without any accompanying social development. It was the culmination of two analogous projects: the nation-state, which occupied the city in its most authoritarian and military incarnation, and modern architecture – its most eloquent collective representation. From the 1970s, the progressive failure of the nation-state led to the termination of its collaboration with modern architecture. Within the remarkably short space of twenty-five years (1936–60) Brazilian modern architecture accomplished an impressive trajectory: from ideological foundation, to maturity, and then collapse, followed by the bankruptcy of the profession itself.

São Paulo, city of the future
Major cities, after several decades of crisis and the collapse of their one-time economic efficiency, are now once again being looked upon optimistically. Following the unprecedented acceleration of international economic relations, they are considered as the anchors around which a new era of production, circulation and consumption will be structured on a worldwide scale. It is argued that the great metropolises, or at least some of them, will replace nation-states as the centres of major investment in

the 'new world order' made possible by electronic communication. But what happens when cities which during the nineteenth century – at a time when European capitals were being rebuilt and modernized – were no more than villages within a decadent colonial order, but which today are inhabited by many millions, find themselves participating in this new world order? São Paulo is one such city that may reveal something of the limits to this purported transformation of cities in a globalized world.

São Paulo was originally built as a modest trading post, supplying food to colonial troops who were then in search of Indians and gold, and it continued in this role for three and a half centuries. With the mid-nineteenth-century shift in coffee production from Rio de Janeiro to the Paraíba Valley and to the state of São Paulo, the town was transformed into a meeting point for the railroads, which transported coffee across the coastal mountain range and down to the port of Santos, whence it was shipped all over the world. By the early twentieth century, the city was starting to change rapidly, and to expand spatially as its population grew. Over the last century, the population has increased approximately 270-fold, to around ten million today, and the urbanized area has increased approximately 400 times, to about 1,500 square kilometres.[12]

Even these estimates are conservative, though, for the area of greater São Paulo has around sixteen million inhabitants, and includes neighbouring cities that serve as dormitories for São Paulo itself. In effect, the city has no limits – one can travel 100 kilometres in any direction from its centre, crossing several administrative boundaries, and still be in the city's grasp. Medium-sized cities – Campinas, Santos, São José dos Campos and Sorocaba among them – between 80 and 100 km from the centre of São Paulo are, economically, still part of São Paulo itself. Up until recently, the history of the city's growth has been one of a constant centrifugal movement, as the city takes more and more land while, at the same time, occupying it at lower and lower densities. The decline in the population density of São Paulo has been striking: in 1914, the city's average density was 110 persons per hectare (pph), but, by 1930, had dropped to 47 pph; today it has stabilized at around 66 pph. While the population growth of the city occurred at a steady 5 per cent per annum for most of the twentieth century, this has dropped today to less than 0.5 per cent. What we see now is no longer the explosion of the city, but a movement of implosion. The symptoms of this implosion can be seen in a variety of changes taking place in the region today: in particular, the growth of *favelas* and the migration of people to them; the relocation of businesses and commerce to new districts far removed from the old centre of the city; and the attempts to recuperate the value of urban areas rendered derelict by these processes.

São Paulo is no longer a city identified, as most cities in the past were, by what is permanent, but rather by continuous change. Within the space of a century, the city has been rebuilt no less than four times, first in adobe, then in brick, then concrete and now glass and steel. But it is not only that the physical appearance of the city is characterized by constant movement, so too is its social composition.

Dom Pedro II Park, Tamanduateí River, São Paulo, 2001. Aerial view showing the metro line in the foreground and the Dom Pedro II bus terminal by Paulo Mendes da Rocha and MMBB Arquitetos in the background.

Serra da Cantareira,
São Paulo, 2001. Part of
the northwards expansion of
the city, which can still be
seen in the background,
these *favelas* (shanty towns)
occupy the surrounding rural
landscape displacing the
natural forests (above and
opposite).

The peculiarity of São Paulo, as of many Latin American cities, is its segregated population. When slavery was abolished in Brazil, at the late date of 1888, the landowning and governing élite took the view that former slaves were unsuited to paid employment, and the federal government actively encouraged immigration from Europe to take the place of slave labour. Considered inadequate for work – and, indeed, for modern life generally – and denied the right to own land, the enormous freed black population had no place in the Brazilian social order. The former slaves' only form of subsistence, as small-scale urban street vendors, was prohibited, and the only space they could occupy was on the periphery. Here they were tolerated, although their settlements were illegal, unregulated and always liable to eviction should investors become interested in the land they occupied. From these disorderly settlements came the supply of maids, small service providers, retail employees and factory workers. But, whereas in Europe and the United States urban reformers included the totality of the city, poverty as well as wealth, in their plans, this was not the case in Brazil, where the areas occupied by the poor did not form

part of the city that was to be regulated by possible reform movements. Thus, the Brazilian city was born as a dual society, in which pre-modern social relations, inherited from the colonial structure, were updated, but not fundamentally changed, to fulfil new roles in modernization. The spatialization of this social structure was based upon the precarious situation of these workers, and their invisibility in social terms. They were granted not rights, but only favours. The land did not belong to them, but they could occupy it illegally, guaranteeing that it was always available for future profitable uses. It was, and still is, a curious situation, where, in three-quarters of the city, the law is treated as an exception, and its infraction becomes the norm.

This polarity between the norm and the 'extra-legal' still exists and creates enormous differentials in the cost of land. Land values are determined not just by physical characteristics, or proximity to the city centre, but by whether they lie within the regulated or the unregulated sectors. Over the last decade, huge self-built settlements have appeared on the outskirts of the city, outside the legal regulation of land use and occupation. With the acquiescence of the authorities, the illegal status of such areas was

High-Speed Urbanisation

preserved in anticipation of a 'speculative attack', or simply so that they might be perpetuated as zones of social and urban exclusion. Plots in the devalued, extra-legal, suburban areas permit higher profits to developers than those within the regulated areas, and both landowners and financial bodies have had no interest in bringing to an end the existence of these extra-legal settlements. The spatiality of the city is thus determined by the perpetuation of the polarity between regulated and unregulated land.

The *favelas,* built as illegal settlements and tolerated as outside the framework of urban and building regulations, have grown in recent years at a pace far in excess of the rate of population growth. In the 1990s overall, the decrease in the rate of population growth in the country as a whole, combined with the expansion of several urban centres, alleviated migration pressure on the two main metropolises, São Paulo and Rio de Janeiro, yet the region of São Paulo nevertheless retained 40 per cent of Brazil's *favelas.* The most recent data, from the 2000 General Census, indicates that the number of such shanty towns within São Paulo increased

by 4.6 per cent between 1991 and 2000, while in the neighbouring district of Guarulhos it increased by 112 per cent. The much lower growth in São Paulo does not indicate a limit to growth or stability, for, in one São Paulo *favela* alone, during the same period, the number of inhabitants grew from 370 to 6,000.[13]

Between 1994 and 1998, the number of families living in *favelas* in the city of São Paulo grew by 47 per cent.[14] Without significant growth in the city's overall population, the 1990s saw an immense migration of its inhabitants within its territorial boundaries. In a 1993 census by the municipal government, 39 per cent of *favela* residents reported that they had given up paying rent in legally regulated housing, and transferred their abode to a shack in a *favela.* This growth in the occupancy of the shanty towns took place at the same time as the city administration in São Paulo had, with some violence, removed several *favelas* close to areas of the city with high land values, in order to permit the construction of roads and commercial properties. And there is more data giving evidence of this internal population migration. The 'Map of Social Exclusion',[15] which indicates differences in the quality of life in São Paulo's districts, shows an emptying of the regulated,

Berrini Avenue, São Paulo, 2004. New and rapidly developing area of the city previously occupied by *favelas*.

legal areas of the city towards the unregulated outskirts. Between 1991 and 1996 there was an increase of 470,000 inhabitants in the 53 districts where quality of life was deemed to have worsened, while within the 37 districts where the quality of life had improved, there was a decrease of 260,000 inhabitants.

What is the dynamic behind this constantly shifting social and spatial structure of the city? In the case of São Paulo, there are two factors causing this perpetual change: economic gain and social segregation. We have already examined some aspects of the process of social segregation, and can now look at the pattern of investment in commerce and business. The historical centre of São Paulo, where banks, the judiciary and the stock exchange were located, has seen the exodus of these activities to other parts of the city, leaving behind only specialist shops and some justice-related activities. Today, there are many empty buildings, both public and private, some of which have been occupied by squatters. Business, luxury housing, shopping malls, and culture and leisure spaces have all migrated, in particular towards the south-west of the city, where land is cheaper and

more plentiful, and where investment produces higher rates of return than development in the centre.

This is not simply the relocation of activity from one centre to another, but rather a process of continuous movement – as business constantly seeks out new investment opportunities, made available by the existence of cheap land and sustained by regulations favourable to redevelopment at high densities. The authorities provide the infrastructure of roads and services to make these new developments possible, but take no interest in the resultant organization of space. Low-rise houses, squeezed on to small plots of land between narrow streets, are transformed overnight into business centres, without regard to the quality of the space. Tall buildings rise on land assembled from small lots, leaving between them surviving remnants of previous development and areas of waste, but there is no overall urban strategy. From the urbanistic point of view, the *Paulista* bourgeoisie builds a 'poor' space: one that is badly designed, exploits occupation to the full and is the result of altering legislation to obtain bigger profits. At the same time, increasing violence, the result of a massive degree of social exclusion, pushes the wealthy inside their homes, where they

are protected by alarms, electric fences, surveillance systems and armies of security guards (Brazil's fastest growing employment sector).

As intimate space becomes overvalued by these means, so public space deteriorates. The result is a pattern of development more ruthlessly laissez-faire than anything in pre-Haussmann Paris, or in the industrial cities of Britain prior to the Public Health Acts. The city creates roads to serve these new developments, but that is all: the rest is left to the 'laws' of supply and demand. Whereas the old centre was characterized by broad sidewalks and squares, and buildings were integrated with exterior space, by the time one reaches the new developments on the south-west border of the city (Avenida Berrini and Marginal Pinheiros) sidewalks have shrunk to 80 cm in width, on which posts for cables and boxes of electrical equipment jostle with pedestrians for available space. Although this district is one of the largest areas of new construction in the whole of São Paulo, its implementation has taken place without any plan. Dozens of new buildings, sophisticated and equipped with high security, burst on the scene each year in old residential neighbourhoods without any infrastructure or services. As long as this speculation bubble lasts, groups of small, lower-middle-class houses are bought up to make way for the new super-valued enterprises in these areas. Immense *favelas*, which had been tolerated on land near the Avenida Marginal Pinheiros, were cleared in order to construct a new avenue to serve the interests of investment.

The city authorities are towed along behind this process of speculation, building new thoroughfares, channelling rivers and pulling down *favelas* in order to make the developments viable. The urban space that results is desolating. Congested avenues, narrow streets, leftover lots and old single-family houses abut shiny new hotels, shopping malls and offices, all of which are accessible only by car. The result of this 'frontier mentality' to the consumption of land has been the deterioration of the inner city.

The succeeding city administration, headed by Marta Suplicy (Worker's Party, 2001–4) tried to partly reverse this process of expulsion of the poor population from the city centre, by promoting social-housing projects – either in new buildings or in renovated ones. These interventions, however, were very timid in relation to the dimension of the

Dom Pedro II Park,
Tamanduateí river, São Paulo,
1996 (above).

Plaza of the Flag, São Paulo,
1996. Aerial view of the
centre with the hills in
the background towards
which the city is expanding
(opposite).

problem. Their main value lay in using small areas within the urban fabric of the city without creating either ghettos or distant dormitory areas on the outskirts, as had traditionally been the case with such developments.

Recently, therefore, it can be seen that the municipal authorities, and some banks, have initiated attempts to reverse the decline of the city centre. Expenditure on the conversion of disused industrial buildings to cultural uses, and on the renovation of historic buildings, has been aimed at enticing investors back into the central areas. Projects such as the restoration of the Convent of Light – the city's most important building from the colonial era – the renovation and enlargement of the National Art Library, and the conversion of the former Júlio Prestes Railway Station into a concert hall for the State Symphony Orchestra would, it was hoped, encourage other investors. Yet, even if this regeneration strategy were to be successful in attracting speculative capital back into services and housing within the central area, the market created by such investment will necessarily exclude the area's present inhabitants, whose reasons for living in the centre are low rents and low transport costs. There would be a repetition of the pattern that occurs throughout São Paulo, a city where the only significant improvements are brought about by private investment: as the value of a particular region is increased, those who originally lived there are forced out and the net population declines.

São Paulo allows us to see the mechanics of the bourgeois city more clearly than elsewhere, because they operate there nakedly, without the restraints and controls that are found in other parts of the world. Although Western cities have undergone a process of continuous dispersal since medieval times, extending their boundaries over the surrounding countryside, regions and, ultimately, into their overseas colonies, those cities had a defined urban space and urban landscape that preserved their apparent integrity, and to some extent restricted the aggressiveness of land speculation. The global city of today is not a new kind of city, but rather an acceleration of the fragmenting tendencies of these Western cities.

While some doubted that São Paulo, with its precarious social and urban economy, could become a global city, it is precisely this precariousness, created by its extreme social segregation, and by the constant migration of its business districts, that has enabled it to become such a city. Older settlements, rooted to a fixed historic centre, have found it harder to adapt to the kind of 'de-territorialization' produced by electronic communications and global capital movements; if they have succeeded in maintaining their world position, it has been by taking advantage of any lack of restrictions; of the relative weakness, or absence, of traditional models of the city; of mobility; and of the fluidity of development in cities elsewhere. São Paulo supremely demonstrates these features. It transforms itself continuously, unrestrained by attachments to traditional ideas of the city – but the cost of this is the enduring segregation of a property-owning from a property-less class, which is fundamental to São Paulo's position as a world city.

CHAPTER FOUR
THE MODERN BRAZILIAN HOUSE
BY JOÃO MASAO KAMITA

Jorge Machado Moreira,
Antonio Ceppas House,
Rio de Janeiro, 1951–8.
Understanding the
architectural project as a
collaborative enterprise,
Moreira frequently worked
with other artists and
architects, such as in this
project for a private residence,
where Roberto Burle Marx
designed a mosaic panel for
the entrance hall (opposite).

THE MODERN BRAZILIAN HOUSE

At the second meeting of the Congrès Internationaux d'Architecture Moderne (CIAM), in 1929, the German architect Walter Gropius, reflecting upon the 'Sociological Principles of the Minimum Dwelling', described an evolutionary framework of social systems: from the tribal clan, through the patriarchal family, to the consolidation of modern bourgeois individualism. In his analysis, Gropius focused on the historical development of the family since the eighteenth century, when, as result of the new division of labour, the patriarchal structure started to lose its character as a closed, self-sustaining unit. Functions that had previously been family obligations – such as education, sustenance, health care and provision for the elderly – were, in modern society, handled by the state. Craftsmanship, originally based on the family unit, began to disintegrate with the invention of the machine and the consequent transformation of the systems of production brought about by the Industrial Revolution. The next step, foreseen and welcomed by Gropius, was the phase of 'collective individualism', where individual and collective needs are balanced – the constructivist utopia, in which modernist housing would be the established norm.

In this account, the modernist housing unit, the *Standarte*, had to respond to the modern imperatives of economy, hygiene and efficiency, by offering well-lit, specifically designed dwelling spaces equipped with technology to improve the life of 'the modern man'. The housing issue was seen from an urban point of view, in which the standardized and functional dwelling unit would meet society's collective needs whilst seeking to balance the quantitative demands of production with the qualitative requirements of the architectural profession. Primary attention was therefore paid to housing developments, and to research on the industrialization of the building industry. Gropius' minimum dwelling, like Le Corbusier's 'machine for living in', was an idealized representation of the modern home: generic, but sanctioned by the indisputable strength of the *Zeitgeist*. In this intersection between the 'rigorous' analysis of present conditions and hopeful predictions for the future, the modernist house had the task of informing and convincing an unprepared society of the viability, the necessity, indeed, of the inevitability of 'the New'.[1]

In Brazil, the first prototype of the ideal modernist house was designed by Gregori Warchavchik, a Russian architect who had recently migrated to the country. The house was put on show in São Paulo in 1929, as an example of a new way of building and living. In addition to its pure prismatic volume and functional plan, the architect designed the dwelling's interiors (wardrobes, furniture and fittings), according to the Bauhaus model of design. The public controversy generated in Brazil by 'the Modernist House' and its revolutionary ways of living, brings to mind the impact of Adolf Loos' silent and 'anti-monumental' house designs in 1920s Vienna.

Compared to the West, there was in Brazil, however, a fundamental historical difference, which served to moderate the universalist principle, inherited from the Enlightenment, underlying the

Walter Gropius, Törten Estate, Dessau, 1926–30. Commissioned by the city authorities, Gropius expanded on the idea of standardization with these prefabricated housing units in an experimental urbanisation for workers (above).

modernist project. Relative to Europe, industrial development and urban growth in Brazil lagged behind architectural modernity, and the lack of ties to the demands of industrial production, or the pressure of a housing crisis, freed Brazilian architects from any obligation to focus on standardization. At least, this was the case between the 1930s, when modernist architectural ideals were introduced to Brazil, and the 1960s, when industrialization finally became more widespread. During this period, Brazil's housing programmes remained relatively untouched by the pressures of industrialization, leaving a path open to free architectural experimentation and to the recuperation of traditional values associated with dwellling, shelter, protection, family, retreat and intimacy.

In most cases, then, the design of houses became a kind of workshop for innovation in forms, construction and technology. The private house – often belonging to the architects themselves – would work as a kind of experimental model for poetic investigations or, to use an analogy with painting, it would represent a kind of architectural 'still life'. However, this kind of experimentalism revealed the dilemma of Brazilian modernity: some reacted enthusiastically, in view of the promise of progress and knowledge; others accepted it only partially, recognizing the inherent social benefits but suspecting that the frenetic rhythm of technical development might disrupt established cultural values.

This dilemma defines the first phase of Brazil's architectural modernity. Its paradox was that while aiming at achieving modernity in the sense of a universal cosmopolitan ideal – whether in the arts, music or literature – it at the same time asserted the uniqueness of a culture that could not be reduced to dependency on external influences.

In the development of modern residential architecture in Brazil, therefore, we see as a result, firstly, the adaptation of Functionalist housing models – Le Corbusier's 'machine for living in' and the Bauhaus 'minimum dwelling'; and, secondly, the relative permeability between the traditional house and the modernist house – in their functional programme, use, and construction elements and techniques.[2]

Balanced antagonisms: the experience of tradition in modernity

Brazil's most thorough sociological study of the dwelling is undoubtedly Gilberto Freyre's *Casa Grande & Senzala*, published in 1933. In this book, the author gave a detailed outline of social relations within the Brazilian patriarchal family, focusing on the dwelling unit at the core of the agricultural estates of colonial Brazil, which comprised the *Casa Grande* (the master's house) and the *Senzala* (the slaves' quarters). The *Casa Grande* hosted a variety of activities carried out by slaves in a situation of close proximity to their masters. Freyre suggests that in colonial times the first civilizing attempts owed more to family organization than to the distant Portuguese state or to the Catholic Church, whose presence and actions were insufficient to impose a different logic of colonization. The persistence of nearly four centuries of this regime,

Gregori Warchavchik,
House in Santa Cruz Street ,
São Paulo, 1929–30. With
this project for a house in
the new modernist style,
Warchavchik was the first
to introduce Modernism
and modern living ideals to
Brazil (above and right).

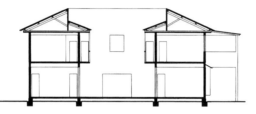

Lucio Costa, Argemiro
Hungria Machado House,
Rio de Janeiro, 1942.
Section and first floor plan
(above and top left) showing
the central courtyard around
which the rooms were
arranged. View of the facade
with its long strip of windows
and vertical *brise-soleil*
(above right).

with the family at its centre, became so deeply
rooted as to have a direct influence on Brazil's
cultural formation.

Rather than portraying the conflicting
relationships between masters and slaves, Gilberto
Freyre dwelt on the fluid borders between these
two realms, highlighting the variety of interchanges
that, one way or another, became part of Brazil's
cultural background. In *Casa Grande & Senzala,* he
analysed the way in which race, religion, sexuality,
cuisine and architecture all reveal a permeability
that overrides class and racial antagonism, as
noticed by Ricardo Benzaquen.[3] The embryo of
Brazilian culture lies in this unexpected and, to a
certain extent, uncontrollable merging of different
worlds.

Within the master's house, however, a degree
of antagonism was to be found in the very plan
of the dwelling, where, for instance, the external
balconies offered a generous opening on to
the landscape while the inner rooms faced the
internal secluded courtyard. This 'balanced
antagonism' summarizes the traditional typology
of the typical Brazilian dwelling in its dual aspect:
an opening-up towards the exterior and isolation
within the interior.

The house of the patriarchal family, despite
its coherence and practicality, was obviously still
bound by the logic of the authority of the clan chief,
and the legitimization of slavery. The challenge
was to overcome these archaic features without
rejecting the cultural significance of the experience
of such a 'tropical space'. In short, the concern of
Brazilian modern architecture would be to reconcile

the individual and collective achievements of
modern democratic society with the feeling of
discretion and privacy that were present in those
previous domestic examples. This passage between
tradition and modernity would corroborate the
theory of the malleability of Brazilian culture, and
thus suggest that it was possible to be modern
without losing one's cultural identity.

This ideal was prevalent in intellectual circles,
although first spelt out by the sociologist Gilberto
Freyre, and was well known in other fields, including
architecture. The Nativist project of Lucio Costa,
and other architects associated with him, sought
a continuity with the Brazilian housing tradition,
also defended by other modernist thinkers linked
to the Office for the National Artistic and Historic
Heritage. Rather than an open and explicit contact
with the exterior, this approach to architecture
saw the ambiguous relationship between inside
and outside as the main aspect that was worth
recovering from colonial houses. Generally, these
houses were organized around a central courtyard.
The frequent use of trellises and wooden venetian
blinds, to protect the windows and doors of the
house and courtyard, emphasizes the introspection
of the internal spaces. As a result, the volume
becomes more 'veiled', and the use of the pitched
roof increases the restraint of the form.

These values subsequently found expression
in the residential architecture of Lucio Costa, the
founding father of the 'Nativist' trend. The calm
and silence of Costa's Argemiro Hungria Machado
House (1942) in Rio de Janeiro were impressive.
Dealing with an urban plot set on a corner, Costa

chose to place the house away from the thoroughfare, and to locate the main entrance on a side street. By doing so, a large area was freed up for a front garden. With these two decisions, Costa achieved the desired detachment of the house from its urban surroundings. To further such isolation, he designed the building as a self-enclosed block organized around an internal courtyard, on to which all of its rooms opened. Large sliding doors enabled the integration of the living and dining areas with the ground-floor courtyard, thus assuring cross ventilation, while, on the first floor, the courtyard void gave privacy to the bedrooms. What is interesting on this floor is Costa's decision to place two opposing windows in the corridor, both looking in towards the courtyard, and then covering them with a trellis. Why protect windows that open on to an already private and intimate space, if not to complicate the relationship between the inner and outer spaces, whose clear continuity was one of the fundamental rules of modernist architecture?

If, in the Argemiro Hungria Machado House, the urban location was a determining factor in the design choice, in the Paes de Carvalho House (1944), also in Rio de Janeiro, such restrictions were not present, as the residence was set on a vast, open piece of land on the banks of a lake. To make the most of the view on to the water, Costa laid out the main areas of the house (living room, bedrooms, kitchen and services) in a long wing, while placing the guests' area and the chapel in an annexed block. An open courtyard connects the two parts of the house. The concept of articulated volumes resulting from this combination of semi-independent wings

would seem to epitomize the open and extrovert character of modern Brazilian architecture of that period. However, this was not exactly what happened here. Despite its asymmetrical layout, the house retained a feeling of seclusion and introversion – not only through its enclosing elements, such as the trellis, but, above all, by the way in which the courtyard articulated the spaces by drawing their various areas towards its core. Such a sense of centrality explained the architect's decision to enclose the open area with a tall wall on one side, and with a light wooden fence, protecting the interior, on the other.

Characteristic elements of colonial architecture were used in both these houses (flat roof, planked floors, balustrade, lattices protecting the openings), co-existing with modern Functionalism and its clean and ascetic forms. However, there was a direct reference to the colonial master's dwelling as discussed by Freyre: the presence of the chapel, adjoining the house. If the sliding trellis in the openings of the Argemiro Hungria Mendonça House remind one of the face-to-face windows of the colonial, urban *sobrados*[4] encountered along the narrow streets of historic Brazilian towns, here, the inclusion of a chapel is a direct throwback to that rural Brazilian domestic prototype: the farmhouse of the large estates.

The plastic rationality of the functional house
Despite the initial impact of Warchavchik's International Style architecture, the adherence to the ideals of modern life by rationalist Brazilian architects did not lead, as in European rationalism,

Lucio Costa, Paes de Carvalho House, Rio de Janeiro, 1944.
The main facade (above left and see plan, below) was designed as a long wing facing the landscape. Two doors gave access and views into the inner courtyard contrasting with the trellissed windows designed to filter the light (above right).

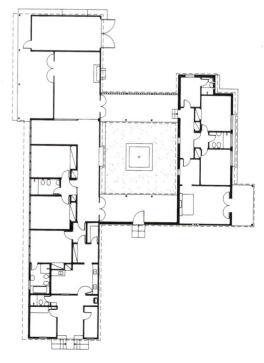

to solutions such as German asceticism or French Purism. As was the case with other types of building, the single-family homes of Brazil's most prominent modern architects – Affonso Eduardo Reidy, Jorge Machado Moreira, Álvaro Vital Brazil, Rino Levi, Oswaldo Bratke, and Lina Bo Bardi – all followed a tendency to emphasize the plasticity of form, but without disregarding functional considerations.

One of the best examples of the equation between form, function and technology can be found in Jorge Moreira's Antonio Ceppas House (1958) in Rio de Janeiro. Designed as the home of a couple with five children, the house was located in a long, narrow urban plot. This led the architect to set the external walls of the house against the site boundaries. The void that constituted the entrance hall worked as the house's main spatial device: the opening began on the ground floor and reached up to the second floor. In this central area of the house, the architect carefully organized the various entrances (social, private, services, leisure) to establish a skilful and functional network of circulation, whose diversity hindered neither the unity nor the dimensions of the main living areas. A

keen adjustment between functional dynamics and spatial stability best described this work

The variety with which Moreira imbued the internal space, where each floor had its own characteristics, was not echoed by the balanced restraint of the house's main elevation. Treated as a compact whole, the facade was defined by an emphatic basic rectangle, subdivided into different levels that mark the intermediate floors, and was complemented by the set-back areas of the ground floor and the terrace. The freestanding and detached frontal plane was the main element of the composition, whose unity was emphasized by the layout of the screening elements. Skilfully, Moreira disrupted the predictability of the facade, traditionally divided into horizontal bands indicating the separation of the floors, by creating a disproportion between the horizontal line of the windows and the verticality of the *brise-soleil*. Le Corbusier's teachings, where the facade was treated as if it were actually a pictorial plane, were here evident.

Just as the unity of the main facade was achieved through complex means, the plan's complexity, despite the variety it included,

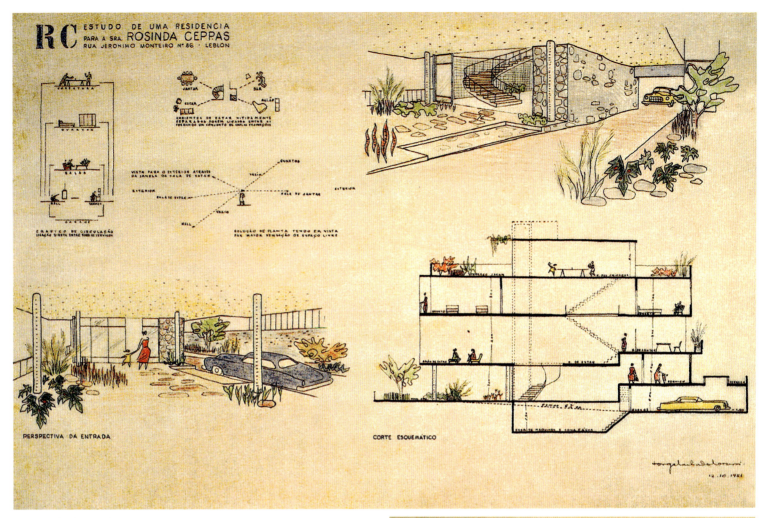

Jorge Machado Moreira,
Antonio Ceppas House,
Rio de Janeiro, 1951–8.
The main spatial device in
this project was the double-
height space that reaches up
to the second floor, as seen in
the four studies on this page.
Functionality was a main
concern for the architect,
who carefully planned the
circulation routes (see
diagramme and section
above) to flow around the
space of the house. The
facade sheltered this
dynamic interior behind
a plane of *brise-soleil*
(opposite).

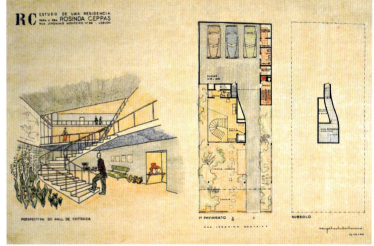

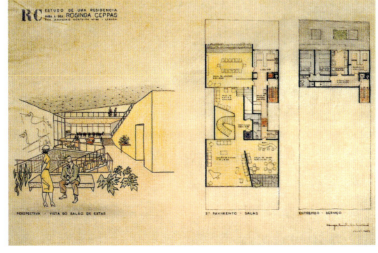

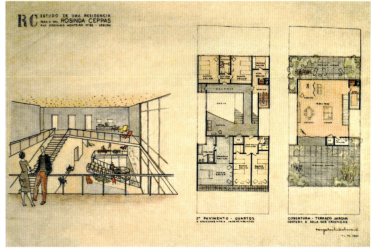

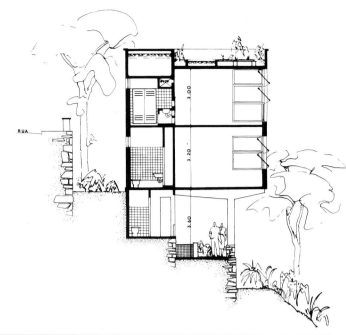

Álvaro Vital Brazil, Álvaro Brazil House, Rio de Janeiro, 1940. Raised on *pilotis*, the house was adapted to the terrain avoiding the need to clear the surrounding vegetation (above left and section, top right). The living room afforded views of the mountains and the bay of Guanabara (above right).

shared the elevation's balanced poise. The same rationale underlay the combination of different elements, plan and elevation, resulting in a simple and intelligent unity. The building's technological refinement, together with the meticulous precision of its spaces and the purity of its form, made the Ceppas House an example of modernity par excellence.

One could very well analyse the output of this rationalist trend, starting with the house Álvaro Vital Brazil built for himself in Rio de Janeiro in 1940, given their shared similarities of architectural approach and volumetric solution, but for now we shall focus further on the work of Affonso Eduardo Reidy.

Similar to Moreira's projects, in its combination of conceptual beauty and functionality, Reidy's Carmen Portinho House (1950), also in Rio de Janeiro, had, as its basic principle, the transparency of forms. The design of this small dwelling set out to meet the needs of a client with a distinct personality. Dynamic, active, modern, heedless of social conventions, Carmen Portinho was one of the first women to distinguish herself in a field usually dominated by men: engineering. In short, she was a

woman who followed her vocation and valued her work, and, typical of the urbanite, needed an intimate place to recover from the stress of modern life. The programme of her house responded uniquely to the requirements of its sole inhabitant, resulting almost in an agenda of 'minimal dwelling', comprising simply living room, bedroom, kitchen, study, servant room and garage.

Here, the formal abstraction of modernist language prevailed, based on the house's geometric rationale: the combination of two trapezoidal prisms on a hillside site. Compared with Lucio Costa's formal introversion, the Carmen Portinho House was definitely extrovert, with each part functionally distinct. The service areas and garage were separate from the wing reserved for the owner; on the ground floor, one part of the house rested directly on the terrain while another hung over the slope, anchored on *pilotis*; in the volumetric composition, each area corresponded to a trapezoidal prism; and finally, on plan, the two areas were arranged into an L shape.

However, the most marked difference between the work of Reidy and the pioneering Lucio Costa lay in their use of the inner courtyard: while the role of Costa's courtyards was to encourage family

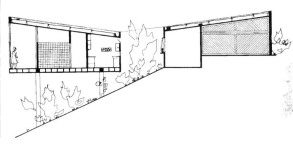

Affonso Eduardo Reidy,
Carmen Portinho House,
Rio de Janeiro, 1950–2.
Designed as two separate
volumes linked by a wooden
ramp and a covered corridor
(see section, top right),
the house was accessed
from street level (top left).
The 13 metre wide glass
facade was designed to make
the best of the surrounding
landscape (above right).

conviviality, in Reidy's work they had an exclusively functional role – to bring in light and ventilation to the surrounding rooms and, like the other formal devices described above, to act as dividing area between different spaces. In the case of the Carmen Portinho House the courtyard is not even a useful area of the house, because it is inaccessible to its inhabitants.

In the house she built in São Paulo from 1949 to 1951, for herself and her husband Pietro Maria Bardi, architect Lina Bo Bardi established a typology close to that of the Carmen Portinho House. Once again, the building was located on the top of a hill, the social and intimate areas resting on *pilotis* while the service area was set directly on the ground. The dwelling was known as the 'Glass House', due to the transparent envelope enclosing the library, living room and dining room, which was intentionally designed as an open gallery to shelter the couple's study and art collection – they were also involved in the project for the São Paulo Museum of Art (see p. 82).

The feeling of emptiness in the volume was reinforced by the slender steel columns, by the incisions on the slabs for the staircases, and by the absence of artificial lighting. Everything came down to the plans of the floor and the roof, supported by skeletal *pilotis*. However, the complete transparency of this 'living-belvedere'[5] contrasted with the closed and regular partitioning of the bedrooms and service areas, which had minimal fenestration facing the back of the house. A long, narrow, court separated these two areas, playing a role similar to that of Reidy's functional courtyard.

The singularity of these two residential programmes – the house-apartment for an emancipated professional, and the house-atelier for owners active in the field of culture – did not prevent them from displaying some common notions that reflected the relationship between public and private in modern society. Spaces for collective conviviality and the demands for individual shelter and intimacy were not only respected but, above all, balanced in an elegant and economic way. The ideal of sociability based on transparent relationships agreed with the modern, truly democratic, creed of universal principles, without denying individual freedom.

Inhabiting landscape
The subsequent loosening of the rigid Functionalist

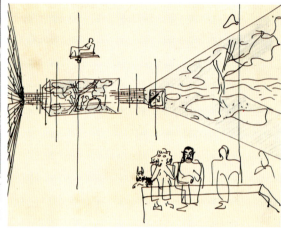

Lina Bo Bardi, Glass House,
São Paulo, 1949–51.
In her first project built in
Brazil, Bo Bardi emphasized
the relationship between
architecture and nature. The
entrance was located under
the main glazed volume
(opposite below left and
opposite above left) opening
into the living-room, where
views of the landscape
predominated (opposite
right and above right) over
the interior. Recent pictures
from the 1990s show views
of the central courtyard from
inside (above left) and from
the access stairs (above
right), where the maturity
of the vegetation is notable.

models for domestic buildings unfolded in several ways. Besides striving to represent a technological and aesthetically advanced product, the Brazilian modern house displays an uncommon inclination to interact with the exuberant tropical nature of its surroundings.

It can even be said that this emotional bond between architecture and landscape represents an alternative way – certainly more peaceful and civilized – of interacting with nature, after almost four centuries of predatory colonial exploitation. It is a kind of reconciliation between Nature and Culture, a pacification of differences – hence the hedonistic feeling of well-being experienced in these built environments. This desire for interaction with nature creates a predominant feeling of openness and transparency and, from the formal point of view, it signals a preference for an inventive articulation of volumes: the interlinking of curves and diagonals with straight lines, for example, and the uninhibited treatment of the space-defining partition walls.

The dominant architectural feature of this approach was the organization of the functional programme around different wings, according to sunlight, ventilation and circulation. Each area – social, private and services – was given a unique volumetric configuration, mainly through the formal treatment of the roof planes. The extended volume with an inverted roof, for which the model is Le Corbusier's Errazuriz House of 1930, became the solution for many Brazilian projects, such as the Juscelino Kubistcheck House (1943) built in Pampulha by Oscar Niemeyer, or the above-

mentioned Portinho House by Affonso Eduardo Reidy.

However, no architect explored this typological composition as extensively as Sérgio Bernardes. His Jadir de Souza House (1951) and Lota de Macedo Soares Country House (1953), both in Rio de Janeiro, articulated two prismatic volumes with a trapezoidal form, thus obtaining a functionally legible composition – formally lively, and interacting with its surroundings.

This way of organizing the programme, aiming at a composition of multiple volumes, stems from the first of the types described by Le Corbusier in his book *Précisions sur un état présent de l'architecture et de l'urbanisme*: the picturesque composition. The impulsive sensuality of such an approach was less to Le Corbusier's own liking than the fourth type, which he considered the synthesis of the previous three: an external pure form combined with a free-composition interior, whose model is the Villa Savoye. The projects of Brazilian architects, if compared with Le Corbusier's preferred type, display less of his idealistic bias in favour of an immediate interaction with the landscape. Their free movement over the landscape, the unconstrained unfolding of form, and the easy expansion over a free surface, all express a feeling of contentment with the lively availability offered by the 'free' territory of the New World. Enjoying geometry in the landscape is what these projects were primarily about.[6]

In the case of projects designed by those architects closer to the rationalist tradition – such as Reidy, Moreira, Lina Bo Bardi and Vital Brazil –

Oscar Niemeyer, Canoas House, Rio de Janeiro, 1953. Views of the upper floor with the pool and the curvilinear roof slab (above left), the kitchen (top right) and the lower floor (below right).

formal freedom was balanced with a functional programme. The more this equilibrium was unsettled, the more the idyllic relationship with the landscape became idealized, as happened in Oscar Niemeyer's architecture, such as his Pampulha buildings at Belo Horizonte, built between 1942 and 1943 (see pp. 118–21). Whereas the architect's drawing was here immediately imprinted on concrete,[7] thus generating an exteriorized spatiality, in the case of his house designs, he seemed to yield more to functional specifications. This is not to say that Niemeyer was conceding to a Functionalist attitude – he was, in fact, formulating his criticism of such an attitude precisely at that time.[8]

One may say that, when confronted with the problem of the house, Niemeyer's approach was closer to that of Lucio Costa, designing his spaces with an evidently affective sense.[9] His borrowing of the simple scale and repertoire of Costa's Nativist houses, can be seen in the first residence he built for himself, in 1942, and in his Francisco Peixoto House (1943) in Cataguazes, in the state of Minas Gerais.

Everything leads us to believe that Niemeyer

associated the house with domestic values, such as the feeling of well-being, tranquillity and rest. Yet, for him, the silent intimacy of the home did not mean enclosure and darkness. On the contrary, it meant light and openness. In his celebrated Canoas House (1953) in Rio de Janeiro, also his own residence, the architect skilfully combined the openness inherent in the modernist plan with the intimacy of the traditional home.

At first sight, the house appears nothing but a flat, sinuous roof slab, supported by pillars, located on a level and elevated terrain, and surrounded by mountains and forest. The free shape of the roof slab rules the design, given the minimum presence of the enclosing walls: these are limited to two freestanding, wide-curving walls that define the living room on the right and the dining room on the left. With the exception of the kitchen area, set opposite the living room, the remainder of this floor of the house, is enclosed only by large glass panes. The feeling of openness is complete, as if the emptiness of the terrain traverses the house and continues through the forest and down to the distant sea.

Architecturally, the house has two basic elements:

a granite floor and a roof slab, both bright planes vibrating amidst the surrounding green. The slab acts as a large canopy, going beyond the perimeter of the interior, to protect it from excessive sunlight as well as forming a balcony that acts both as an extension of the living room and, near the pool, as a social area. The pool, with its equally sinuous outline, emphasizes the organic shape of the roof; the architect reaffirms this interaction by incorporating the granite rock that extends from the swimming pool into the 'house-tent' itself.

Inside the house, the rock's curve leads to the staircase serving the lower floor, where the bedrooms and study are located. The layout of this level is adjusted to the topography, in sharp contrast with the free plan of the upper floor. This division between public and private in residential programmes is not new, as was seen in Reidy's and Lina Bo Bardi's houses, above. What is unusual in this house is that some of the silent intimacy of the private areas seems, gently, to enter the public areas. In spite of the glass pane that envelops the ground floor allowing the interaction with the exterior, a certain feeling of privacy is preserved. The curved plan of the living room provides

intimacy, but does not hinder the connections to other rooms. Indeed, the whole house captures an atmosphere stoically adjusted to the needs of its dweller, hence the modest size of the rooms, the purity of the layout and the minimal presence of domestic appliances. Luxury, waste, the gratuitous – these are not attributes of this house.

The key to this harmonic adjustment between inside and outside is undoubtedly the intelligent setting of the house. The clearing is surrounded by the thick vegetation of the adjoining hills, and the access road is on an upper level. To arrive at the house, one has to follow a winding road until reaching the site. The house is thus completely isolated, which is why one feels protected despite the transparency of the volume. Indeed, in that space, everything is interior, and the enclosing role is played purely by natural elements. Thus, one can say that this house is not only the building itself, but a whole set of various elements: the plateau, garden, swimming pool, granite rock and the floating canopy over the inner spaces. The architect has set everything in close contact, establishing endless exchanges between architectural and natural elements. If it is possible to speak of a

Oscar Niemeyer, Canoas House, Rio de Janeiro, 1953. External and internal views of the living room and the rock around which it was designed (above and top).

Rino Levi, Milton Guper House, São Paulo, 1951–3. This project gave its back to the street (see facade, above left and plan, opposite below left) facing out onto the inner garden, which was adjoined to the living room by a pergola (opposite above and below right, see also elevation, above).

tradition of the Brazilian house, going back to the first colonial dwellings, that operates on this kind of symbiosis between building and landscape, Oscar Niemeyer's Canoas House represents the fullest evidence of its continuation.

Unbalanced antagonisms: the politics and poetry of the brutalist house

After the new ideas introduced by Gregori Warchavchik in the second half of the 1920s, three architects have had a major role in the consolidation of modern house design in São Paulo from the 1940s onwards: Rino Levi, Oswaldo Bratke and Vilanova Artigas.

The designs of these architects had in common the way they represent the urban experience, as well as a new logic of the production and circulation of goods. Levi's and Bratke's answers to these problems were, perhaps, more pragmatic and technical, while those of Artigas tended to the ideological and poetic.

Houses such as the one Levi built for himself between 1944 and 1946, and his Milton Guper House (1953), all in São Paulo, revealed the difficulties and challenges of the small and irregular

corner plots that the architect was dealing with. In both cases, Levi alternated green, open areas with built ones, aiming at creating a courtyard for each of the several sections of the programme. In this way, the layout of the 'plan in parts' with interconnected wings, spread out over the site – as was usual in other projects in Rio de Janeiro[10] – but, curiously, the gardens here had the opposite effect: rather than offering the opportunity for continuity between architecture and landscape, they worked as barriers to protect and isolate the houses from the street.

Oswaldo Bratke's concern was more constructional. The residences designed in the 1950s, such as his own house (1951) and the Oscar Americano House (1952), both in São Paulo, represented the epitome of such an approach . They were clearly laid-out, comprising a spatial grid – made up of pillars and beams, slabs, and hanging floors – which defined both the plan and the volumes of the house. Once this independent structure was set, the architect's main preoccupation became the partition walls, whose logic was rigorously dictated by the needs of the programme. The internal spaces were distributed in

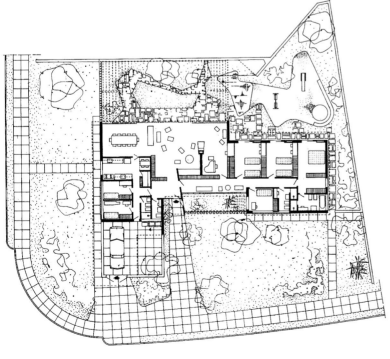

Oswaldo Bratke, Oscar Americano House, São Paulo, 1952. The plan was based on a dynamic grid combining empty and built spaces (opposite below left). View (above) and detail of the east facade (opposite above right) with terrace (opposite above left). The pavement on the north-west facade had mosaic tiles designed by Livio Abramo (opposite above right).

disciplined but flexible way, giving prominence to the inner gardens; and extreme care was given to problems of ventilation and solar gain. Following a perfect planning logic, Bratke used a variety of means in the definition of his enclosing partition walls. The results were dwelling spaces enriched by light-and-shade effects, ventilated and comfortable – in short, spaces highly suited to the weather and the landscape. With such a design method, Bratke managed to combine, as Jorge Moreira also did, regularity and flexibility in the same equation – solving, with a remarkable economy of means, the demands of the rationalization of the building industry, without prejudicing the needs of the houses' interiors. Finally, he proved that standardization was not incompatible with flexibility and variety of forms.

Vilanova Artigas' architecture, like that of Levi and Bratke, took account of both the urban circumstances and the constructional features of each project. What was different about Artigas' work was the critical and incisive character of his proposals, which questioned the architect's social function and status.

While most of Rio's architects maintained an attitude that could be categorized as 'apolitical, neutral, technical', seeking collective well-being and the affirmation of a positive and self-sufficient culture – although taking advantage, at the same time, of the *Estado Novo* (the authoritarian government of Getúlio Vargas, which held power in the early 1940s) – Artigas openly stated his political commitment. An architect and a communist, Artigas' professional practice did not separate art and politics, and it was this that enabled him to start questioning the use, the value, the type and the programme of the bourgeois house (see p. 183).

On one hand, according to Artigas, technical advances had their high social costs, and this was why he was always critical of the ideal of progress inherent in Modernism. On the other hand, he saw the legacy of violence and predatory exploitation from the patriarchal and slave-based society that linked Brazil to its colonial past. For Artigas, the contemporary bourgeois house retained too much of that tainted legacy, hence his commitment to critically review the hierarchy of space, the distribution of the programme, the siting, the functional division and the stylistic rules of the

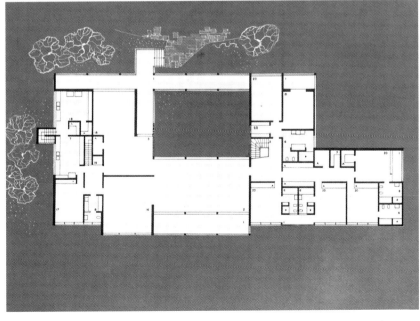

Sobrados, Mariana, Minas Gerais. This row of *sobrados* is a typical example of eighteenth century Brazilian urban architecture, a model which was followed up to the first half of the twentieth century.

bourgeois home. Until around 1940, the typical house for the affluent classes in São Paulo was the two-storey *sobrado*: a model established by central planning, most examples of which were passively compliant with local regulations, and submissively followed the eclectic tendencies then in force. To Artigas, this model was completely outdated; yet, São Paulo's residents insisted on it, provoking him to criticize their 'stagnant and inert' lifestyle, to the point of comparing them as well as building companies, architects and real-estate agents to 'vegetation'.[11]

Although his commitment to achieve a new division of the internal spaces of the house, with the aim of integrating all its areas, dated back to the 1940s, it was only in the Baeta House (1956) that Artigas' typological strategy became clearly defined. There, the architect pioneered the solution that was to become his trademark: the large, unitary covering formed by the roof and blind facades, supported, in this case, by six columns. Sheltered by this synthetic structure, the internal spaces flowed without restrictions, their differentiation achieved through the articulation of different levels – as in the case of the living room, to which the study

was connected by a flight of stairs. The division of space was comprehensible without the need for partition walls, which would have hindered communication between different areas of the house. Since the openings followed the longitudinal axis of the plot, that is, they opened on to the side boundaries, the front of the house was defined by a huge concrete plane and by the garage opening. Externally, therefore, there was not the slightest hint of the fluid life developing beyond these opaque surfaces. To broaden the interior and resist the exterior was to be the architect's poetic attitude.

Artigas' series of reactions against the traditional bourgeois house reached its climax in the Taques Bittencourt House (1959). Its large roof was established as the fundamental structure of the house, as the lateral concrete panes reached down to the ground, converting the three-part configuration (beam-column-beam) into a structural portico, in which the components could no longer be disengaged, since they now formed a single element. Once the full use of the interior was secured by the use of such a primordial envelope, the architect had all the internal space at his disposal.

To start with, he operated a provocative reversal,

The Modern Brazilian House

João Batista Vilanova Artigas, Baeta House, São Paulo, 1956. Preparatory sketch showing structural solution (above), view of blind facade parallel to street (top), and the living room (below).

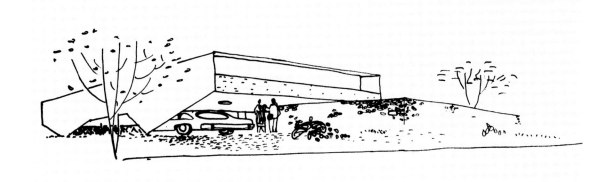

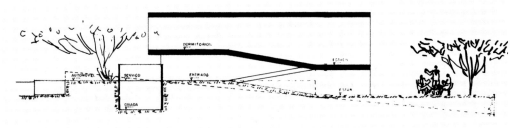

CORTE ESQUEMATICO

João Batista Vilanova Artigas, Taques Bitencourt House, São Paulo, 1959. The structural system (see perspective, top and section, above) in this project allowed for all activities to be sheltered in a single space organized around a central courtyard lit from a bove by an opening in the roof slab.

by setting bedrooms, kitchen and service areas to the front of the plot, while leaving the back for convivial spaces. A feeling of expansion and spatial interconnection was produced by introducing an internal garden between these two zones, towards which their outer rooms faced.

The internal spatial flow, with no walls acting as barriers, was emphasized as a zone of conviviality and free social interaction in contrast to the external space of the city, divided by physical and symbolic barriers expressive of the logic of the speculative property market and of the exploitative character of capitalism. In this sense, the interior acted as a rectified space and, contrary to the usual typology, the living areas were organized away from the facade and the street.

Artigas' strategy of placing a large roof over inteconnected spaces was intended to increase the convivial areas of the programme, which led to its being repeated in other projects, particularly in schools, such as the celebrated Faculty of Architecture and Urban Studies of the University of São Paulo (see p. 178). Obviously, the political message implicit in the proposal of these interactive spaces was a rejection of space as private property, or 'merchandise', and its alienation from the sphere of public interests.

Contrary to the optimism of the 1940s and 1950s – of which the construction of Brasília was the strongest expression – in the 1960s, Brazilian architects were faced with the dual phenomena of mass consumption and industrialisation, as well as the political tragedy of the military dictatorship and an ever-increasing number of marginalized

people migrating to the cities. The critical architectural approach, defended by Artigas since the beginning of the 1950s, now became an imperative: one could not, in such a troubled context, remain naive or apolitical. In this sense, one can observe some correlation between Artigas' criticism of the ideological basis of the Modern Project and the revision of principles initiated by the breakaway Team X group at the 1956 CIAM conference.

Artigas' Brutalism opened paths that would be followed by younger architects – such as Carlos Milan, Fábio Penteado, Eduardo de Almeida and, above all, Paulo Mendes da Rocha – who would absorb the master's critical attitude and architectural approach. These designers carried on with austere and compact forms, the use of advanced building technologies, land-works, and vast internal spaces, while Artigas' political criticism would find – in Sérgio Ferro, Flávio Império and Rodrigo Lefèvre – even more radical followers. These two groups had in common the rejection of architecture as a mere 'luxury item', the denial of the alienated compliance of architects towards the construction market, and the repudiation of the nebulous and self-centred aestheticism of the then current trend of Formalism. From Mendes da Rocha's 'rationalized *favela*'[12] to Ferro's experience of collective housing construction, the common point was the belief in architecture as 'a way of knowing reality'.

Other followers of Artigas were less committed to the general transformation of the production system, whose end result was the

inevitable migration of architecture into politics, but nevertheless remained faithful to his critical approach to design.

Following Artigas' combination of logical and ethical construction, Carlos Milan looked for economy of means and the standardization of the building process. Strict modular division of the plan, together with the rationalization of the construction process and the use of prefabricated components – or pieces cast in situ – gave Milan's houses an unpretentious scale, which avoided rhetorical structural expressions. This was exemplified by the Antonio D'Elboux House (1962–4) in São Paulo, a two-storey residence supported by *pilotis* on a steeply sloping plot. The exposed concrete structure of the external walls formed a diagram of slabs, beams and pillars, and the spaces in between them were filled with different materials: wall panels, with a textured render finish; precast concrete windows, with iron frames, glass panes and precast concrete blocks.

Such a method of deconstructing the building into its basic elements, with the object of standardizing these components, was close to Joaquim Guedes' approach. However, while Milan was inclined to use a regular volume raised on *pilotis* (an obvious legacy of Artigas' re-reading of Le Corbusier), Guedes' forms changed with every new project. Consistent with his methodology of distilling the rationale for each design from its specific circumstances, he rejected the use of a fixed or constant architectural vocabulary.

Taking a strong analytical approach, Guedes selected every functional, structural, and even cultural, detail in relation to each specific building project: the architect's position, technical and economic viability, the client's circumstances, and the features of the particular residential programme, making the result a series of localized solutions.

In Guedes' architecture, the challenge was to maintain sufficient unity of the whole, so that the architectural form did not become a disjointed collection of fragments. The expressive tension in his work resulted from the confrontation of the circumstantial with the singular. The bigger the challenges imposed by the increasing complexity of the project's process, the bigger the stimulus to formal invention. In his best projects, Guedes took this tension to its limit, as in the Cunha Lima House of 1958-63 in São Paulo.

The sloping terrain and the increasingly complex programme for this residence – which required, in addition to the usual rooms, a study, a wine cellar, equipment and machines for the swimming pool, a sauna, and the later annexation of the adjacent terrain, onto which extended the kitchen and service areas – contributed to the gradual generation of solutions that suited both the small amount of space available and the difficult topography. Guedes decided to organize the house on four floors, resting on *pilotis*. He supported the floor slabs with inclined beams, creating a ramified and dynamic structural system, while the subsequent extension of the kitchen provided the house with an unusual inverted-pyramid box, used to collect water from the roof. Each specific problem seemed, therefore,

João Batista Vilanova Artigas, Taques Bitencourt House, São Paulo, 1959. Ramps leading to the higher levels and attached to the load-bearing walls offered a view into the central courtyard (above).

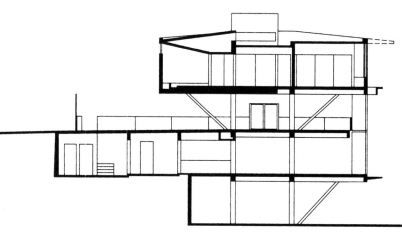

Joaquim Guedes, Cunha
Lima House, São Paulo, 1958.
Views of the north-west
facade (above). The long
section shows how the
house was adapted to the
difference of level in the site
(above right).

to require a particular formal solution. Although
the composition vaguely resembled a rectangle,
the variety of the many design elements, by
attracting the observer's attention, contributed
to disrupt the unifying power of the house's
overall form.

In the house built for engineer Waldo Perseu
Pereira (1967-9) in São Paulo, Guedes achieves the
same tense balance as in the Cunha Lima House,
although with a different, more expansive spatial
development. The programme also had some
complications since, besides the couple and their
children, the owner's father required a private
apartment with an independent entry.

The triangular corner plot suggested the
development of volumes following a slope to
the north, bordering the back street. Guedes set
at the higher level, the independent accesses to
the house and the private apartment and, on a lower
level, the main house and the services area. Seen
from the street, the building presents a regular and
horizontal appearance, as if it had only one storey.
Nothing anticipates what follows when one
descends the stairs towards the two storeys below
and starts to experience the succession of spaces

unfolding in increasing magnitudes until one
reaches the lowest level, where the various living
areas are organized in a radial sequence giving a
strong feeling of openness.

This way of designing the plan according to
the suggestions of local topography is reminiscent
of Alvar Aalto's typology, as Guedes himself
acknowledged. More than a formal issue, what
is important is the flexibility of Guedes' method,
which allows the incorporation of suggestions
from other design vocabularies. Aalto's Nordic
empiricism, with his quest to take into account
the site's physical conditions, is akin to Guedes'
analytical modus operandi.

Another fundamental principle that similarly
interferes with the house's planning, is what Guedes
calls 'the client's culture'. Attention to the particular
characteristics of taste, social class and psycho-
physiological needs of the clients, allows him to
insert the architectural object appropriately into
the social and territorial context of its inhabitants.
Other architects, more associated with architecture
as a social project, sometimes criticized this
anthropological attention to the client's context,
but, for Guedes, to set aside one of the terms of the

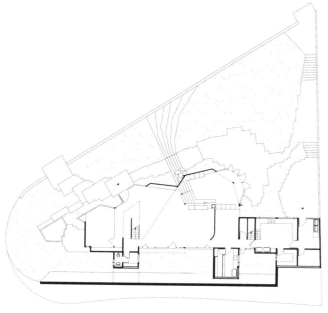

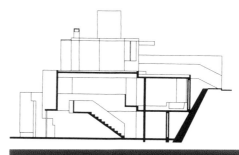

problem for ideological reasons was to corrupt the whole process of design – a process which he tried so obstinately and rigorously to define.

Unlike Joaquim Guedes' analytical approach, Paulo Mendes da Rocha's design strategy, as Sophia Telles suggests,[13] operates through 'condensation'. Far from being minimalist, in the sense of a reductive procedure, it starts from a synthesis of the two elements at the core of his whole production: the connection between the ground and the roof plane. The rationale for his uninterrupted roofs, generally a structure of waffle slabs, was to provide spaces capable of concentrating, in a common area, several activities: living, dining, studying and cooking. Concrete, built-in furniture and low concrete partitions helped to define different areas. The intelligent way in which the architect built elements of furniture into the external walls and internal partitions represented, in the opinion of many, the essence of Mendes da Rocha's act of 'condensation'.

In his own house, built in 1964 in São Paulo, Mendes da Rocha broke down the identity of the wall by embedding concrete tables, closets and long benches in the external walls, and alternating these elements with horizontal fenestration. One of the most remarkable built-in elements is the dining table, which protrudes from the external wall exactly below a window. In this way, both wall and window are 'displaced' from their traditional positions. Seen from the outside, such shifts turn the facade into an array of assembled, constructive parts, seemingly devoid of any anthropomorphic connotations.

In perceptual terms, the traditional Euclidian spatial references (horizontal, vertical, high, low) lose their stability, since the architectural elements are here displaced from their usual positions, and take on more than one possible meaning depending on the role they perform in the design as a whole.

On the other hand, the 'condensation' of Mendes da Rocha's designs can result in the opposite effect – that of homogenization of spaces. This is true in the case of the bedroom area of his own house, in which the long, narrow and almost repetitive spaces turn the bedrooms into veritable alcoves of the main living areas. Similarly, the centralization of the plan is echoed in the

Joaquim Guedes, Waldo Perseu Pereira House, São Paulo, 1967–9. View of the west face (above left) and the living room and mezzanine (above right), and drawings showing the groundfloor plan (top left) and the cross section (top right).

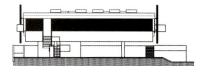

predominantly rectangular synthetic volume.

At the time, the originality of the house's plan was much debated. The location of the bedrooms was considered particularly radical: they sat in the centre of the plan, flanked by the living/dining wing on one side, and by the gallery/office wing on the other. In this way, the wings formed a continuous circuit around the sleeping area, and all the bedrooms could themselves become passages to the other areas of the house, especially given that their partitioning walls did not reach the ceiling, allowing the whole internal space of the house to be perceived as a continuum. Artigas' 'community' ideal was here presented in its most obvious and radical form.

The way in which the building was set on the ground was also typical of Mendes da Rocha's approach. The rectangular volume was raised on four *pilotis*, but the embankment that bordered the corner concealed these supports, giving the appearance from the street that the house lied directly on the ground. The interesting aspect about using the ground surface as part of the design strategy was the apparent contradiction it created with Le Corbusier's *pilotis* principle. Whereas Le Corbusier's intention was to affirm the plastic form in the landscape by physically raising it on *pilotis*, here, the use of the embankment draws one's attention to the original ground surface, a reminder of the modest hill that existed in that location before urban expansion.

In the António Junqueira House (1976–8) in São Paulo, the ground surface of the site was taken as an integral element of the design. Mendes da Rocha

set most of the house below road level, while the roof slabs appeared almost as extensions of the street, and, consistent with this effect, were treated as roof-gardens. The brief required the housing of a large library, which was accommodated in a separate volume, the only part of the project to rise above ground level, as the sole survivor of a traditional architectural vocabulary. It took the form of a structural portico, whose opening was closed by an oblique and loose plane, a pure architectural element, reminiscent of the primordial meaning of the act of building: to shelter a surface. The similarities of this house with Mendes da Rocha's famous Brazilian Museum of Sculpture (1985-95) are evident (see p. 54).

In the Millán House (1970), also in São Paulo, Mendes da Rocha took a rather different design approach. Here, the architect completely enclosed the boundaries of the plot with concrete ramparts, then divided the site with a sinuous wall separating the open-air courtyard from the inner areas, and located the bedrooms within suspended pavillions interconnected by a bridge, leaving the ground floor for the service and living areas. The innovative idea was to set volumes in a space which was conventionally recognized as internal.

In this project there were no external windows; natural light entered through a skylight in the roof slab. The most spectacular space was the double-height hall, lit from above, surrounded by the imposing sinuous concrete plane and dominated by the curving stairs leading up to the internal bridge that connected the suspended volumes of the bedrooms. As with Mendes da Rocha's own

Paulo Mendes da Rocha, Mendes da Rocha House, São Paulo, 1964–6. Views from street level (above left) and of the entrance (above right), first floor plan (below) and elevation (top).

Paulo Mendes da Rocha, Antonio Junqueira House, São Paulo, 1976–80. Views from the street showing the library and concrete screen (opposite top right), access to the library (opposite bottom left) and a side view of the libary with the rooftop garden (opposite bottom right).

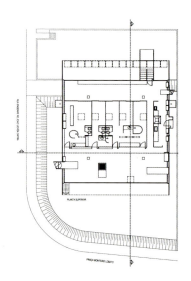

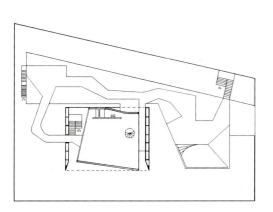

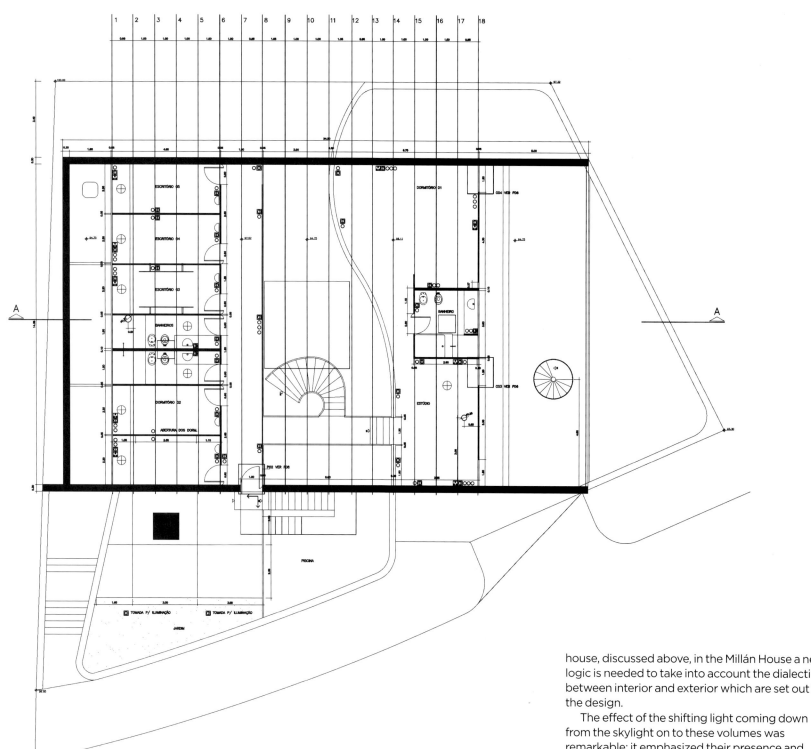

house, discussed above, in the Millán House a new logic is needed to take into account the dialectics between interior and exterior which are set out in the design.

The effect of the shifting light coming down from the skylight on to these volumes was remarkable: it emphasized their presence and continually changed the surrounding spaces. Here, there was a reference to Le Corbusier's skilful use of light, to enhance planes and volumes and, at the same time, destabilize perception of them by the continuous shift of natural light.

For Paulo Mendes da Rocha, the design of houses provided ways of thinking about architecture as a form of knowledge that challenged the usual notions of programme, setting, inside and outside, void and volume, structures and enclosures. By unsettling such notions the architect has played a self-reflective game with the basic elements of the architectural task.

The radicalism of Mendes da Rocha's residential projects lies in the way it overcomes the tendency, common in Brazil, to associate the house with the psychological dimension of intimacy, and to think of the dwelling unit as privacy and protection against

external threats. Mendes da Rocha's approach reassesses the concept of domestic life, and of what should be considered familiar, emotional and close at hand. However, it is still possible to detect glimpses of intimacy in his work, albeit an intimacy linked to one's own private consciousness rather than to moral conventions or established habits. This kind of 'house of the mind' reaffirms Mendes da Rocha's – and, before him, Vilanova Artigas' – view of architecture as a form of knowledge.

By stripping the house of any affective and psychological projections, Paulo Mendes da Rocha boldly assumes it to be a public, rather than private, entity, hence the severe and impersonal aspect of his designs. It becomes clear that for him, the public realm is not confined only to what takes place in external and open spaces, but rather is constituted through the relationships of those who share the same space, and who, at the end of the day, constitute society.

Paulo Mendes da Rocha, Millán House, São Paulo, 1970. First floor plan (opposite), showing the sinuous wall separating covered and open-air areas. Views of the living room and skylight in the central double-height space (above left) and access to the rooftop garden (above right).

CHAPTER FIVE
REINVENTING THE BUILDING SITE
BY PEDRO FIORI ARANTES

Oscar Niemeyer, National
Congress under construction,
Brasília, 1958. The Chamber
of Deputies is sheltered by an
inverted dome positioned on
a white plane, in symmetry
with the dome of the Senate.
While domes are pure
architectonical forms – almost
perfect from a structural point
of view – inverted domes are
difficult and costly to build
(opposite).

REINVENTING THE BUILDING SITE

Starting Point

Brasília, the highest point of modern Brazilian architecture, was both its crowning achievement and the most striking illustration of Brazil's underdevelopment.[1] The construction of an entirely new capital city in the uninhabited interior of the country, undertaken on an unprecedented scale, starkly illustrated the enormous contrast between modernist design and outdated and unsafe methods of production. Far from being an anomaly, this was quite in keeping with the singular combination of modern architecture and developmentalist states on the periphery of capitalism.

While Brasília's daring forms expressed the nation's desire to put itself onto the same footing as the major economic powers, the large building sites gave ample evidence of the backwardness of production. The discrepancy between the facade of modernity and the reality of Brazil's economic base exposed the artificial character of the new capital city and, by extension, of peripheral modernization itself.

For the generation of architects who graduated during the construction of Brasília, at the end of the 1950s and the beginning of the 1960s, this perception – of a discrepancy between the progressive intentions of those who planned the new city and the exploitation and violence suffered by the workers on its building sites – was evident. For some, this perception led them to develop new building practices and even a whole new theory of architecture in a kind of settling of scores with modern Brazilian architecture.[2]

In the first half of this chapter, we shall follow the debate between the main São Paulo modern architect, João Vilanova Artigas, and his three dissident disciples, who were critical of the prevailing modern approach to building, and who worked together until their arrest in 1970: Sérgio Ferro, Rodrigo Lefèvre and Flávio Império.

Classmates from the secondary school and the architecture course, Ferro and Lefèvre had privileged contact with the construction of Brasília. Ferro's father was a Social Democrat Party politician, an ally of Juscelino Kubitschek, President of Brazil from 1957 to 1960, and also a building developer for the new capital. These connections enabled the three architects to plan and construct residential buildings in Brasília, even while they were still students. What they witnessed on frequent visits to works in the new city led them to reflect on architectural practice, and to look for alternative paths.

Ferro and Lefèvre were critical of the official reports of the miraculousness of the construction process in the capital city. In testimonies given years later, both recounted the actual nature of the labour relations on the building sites.[3] There was ample evidence of at least four forms of exploitation to which the Brasília workers were subjected:

1) Devaluation of labour. The vast majority of the capital's builders, known as *candangos*, were impoverished rural or landless workers from the poorest parts of Brazil, the scrubland of the northeast. The Brasília building sites were planned for the extensive use of unskilled labour carrying

Reinventing the Building Site

Oscar Niemeyer, National Congress under construction, Brasília, 1958. The epic story of the construction of the new capital hid the tragic fate of many of the workers that took part in it: their exclusion from the city that they helped to build (opposite above).

Oscar Niemeyer, Cathedral under construction, Brasília, 1958. The difficult and complex construction process to which inexperienced rural workers were subjected in this project highlighted the contradictions between the design's good intentions and the actual working conditions on the building site (opposite below).

out strenuous work. As such, the construction of Brasília represented the climax of the devaluation of labour that had occurred in civil construction, a process begun decades earlier, and unwittingly taken further by modern architects.

2) Super-exploitation. The workers were subject to long working days, low salaries, poor food and epidemics, and at risk of death on account of minimal safety procedures. The 'continuous shifts' demanded in order to complete work on time, sometimes involving working two or three days without stopping, increased the workers' vulnerability. The dangers were exacerbated by the primitive production techniques employed in the construction of monumental buildings. Workers' organizations were repressed, and dozens of labourers were murdered.

3) Deletion. Niemeyer's polished white facades, which made the capital's buildings look almost ethereal, wiped out any trace of the human effort that had brought them into existence. The works exist apparently independently of those who produced them, a result intensified by the architect's prominence. This apparent autonomy, not only signifies the fetishism of the commodity, but is also a manifestation of a tendency to abstract social relations and of the state's control over social reality.

4) Segregation. Workers were forbidden to remain in Brasília after it was built. They were prevented from living in proximity to their work simply on account of the fact that no place had been planned for them: Brasília's Master Plan had not included low-income housing. The builders had

to remain in their camps, which were to become precarious satellite towns, separated from the city by a green belt.

These observations are not merely a litany of the brutality present in the construction of Brasília, but are characteristic features of how capitalism works in a peripheral country. For two decades, Brazil was the country with the highest economic growth in the world, an achievement obtained by the mobilization of an impoverished workforce and its inclusion in both modern and archaic circuits of capital accumulation. The accelerated modernization of post-war Brazil occurred without significant internal investment, and thus depended on constant foreign investment and primitive methods of creaming off profits – in agriculture, in mining and, indeed, on large building sites.

The Brasília building sites were, therefore, no exception, but a microcosm, in one single highly symbolic location, of how Brazilian modernization went about its business, manifesting all its ambitions, inequalities and human cost, and, by extension, those of the dynamics of worldwide capitalist expansion also.

The deletion of the traces of labour for Brasília, a process in which architects were accomplices, amounts to a deletion of history itself, and calls into question the whole direction of architectural production in Brazil. Scrutiny of the architects' participation in this process gave rise to the thoughts and actions of the *Arquitetura Nova* (New Architecture) movement, whose brief history we shall now appraise.

Oscar Niemeyer, National
Congress in construction,
Brasília, 1958. The construction
of the National Congress,
especially that of the inverted
dome, emphasized the
opposition between the
suppleness of Niemeyer's
design and the the heavy
workload demanded of those
building it.

The 1960s

In the 1960s, the Faculty of Architecture and
Urbanism at the University of São Paulo (FAU-USP)
became the most important architecture school in
the country, with its own pedagogical project,
distinguishing its courses from those of engineering
and fine arts, and the highest level of debate about
the direction to be taken by post-Brasília modern
Brazilian architecture. Most of the Faculty was
involved in the debate, which lasted the entire
decade. Orchestrating everything was the school's
grand master, the architect João Vilanova Artigas,[4]
and his three main disciples: Sérgio Ferro, Flávio
Império and Rodrigo Lefèvre – the Arquitetura Nova
group.[5]

Broadly speaking, on Artigas's side were those
who believed that through the study of design
social problems could be overcome, whereas on
the other side, were those who maintained that it
was through the study of the building site that
thought and action in building practice could be
united. Or, as Sérgio Ferro saw it, 'the confrontation
between the search for development of productive
forces (Artigas) versus the critique of the
exploitative relationships of production (Flávio
Império, Rodrigo and me)'.[6]

The beginning of the 1960s was a time of great
excitement and there was a belief that a new phase
of development could unfold positively in Brazil.
The Presidency of João Goulart (1962-4) aimed
at fundamental reforms, including land reform,
while trade unionism was gaining strength through
mass mobilization. At a meeting of the Institute of
Brazilian Architects in 1963, architects discussed,

for the first time, the possibilities of urban reform in
the country. Ideas of social change were sweeping
through Latin America, aroused by fast-moving
industrialization and the rise of a new working class,
as well as by the historic opportunities presented by
the 1959 Cuban Revolution.

It was in this context that the architect João
Vilanova Artigas – like Niemeyer, and so many others,
a member of the Brazilian Communist Party – carried
out his most important project linked to the idea of
a new pedagogy in 1962: the new FAU-USP building
itself. A modernist manifesto, an immense
parallelepiped on stilts, its internal spaces were laid
out under a large translucent, reticulated roof,
clustered around a central hall measuring 1,000
square metres by 13 metres in height. A series of wide
ramps surrounding the great hall leads to each floor,
linking the levels containing the main auditorium;
the models and prototypes workshop; the Students'
Union, where the café and museum are located; the
library and archives; the teachers' room and
interdepartmental workshop; the open studios,
illuminated from above; and, finally, the classrooms.
In the original plans, the classrooms were the only
enclosed spaces, and the interior of the building was
like a promenade, rising through the areas of study,
creation, leisure and sociability, led finally to the
moment of reflective synthesis in the studios at the
top. The building as a whole, with few outside
windows and lit entirely from above, is reminiscent
of a small town, conceived in such a way as to
demand from students and teachers the intellectual
breadth and creativity required to produce a
new country.

Reinventing the Building Site

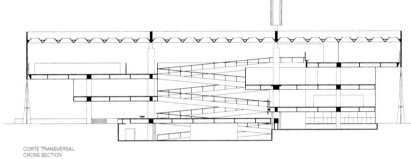

CORTE TRANSVERSAL
CROSS SECTION

João Batista Vilanova Artigas, Faculty of Architecture of the University of São Paulo, São Paulo, 1961–9. This project is like a miniature city, lit through a transparent roof (opposite above right) supported on *pilotis* (opposite above left and below) and organized around a large hall where some of the most important events in the faculty take place (above right; see section, above left).

The course itself, originating in the Technical School, from which it had separated in 1948, had previously concentrated on engineering disciplines. Inspired partly by the experiences at the Bauhaus and the Ulm School, the course underwent radical reform, shifting the axis of teaching towards creative workshops. Alongside Building Projects and Urbanism, Design Studies was now fully incorporated into the curriculum. This centred upon the key discipline of Industrial Design and was supported by the reformulated area of Visual Planning, a field previously considered closer to 'fine arts'. At the same time, new emphasis was placed on History, and various humanities teachers were brought into the Faculty, giving rise to the formation of three departments : History, Technology and Design. This structure became the model for most architecture courses in Brazil.

For Artigas, the school was to produce not only integrated individuals, as Bauhaus director Walter Gropius had proposed, but agents of innovation, capable of operating in a whole gamut of processes. They were to be professionals uniquely ready to respond to the various needs required by the modernization process in Brazil,

from the design of the simplest objects to major urban and territorial structures.

In 1962, the year that the curriculum was reformed and the new building project designed, the newly graduated Sérgio Ferro, Flávio Império and Rodrigo Lefèvre became teachers at the school. In the following year, they launched a manifesto, published by the Students' Union. Entitled 'Initial Proposal for Debate: Possibilities for Action', the young teachers' programme questioned the positive and uncritical attitude towards Brazilian modernization shown by the vast majority of architects, including the communists. As far as they were concerned, architectural production was taking place in a situation of con-flict between labour and capital, which required architects to adopt a participatory position, on the side of the workers. This was an ironic demand to make of professionals, who, in Brazil, were well versed in finding progressive justifications for their less than radical practices.

The manifesto shifted the focus of architectural debate from design and aesthetics to the relations of production – a question that was to be expanded upon in all of the group's subsequent texts. They

179

João Batista Vilanova Artigas, Ivo Viterito House, São Paulo, 1962. The house was supported on four points, with four columns and two continuous beams running along the sides (see front facade, above and back facade, opposite left) in order to achieve flexible interiors (opposite right).

believed, for example, that Brazilian architecture's 'mannerism' and its apparent 'irrationality', denounced by Max Bill in Niemeyer's work,[7] concealed questions of class and domination, a problem that would not be overcome by the industrialization of architecture, given that this would only serve to restore and reinforce the domination of capital over labour (see p. 26). Their approach led them to consider how, at a time of developmentalist euphoria, the momentum of Brazilian modernization and the desire to be on a par with the Western economic powerhouses could only serve to obstruct any kind of progressive exit from the country's social impasse.

Refusing to have anything to do with the reforms in hand and the great works they demanded, the manifesto defined a constructive and critical alternative, similar to that of the *Cinema Novo* (New Cinema),[8] whose *raison d'être* was to expose underdevelopment. The 'Aesthetic of Hunger', the *Cinema Novo* manifesto written by Brazilian film-maker Glauber Rocha, addressed two kinds of problem: how the habitual lack of resources in artistic production might move from being a hindrance to being an integral part of the work;

and the obligation to expose the country's social reality, a Brazil nobody wanted to see, and for which no alternatives had yet been dreamed up, let alone built. The aim was no longer to emulate the finished models of the consumer society in the major capitalist countries, but to show the local reality without altogether abandoning a universal perspective: the phenomenon of underdevelopment was to be seen as part and parcel of the uneven development of world capitalism that makes up the reality of everyday life for three-quarters of the world's population.

It was by analogy with *Cinema Novo* that Ferro, Império and Lefèvre named their experiments *Arquitetura Nova. Novismo* in architecture established a field of thought and action at a distance not only from the modern industrial paradigm and its canons but also from proposals based on the 'popular' and the 'vernacular', which they saw as regressive and populist ways out of the dead end of underdevelopment.

The initial basis of *Arquitetura Nova*, articulated in the same manifesto, was the concept of the 'poetics of economy': 'from the utilitarian, constructive and didactic minima came the

Reinventing the Building Site

foundations of a new aesthetic, which they called the poetics of economy'. Following the building of Brasília, this was a bold, clear statement of intent. The extremity of their position, which allowed them not to mind being called '*miserabilistas*', indicated a readiness to recognize the actual housing conditions of the vast majority of the population, and a determination to extract from this a material solution to the housing problem and a critical response to underdevelopment itself.

In practice, the debate between Artigas and his three disciples was played out over projects for single-family houses. From the 1940s to the 1960s, Artigas was the main formulator of principles for domestic architecture in São Paulo. His aim was to define an idea of living that was in keeping with the spirit of modernization, replacing the eclectic mansions of the local bourgeoisie and the antiquated rural models still prevalent in the city.

Artigas's houses - simple and tough, like his concrete furniture - were imbued with moral severity, and an almost puritanical aesthetic and ethic. Their sobriety removed from the bourgeoisie the possibility of transforming their houses into treasure troves, and instead encouraged the middle classes to turn their attention and their capital towards industrializing the country; they suggested, in the manner of Max Weber, an affinity between the capitalist spirit and the Protestant asceticism and work ethic.

In Brazil, where there was a kind of 'anti-work ethic', characteristic of a slave-based society,[9] and the ruling classes tended to fritter their capital away on conspicuous and lavish consumption, Artigas's view was that this pathology needed to be confronted with moral re-education, beginning with the habitat. Design was presented as an instrument that would transform the enslaving and predatory instincts of the influential elites and prepare them to realize the utopias of which they were supposed to be the true bearers.

Paradoxically, this project fitted into the political perspective of the Brazilian Communist Party, for whom the bourgeois-democratic revolution led not by the proletariat but by the middle-classes was a necessary historical step. The act of imagining a reformed bourgeois home was therefore considered a strategic act. Attempts to solve working-class housing, on the other hand, were considered at that time to be reactionary

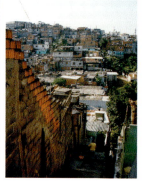

São Paulo, 1997.
Views of illegal settlements, typical of the rapid development São Paulo has undergone. Most of the rural migrants that come to the city in search of better living conditions end up occupying land on the outskirts, lacking proper infrastructure and building their own houses without technical support. This kind of illegal settlement, tolerated by the state, makes up almost half of the entire city of São Paulo.

and better postponed – a point of view backed by a somewhat narrow reading of Friederich Engels's *The Housing Question* (1872), according to which the provision of housing would only diminish the revolutionary impetus of the working class.

The new modernist houses introduced a fresh approach to production. As Artigas explained, his generation fulfilled the historic task of doing away with the archaic practices surviving and imposing necessary changes both in design and in production.[10] It was to be a 'revolution' in the social division of labour on building sites, transferring knowledge and power from the workers to architects – 'as though we were with Brunelleschi',[11] to cite Artigas's apt comparison. In São Paulo, the main losers in this process were the Italian master builders, the vanguard of the city's workers' organization, who had come to Brazil at the end of the nineteenth century, and whose traditional expertise was no longer indispensable. This reduction of the status of labour and its power in the building industry was a process which, as we saw before, reached its climax with the construction of Brasília.

In architectural terms, the guiding principle of Artigas's houses consisted of a unique combination between a large free-standing roof, in itself a representation of the fundamental act of shelter, and the free arrangement of the interior spaces. This was a solution that understood the house as the answer to the human need for protection, yet also open to invention, not only spatially, but also in terms of new relationships between residents. In each house, the layout expressed the tension between need and social innovation.

In order to allow for internal flexibility, Artigas supported the roof only along the edges of the plan, giving it a major structural task for a single-family dwelling, demanding considerable amounts of steel and concrete, often hidden from view. This was a sophisticated and far-from-economical solution, out of the reach of the vast majority of the population.

Ferro, Império and Lefèvre took a radical view of Artigas' proposal and by looking at ways of making it cheaper and more democratic, suitable for low-income housing, partly inverted its meaning. At the time, they were still making houses for friends, almost all of whom were university professors who had agreed to take part in their experiments. The principle of the large roof and open interior was taken to its limits but the choice of new materials and the ways in which they were used – along with a new understanding of the relationships between the technique, the architect and the worker – would lead to divergent aesthetic and political paths.

In the *Arquitetura Nova* houses, the great roof was no longer a box of concrete, but a vault,[12] a change that was no mere formal option, but a move defined by the properties of simple, cheap and easily replicated technology, ideal for popular housing. The vault brought together structure, roof and enclosing wall all at once, creating a totally free internal space. At the same time, it was very economical, as the system worked solely with compression, significantly reducing the need for steel, instead employing commonplace materials, such as beams, rafters and terracotta blocks. The aim was to establish a dialogue with the builder of popular housing in the search for alternatives to self-help construction – the 'do-it-yourself' housing-production system prevalent in the illegal settlements on the outskirts of Brazil's large cities, characterized by the direct administration of residents, self-financing and absence of technical support.[13]

Self-construction, the architecture experienced by the vast majority of Brazil's population, was *Arquitetura Nova*'s starting point, and this was not an issue that had previously been addressed by any but a few of the country's architects. At the same time, *Arquitetura Nova* criticized this form of 'natural' social reproduction of the working class, and rejected the romanticism of its apologists. On account of the poverty of the resources and the urgency with which it was carried out, Ferro claimed in a 1969 text, 'A casa popular (The low-income house)' – at a moment of frantic expansion of the São Paulo peripheries – that self-construction hindered the opportunity to attempt anything more innovative. Technique was not learned, but experienced, like a bird building its nest – hence the 'pre-historic' nature of the work. While self-construction represented the reunion of the producer with the work, in which the former produced use value for his family, it was something of a bitter reunion, the antipoetics of economy: it derived from the minimum, and afforded only the minimum required for survival.

The vaulted roof was a clear expression of the principle of the 'poetics of economy'. Seeking a national basis for low-income construction, and a creative and contemporary solution to the obvious lack of material resources in an underdeveloped country, the possibility of free invention in the arrangement of the rooms under the great roof gave *Arquitetura Nova* the opportunity to introduce a method of learning from the building site. In the future, it was thought entirely conceivable that the layout of the rooms inside the house might be decided collectively by workers, architects and residents, dispensing with a priori design and placing greater value on individual contributions. The building site, protected from the elements by the vault roof, would thus become a workshop. The architect's design would no longer be an imposition, but would merely present situations for collective reflection among the participants in the production. The *Arquitetura Nova* would be the fruit of constant dialogue amongst all those executing the project so that thinking and action would be reunited.

While they were clarifying the working procedures, the desire to give value to each job forced the *Arquitetura Nova* architects to think of new construction details arising from the conditions of the building site. The final result ought to display the signs of the process of human endeavour that had brought it into being, thereby restoring to the building its history. Pointing to a possible new relationship between design and the building site, the *Arquitetura Nova* proposed a genuine democratization of architecture, both in production, by changing working relationships, and in consumption, by looking for means to increase the supply of adequate housing.

In 1964, a *coup d'état* installed a military dictatorship in Brazil, on the pretext that pre-emptive action was necessary to protect the country from the

Rodrigo Lefèvre and Flavio Império, Juarez Brandão House, São Paulo, 1968. The vault roof was treated as two separate structures compromising the economic and practical objectives of the self-managed building site (opposite above right).

Rodrigo Lefèvre and Nestor Goulart Reis Filho, Pery Campos House, São Paulo, 1970 (opposite above left and below left).

Sergio Ferro, Bernardo Issler House, Cotia, 1961 (opposite top left and below right).

Arquitetura Nova, various projects, São Paulo, 1960s. Vault roofs were set up using a frame (right) which was then covered with a roof slab made of curved beams (far right). The architects wanted to protect the building site from the elements with this single structure in order that it could become a collaborative work-shop for everyone involved in the construction process.

João Batista Vilanova
Artigas, Elza Berquó House,
São Paulo, 1967. Planned
around an inner patio and
taking advantage of new
materials, Artigas placed the
concrete slab of this house
on tree trunks (above).

threat of socialism. Not so much a reaction to any actual threat, the dictatorship was in fact more an attempt to strengthen the conservative elements of modernization, widen the gap between the forces of capital and the forces of labour, and thus to boost the growth of Brazilian capitalism. In the process, the trade unions were subjected to interference and repression, while there was terror in rural areas. Salaries were squeezed, the lower ranks of the armed forces purged, university staff subjected to police investigation, student organizations outlawed, liberal churches raided, civil rights suspended, and opponents of the *coup* were imprisoned, tortured and assassinated.

Artigas was arrested by the regime and exiled to Uruguay for one year. When he returned, still subject to police investigation, he remained underground until his acquittal in 1966. In this troubled time, Artigas designed the Elza Berquó House (1967) in São Paulo, saying later that he carried out the design almost as 'a prisoner-architect'. The house is famous because its roof is supported not only by concrete columns, but also by four tree trunks. The load-bearing trunks appear to represent the architect's doubts about the prospects of national development, as well as his feeling that the country's entire past might have been a mirage: 'I made a concrete structure supported on wooden trunks in order to say that on this occasion this whole technique of reinforced concrete, which made this magnificent architecture, is no more than hopeless foolishness.'[14]

Artigas felt that, following the *coup*, the project of the bourgeois house could no longer have the same positive meaning. Everything seemed out of place. Even the communists, perplexed and incapable of providing opposition to the new regime, began to disintegrate, giving rise to a number of more radical groups engaged in armed struggle. The architects who had felt they had been taking part in the construction of the country were now asking themselves what the consequences of the *coup* would be for modern architecture. Would the military be ready to exhume neo-Classicism as the official style? Would architecture schools be closed down and modern architects persecuted, as had happened under Nazism and Stalinism? But contrary to their fears, the increased economic growth meant that they were once again called upon to collaborate in the country's modernization, designing new cities, major infrastructure projects and all kinds of buildings.

In 1967, Artigas accepted an invitation to build a housing project for 60,000 people in Guarulhos, near São Paulo. With the backing of the military government, he had the opportunity to combine his programme for the *casa paulistana* (the typical São Paulo house) with mass-production design, a development not without irony, as this was the same government that had cancelled people's rights, including those of the architect himself, who was later forced to retire.[15]

The project was presented at FAU-USP in 1968, the year of a hardening of the regime and the withdrawal of further rights, including freedom of speech. The presentation of a work of such size, commissioned during this period of harsh repression, made it at least necessary to address

Reinventing the Building Site

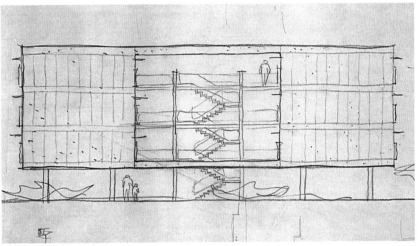

João Batista Vilanova Artigas, Paulo Mendes da Rocha and Fábio Penteado, Zezinho Magalhães Prado Housing Development, São Paulo, 1967. Faced with the task of housing 60,000 people Artigas organized the complex in eight *freguesias* (top), each one of which grouped thirty-two blocks (above left and right), a shopping centre and a school.

certain paradoxes, including the significance of large-scale social housing production being managed by a dictatorial and anti-social state.

The promise of a house for every family became one of the main rallying cries of a regime that habitually exploited the ambivalent feelings of the working class towards small property owners. What, prior to the *coup*, might have seemed forward-thinking experimentation given the lack of public initiatives, now acquired a different political meaning. Sandra Cavalcanti, future chair of the *Banco Nacional de Habitação* (BNH - National Housing Bank), spelled out the state's intentions in a letter to Castello Branco, dictator from 1964 to 1966: 'We feel that the 'revolution' will require vigorous joint action alongside the masses. They are orphans and they are upset. I believe that solving the problem of housing, at least in the major centres, will work as a soothing balm to their civic wounds.'[16]

Far from solving the housing problem, the BNH was, in fact, an important component in the wheel of economic accumulation. It appropriated resources from the newly created Severance Indemnity Fund for employees to finance large building sites, under the control of increasingly powerful Brazilian developers. This building-works policy, based on the extension of infrastructure networks for large housing complexes on the outskirts of cities, and on ample financing for the middle classes, made a decisive contribution to the 'miracle' of Brazilian growth in the 1970s.

Unlike Ferro, Império and Lefèvre, whose solutions to low-income housing involved simple techniques and materials, Artigas wanted to show that modern industrial construction techniques in Brazil were reaching a historic moment of democratization, even during a period of harsh authoritarianism. The research into construction systems and materials for the Guarulhos Housing Complex was conducted in unprecedented depth. The thickness and treatment of concrete, the cladding of walls and floors, partitions and window frames, the plumbing layouts and equipment, everything was studied in new ways, with mass production in mind.

In truth, the architects involved in the project knew that there was no industrial infrastructure capable of carrying it out, and the expectation was that the sheer size of the work would stimulate the creation of such an infrastructure. The developers, though, showed no interest in the proposal – their concern was not the economy of labour but, quite the contrary, the bulk purchase of a workforce at low cost. The BNH at first refused to approve the project, under the pretext of guaranteeing jobs to larger numbers of workers. In the end, the housing complex was built, partly using traditional methods, with the extensive use of unskilled labour. As well as showing what was to come in terms of housing solutions, the Guarulhos Housing Complex revealed, yet again, ten years after Brasília, the inherent contradictions between design and the building site in modern Brazilian architecture.

Gradually distancing themselves from the master – and, indeed, from architecture – Ferro, Império and Lefèvre moved into the fields of painting, scenography and criticism, in search of

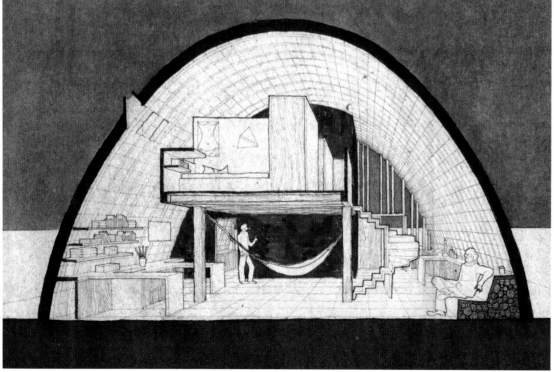

Reinventing the Building Site

Rodrigo Lefèvre, Dino Zamattaro House, São Paulo, 1971. The single vault model was chosen both for practical and economical reasons as well as for the new sense of space that it allowed. The shape of the vault meant that furniture had to be located near the edges (opposite below right), where it could be used by a sitting person, and the rooms had to be accomodated in the double height space in the centre (opposite below left) and lit by windows inserted in the slab (above).

alternatives that were not tainted by association with the military dictatorship. Ferro and Lefèvre left the Communist Party in 1967 and, with Carlos Marighella, joined armed resistance groups against the regime, until their arrest in 1970. In prison, Lefèvre planned the Dino Zamattaro House (1971) in São Paulo, the most accomplished version of their vault-roofed house project.

After his release from prison, Ferro emigrated to France and became professor at the École d'Architecture de Grenoble, where he wrote the last *Arquitetura Nova* essay, entitled 'The building site and the design'. It was published in Brazil in 1976, and released as a book three years later.

Império and Lefèvre stayed on in Brazil, working as teachers in various schools. During the 1970s, Lefrèvre wrote a Masters thesis, in which he proposed a policy of mass construction by *mutirão* (the term used to designate self-built and self-administered housing collectives), with public support and finance. The construction of the house and the whole neighbourhood was to be carried out in a participatory and pedagogical manner. Construction would thereby constitute an educational process, with the building site

becoming a school, in which technical experts and the general public would build a 'new urban culture'.

The proposal of a participatory building site as an emancipating educational process is clearly inspired by the theories of the great Brazilian educator Paulo Freire, best known for his internationally acclaimed book *Pedagogy of the Oppressed*. According to Freire's teachings, literacy moves from being a process of domesticating and mechanizing students towards a means of awareness and liberation. Learning to read and write becomes, most importantly, an act of learning how to read the world and to write one's own history. What was required was an emphasis on the reality of each community and its problem-situations with a view to the formulation of generative-themes with transformative educational properties. For Lefèvre, the generative-theme was the production of the house and the neighbour-hood, which had the additional advantage that it could be directly experienced in reality, through the actual process of housing construction.

After he was released from prison in 1971, Lefèvre worked as a paid architect for a large practice called Hidroservice, for whom he designed hospitals and public administration buildings, among other major works. Companies such as this were a major phenomenon in post-Brasília Brazil until the crisis of the developmentalist model in the 1980s.

Lefèvre died in 1984, Império in 1985, and Ferro still lives in France, working as a painter and professor in Grenoble. On his recent visits to Brazil, Ferro has revisited his theses on architecture, staged individual exhibitions and worked with the *Movimento Sem Terra* (Movement of the Landless), a political organization of rural workers fighting for the democratization of land-ownership.

The story now moves forward to the 1980s, with other architects and new political and social circumstances. The reinvention of the building site as a result of the production of low-income housing, a project that was truncated for the generation that lived under the military regime, was to regain momentum in the 1980s with the new political openness and the emergence of movements that campaigned for housing.

The 1980s
The military regime in Brazil lasted twenty years, and was brought down by social forces that had developed during that period. The acceleration of industrialization, albeit run for the most part by foreign companies, ultimately led to an increasingly strong and well-organized working class, as was the case in the automobile industry. In São Paulo, strikes at the end of the 1970s created a new platform for the capital-labour struggle, and elsewhere there was the rise of the so-called 'new syndicalism',

led at the time by a migrant from the northeast named Luiz Inácio da Silva, better known as Lula.

Nonetheless, the regime's fierce repression of trade unionism took the popular struggle beyond the factory floor. At the end of the 1970s, new characters were coming onto the scene: the social movements on the outskirts of São Paulo, many led by women, campaigning for crèches, housing, healthcare, transport and sanitation. The space of daily life became a political forum, and there was increased debate between social classes, on matters ranging from demands for fairer salaries and working conditions to campaigns for citizens' rights. Such movements were supported by local church-based communities, nuclei of the important progressive role played by the Brazilian Catholic Church, which was linked to the 'Theology of Liberation'.

The convergence between the new syndicalism, grass-roots social movements, the liberal Church and dissident intellectuals resulted in the formation of the *Partido dos Trabalhadores* (PT - Workers' Party) in 1980, with a programme of democratic socialism, critical of the Soviet experience and of the Brazilian Communist Party. In just one decade, the PT became the biggest left-wing party in the Western world (in terms of numbers of votes and membership), winning local council elections in several state capitals and losing the presidential election of 1989 by less than 5 per cent of the total vote. As we shall see, it was only under those councils that were run by the PT, that pioneering experiments by militant architects in alliance with social movements had any chance of becoming

Reinventing the Building Site

public policy, and this was particularly so in São Paulo, where the PT won the local elections in 1988.

It is no accident that the social movements engaged in the struggle for housing had their greatest success in São Paulo, the biggest city in Brazil and the one with the greatest disparity between rich and poor. Homeless organizations played a leading role in the adoption of a new housing policy in the city, the most advanced and democratic policy of this kind in the country, replacing the programme of large housing complexes instituted by the military regime. None of these changes would have been possible without this popular mobilization.

The social struggle of these housing organizations was characterized by the constant play between confrontation and conciliation, between dissension and a desire to integrate. The various occupations of land and buildings were not denials of private property, but rather sought to democratize it. Within a society split between owner elites and propertyless masses – no agrarian land reform whatsoever has taken place in Brazil – such efforts acquire a highly contentious meaning. The struggle for land and housing called into question the foundations of Brazilian conservative modernization and its preservation of those outdated structures which define unequal access to power, property and social opportunity.

The conflict instigated by the housing movements brought into the public arena the debate about conditions for the social reproduction of the working-class and questioned its segregation on the outskirts of the city. São Paulo's enormous periphery, home to almost eight million people, is a veritable 'hidden city' – hidden, that is, from the state, the middle classes and the town planners. It exists almost in secret, deprived of the most basic social rights and of the most elementary benefits of modernity. Public action, when it has occurred, has centred on the production of huge, single-function complexes, leading to 'planned ghettos', a habitat in its purest form, creating only another kind of repression.[17] It is no surprise, therefore, that São Paulo has the largest housing complex in Latin America, Cidade Tiradentes, made up of 40,000 residential units occupied by families that have been displaced from their home towns by public works and by rising real estate values.

The housing movements have therefore tried to break the 'iron ring' that isolates the working class from other classes and spaces in the city. They want to raise awareness – by means of occupations, demonstrations and marches – of the need for action that will ensure their rights, and that will not segregate the poor into precarious and ghettoized territories.

The main feature of housing production introduced by these movements was the *mutirão*, in which future residents take part in construction, reconstituting a kind of traditional popular solidarity. But the schemes also receive public financing and are supported by interdisciplinary offices providing technical assistance to the housing movements. Self-administration means that control is in the hands of the user, who is put in the position of being able to question the normal state housing policy implemented by the building contractors.

Cidade Tiradentes, São Paulo, 1982–92. The largest housing development in Latin America, it was constructed on the peripheries of São Paulo, benefitting real estate companies and developers, an economic model which the popular housing movements are actively opposed to.

The inspiration for this alternative system of production came from another Latin American country, Uruguay, which has been experimenting with *ayuda mutua*, self-help housing co-operatives, since 1968, and where, unlike Brazil, continuity in co-operative housing production policy has ensured highly organized building works, and well-managed community housing complexes and facilities. In Uruguay, it has been anything but a marginal means of producing space, accounting at times for 50 per cent of all housing production.

In Brazil, an explosion of experiments in various fields was translated into actual public policy at the end of the 1980s, when the PT came to power in local council elections. Militant architects drew upon an eclectic variety of architectural references and political tendencies. In general, they looked for alternatives both to the modernist paradigms in architecture and to Brazilian conservative modernization, which had only served to deepen internal social inequity and to increase external dependency. The new groups were far removed from the old communist architects, including Artigas and Niemeyer, and were deeply suspicious of developmentalism – of the country, of the forces of production and of architectural forms. Politicized by the daily contact with the workers, both in political activity and on building sites, they believed they had much to learn from the social movements.

Their architectural reference points were many and varied. One was the Egyptian architect Hassan Fathy, on account of his respect for and preference for working with popular knowledge, in opposition to the developmentalism of the

Egyptian state, as described in his book *Architecture for the Poor.* Another was the controversial Antoni Gaudí, referred to by Sérgio Ferro, for his example of on-site architecture. Others included the English architect John Turner, author of *Freedom to Build and Housing by People,* and Bernard Rudofsky's *Architecture without Architects.* Among Brazilians, they made reference to Gil Borsoi, for his updating of the *arquitetura de taipa* (lath-and-plaster architecture), a Brazilian colonial technique employed for low-income housing in State of Pernambuco; to José Mário and Afonso Risi for their rediscovery of knowledge and pleasure on the building site and the formal perfection of their project for the Claretian priests in São Paulo; to Johan van Lengen, a Dutchman who came to Brazil to work with river communities in Tibá, State of Rio de Janeiro, and who wrote the *Manual for the Barefoot Architect.* Finally, and more surprisingly, they took inspiration from Buckminster Fuller, together with Frei Otto of the Stuttgart Lightweight Structures Institute, for their geodesic spatial structures.

The combination of a third world architecture, participative or vernacular, with the steel structures of German architects, reveals a propensity to look for architectural expression that was both popular and contemporary – not unlike *Arquitetura Nova* in the 1960s. As we shall see, the use of mixed structures, combining exposed brickwork with steel, partially fulfilled this ambition.

As they concentrated primarily on *praxis,* the architects of the *mutirões* did not establish their own theoretical field, as had *Arquitetura Nova,*

and almost all of them were far removed from Marxism. In the relative theoretical desert beneath the exuberance of the *mutirões,* the texts of John Turner were an important reference, although his thesis could also be interpreted as a liberal reading of the housing question, through his advocacy of the enterprising individual over the counterproductive state. This ambiguity has dogged Turner, and his defence of self-construction, at various times, to the extent of making him an ideologue for the UN Habitat and, less openly, for the World Bank.[18] On the other hand, his confidence in free popular initiative had undeniable affinities with the self-administration approach of housing organizations, as opposed to authoritarian state action and large housing complexes.

In the 1980s, architects and the organized masses came together, thereby accomplishing what had been talked of in the years before the military *coup.* Although this did nothing to alter the traditional connection between architects and the dominant classes, it did open up the possibility that some architects by acting alongside the housing movements and the people of the hidden city might question the profession's elitism.

1990s
The operating methods of the militant architects connected with the housing movements were to alter substantially from 1989, with the unexpected victory of Luiza Erundina, of the PT, in the São Paulo mayoral elections. A female migrant from the poorest part of the country, she took charge of running the largest and richest city in South America.

Land occupation by the Paulo Freire Association, São Paulo, 2000. Popular housing movements occupy unused plots as part of their strategy to foster organized urban settlements, democratically managed and funded by the state, and prevent the spontaneous formation of irregular settlements.

Ação Direta, São Francisco VIII Community Centre, for the Movimento Sem–Terra Leste 1 – UMM, São Paulo, 1989.
The shape of this community centre, reminiscent of the architecture of Buckminster Fuller and Otto Frei, highlights the architects' intentions of combining popular architecture and contemporary spatial structures (above).

Many who had taken part in the first *mutirão* experiments, or in the academic laboratories, were now part of the PT party machinery and in a position to make new housing and planning policy either from within public administration, or through the technical advisory bodies set up to aid the housing movements. With the Left in power, the *mutirão* initiatives, no longer in opposition to the state, could be put into practice with government support, although frequent conflicts with the state persisted during this period.

The Housing and Urban Development Department - previously dominated by a techno-cracy far removed from the actual problems of the city, and run by an elite in the pay of builders and politicians - was now administered by a FAU-USP professor and ANSUR co-ordinator, Ermínia Maricato. The local government's new directives were, according to Maricato, to be a total reversal of previous priorities, the democratization and transparency of the administration, universal application of the law, recognition of illegal settlements, land reform, and the urbanization of the *favelas*, all of which entailed running the city from a completely new perspective.[19]

The Office for Low-Income Housing, run by Nabil Bonduki, an ex-FAU-USP alumnus and co-ordinator of the workshop at the Faculty of Fine Arts, produced a new programme of *mutirões*, known as *Funaps-Comunitário*. This programme established *mutirões* as the main form of housing production in the city, and introduced mechanisms to preserve the independence of their builders from the developers, transferring to the former the

management of resources. The programme also regulated the operations of the militant architects, who became legally recognized and were paid accordingly. They were, moreover, required to form non-governmental organizations as technical advisers, which gave them a new professional outlook, but also new ambiguities, related to the emergence of non-profit organizations.

While the PT was in office, 100 *mutirões* and some 11,000 housing units were begun. Of these, only 2,000 were completed during the PT's term in office, while 9,000 were passed on to the next administration. With the election of the extreme right-wing Paulo Maluf in 1992, all *mutirões* were interrupted and building work suspended. Maricato and Bonduki were subject to politically motivated enquiries. The movements now became a platform for the campaign to resume the works, known as the *Fórum dos Mutirões*, which scored its first victories during the administration of Maluf's successor, the also conservative Celso Pitta (1997-2000). It was only in 2001, following Marta Suplicy's victory for the PT, that these *mutirões* resumed operation and were completed.

In ten turbulent years of existence, the *mutirões*, suffering constant setbacks, merely hinted at what participative building sites might achieve in the production of low-income housing. With a more consistent public policy, they could have had a much greater effect on the city.

The *mutirão* has been sustained by the presence of three crucial agents, sometimes in dialogue and sometimes in conflict. The Public Authority, as programme co-ordinator and financial agent,

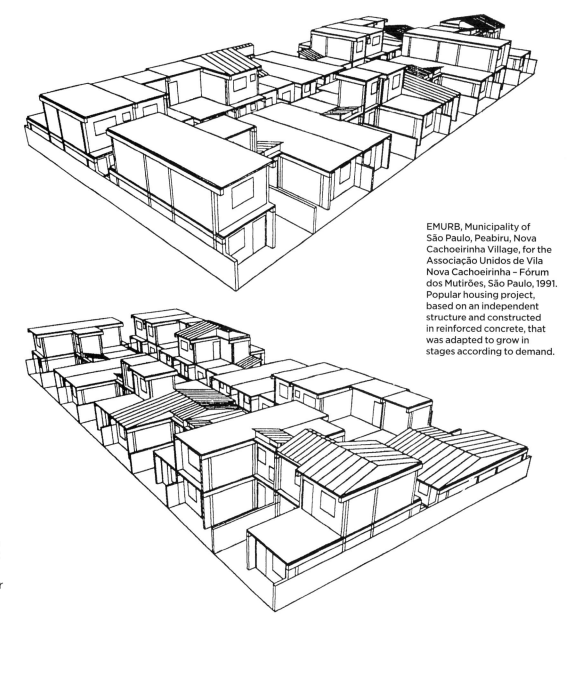

allocates land, carries out and approves technical analyses of projects, executes measurement of building works, verifies settlements of accounts and releases funds. The Housing Movements and their associations lobby the Public Authority for a given policy to be realized, organizing occupations, marches and publicity campaigns. The main such social organization in the city, the *União dos Movimentos de Moradia* (UMM – Union of Housing Movements), is divided into various independent movements, many of which have organized 'origin-groups' that meet in local churches. When a project is won, families of different 'origin-groups' form an 'association'. The Technical Advisers realize projects and monitor works paid for, in part, by public finance. These bodies are made up of independent technical experts, with no connection to the Public Authority, developers or commercial practices. They are interdisciplinary teams made up of architects (always the most numerous group), engineers, lawyers, sociologists and educators and are, institutionally speaking, NGOs or co-operatives.

The projects of the self-help *mutirões* are distinct from normal building and housing production undertaken by developers. In the *mutirões*, producer and building are re-united, as opposed to the brutality and the iron rules that are the norm on building sites run by capitalist concerns. They constantly throw up new experiences, and are often subject to unforeseen pitfalls and tensions, but they do set out new production relationships and a fresh way of realizing architecture.

The guiding principle of the architects in the Technical Advisers' bodies is the collective design

EMURB, Municipality of São Paulo, Peabiru, Nova Cachoeirinha Village, for the Associação Unidos de Vila Nova Cachoeirinha – Fórum dos Mutirões, São Paulo, 1991. Popular housing project, based on an independent structure and constructed in reinforced concrete, that was adapted to grow in stages according to demand.

São Paulo, 1990s.
The presence of women on building sites was one of the changes introduced by the *mutirões*.

of housing units, and the implementation of buildings, open spaces and community centres. Their approaches to assembly, design, models and prototypes are distinct from the uniformity of the standard state-financed projects. *Mutirões* adapt typologies to suit people's way of life. Furthermore, their units are bigger in area than those previously built by the state, 65 square metres on average, and use better-quality materials, such as terracotta blocks and tiles, rather than cement blocks and asbestos roof tiles.

Within the participative projects, the theory put forward by most technical advisers is that each new project should emphasise the interaction of those involved, and allow the development of a strategy specific to each site. The intention is to make the most of the urban conditions in which the projects are inserted and to avoid environmentally damaging site works – a common result of the usual site-clearing process, which almost always requires levelling a large plateau.

Engineers and architects acting as Technical Advisers have tried to adopt rationalized construction systems and labour-saving technology. Productivity gains in the *mutirões* cannot be achieved by merely exploiting the workers even further, since they are the ones running the work. Arbitrary and authoritarian design solutions are thereby avoided and all project decisions are made on the basis of simplifying working procedures, as well as the reduction of both the physical effort and the safety risks of executing the work. Rather than becoming removed from producers and establishing a

rationality that is foreign to them, technique thus becomes human and accessible.

Nevertheless, this does not mean a return to handicraft. On the contrary, workshops for producing components were set up on many building sites, fabricating elements in reinforced concrete, for example. This technology, using water curing, enables economy of materials and produces light, durable components,[20] and is technology easily accessible to builders, although not part of the popular universe of self-construction. On a smaller scale, some Technical Advisers have attempted mixed construction systems, with the employment of steel technology – up to then only used in Brazil on more sophisticated works, as in the case of Copromo, União da Juta and Sanko. In the *mutirão* projects, metal staircases were installed immediately after the foundations were laid, so as to make it easier to build the multistorey *mutirão* structures. The staircases acted as a spine, from which materials could be hoisted up, and enabled the site workers to move around safely. The apartments grew in structural blocks around these staircases. It is a simple, lean system, as it dispenses with scaffolding, formwork, steel reinforcement and the plastering of beams and columns.

The self-help *mutirão* depends at all times on the decisions of a General Assembly. 'Works Regulations' are defined by all parties before construction begins, and are revised and discussed throughout the project, acting as a kind of consensual law capable of mediating conflicts. In order to assist in this task, an Ethics Council

is elected, which ensures everyone's right to a defence and a hearing so that a merely punitive interpretation of the regulations is avoided.

All *mutirões* have co-ordinators and administrators chosen by its members and elected in an assembly. The building site is organized into task-based teams, and on some sites these teams alternate, so that everyone can learn different trades and no one has to work on monotonous or repetitive tasks. Whereas traditional civil construction is an exclusively male environment, in housing movements women are in the majority and provide the main leaders. Their presence introduces a new attitude and they bring elements alien to the traditional building site: a sense of responsibility, learning, teaching and playing, as well as the exchange of experiences on subjects ranging from federal politics to the price of beans, from educational to emotional issues. They avoid the usual hierarchies and orders that men tend to bring from their experience as salary-earning workers.

The environment thus created points to a possible sense of totality and resistance, a space appropriated by social forces, as opposed to the domination of the space by the state and by profit-making companies. The *mutirões* are embryos of a kind of counter-space, in the words of French philosopher Henri Lefebvre. They exist as residual virtualities within the planned and programmed order. At the same time they create men who are no longer fragmented, and for whom social acts and festive meetings are incorporated into work and daily routine, as distinct from the way in which capitalist society tends to seal off leisure as an autonomous realm. The conclusion of each stage on a *mutirão* is celebrated, and days spent laying concrete are often happy times. In this way, self-administered building sites are places where a possible reunion between work and pleasure is achieved – an ideal of William Morris, who believed that, upon reaching such a point, all work would become art.

The experimental utopia put into practice in the *mutirões* often runs into difficulties, however, due to the conditions in which they are realized. Residents build their future homes without being paid, a process that constitutes 'surplus labour'. In addition to working in paid jobs during the week, they have the extra burden of building their own houses at the weekend. The notion of *mutirões* as emancipation has therefore strongly been called into question. One consequence of this self-sufficiency may, ironically, be a general reduction in salary. The savings made by the self-builders work for the benefit of capital itself, which can take advantage of the reduction of costs in the reproduction of the labour force and can, therefore, pay lower salaries.[21]

While this analysis may be accurate for the colossal self-built settlements on the outskirts of large Brazilian cities, it does not take into account the political dimension of the *mutirões*. Workers take on the task of building, with the principal aim of having the control of the production process in their own hands. They attempt new forms of labour with the intention that they spread and develop and as attempts to challenge the prevailing methods of production.

Usina, Mutirão COPROMO, for the Associação Pró-moradia de Osasco, São Paulo, 1990. Surrounded by *favelas* and irregular settlements, this project is like an 'island' of social experimentation. Unlike self-help housing, *mutirões* use good quality materials and achieve much larger built areas. View of construction with steel structural system and ceramic masonry realized by the *mutirão*; staircases were built by an engineering association (above left and right).

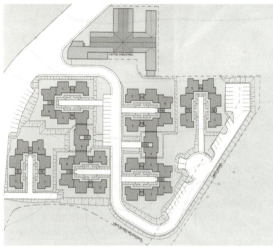

Usina, Mutirão União da Juta, for Movimento Sem–Terra Leste 1 – UMM, São Paulo, 1992. The site plan (above left) shows the layout with a succession of internal plazas within walking distance from all blocks. The three building typologies were discussed and developed with the future inhabitants (top left). Reinforced ceramic masonry and steel staircases were used for the construction (above right).

Thus, despite originating as surplus labour, the *mutirão* is politicized and independently managed by the social movements and their technical advisers, creating the opportunity to confront the usual aspects of capitalist production. The apparently inevitable appropriation of surplus labour by employers has through political action, allowed a glimpse of alternative forms of work. Self-help co-operatives, agrarian land reform settlements and other forms of economic solidarity all meet around these ideals – or that at least, is the idea of those committed to such work.[22]

Even with the political reverses they have suffered, the self-help *mutirões* have produced a further paradox worthy of reflection. Many modern architects had believed that capitalist companies would be the key to the industrialization of construction in Brazil. However, building remained one of the most outdated sectors of the economy, with little incentive to undertake capital investment because of the enormous swathe of low-paid workers with few legal rights. Increases in productivity were achieved mainly by further exploitation, rather than by rationalization or by increasing the productive power of the worker through investment in plant and equipment. Although the self-administered *mutirão* was deemed a pre-modern form of production, with the support of independent technical experts and with access to public funds it was, in practice, capable of accomplishing far more in the way of innovation than were the capitalist building firms.

Ermínia Maricato, the PT Housing Secretary at the time, summed up the paradox: in Brazil, forms

Reinventing the Building Site

of building that appear archaic, such as the *mutirão*, are actually more technically advanced and forward-thinking, whereas capitalist, that is to say 'modern production', appears to perpetuate the archaic. It is important to reiterate that the essential element of the economies achieved through the works of the social movements came not as a direct result of the *mutirão*, i.e. of the unpaid work of future residents, but through 'self-administration', and the adoption of rationalization techniques, transparency and democracy in management and non-profit operation. The *mutirões* were, consequently, lauded and used as a reference point to contest the spreadsheets and construction standards of housing programmes carried out by developers and received the support of the Brazilian Association of Industrialized Construction. They have, at the same time, been criticized by construction companies with which they have competed for public funding.

Lula, the sheet-metal worker who founded the PT in 1980, scored a historic victory in the Brazilian presidential elections of 2002. This established a platform of enormous possibilities, and an even greater number of contradictions. Elected after a decade of neo-liberal policies, Lula inherited a country ravished by poverty and social inequality, as well as a framework of financial dependency that restricts the possibilites for institutional change. Brazilian society has never been so split between the globalized and the disposable. The government will therefore have to adopt strong positions if it is to confront historical questions of the country's structural injustices and external dependency.

One of the Lula administration's innovations has been the creation of the Ministry for Cities, aimed at addressing urban, housing, transport and sanitation issues, and at reversing the dismantling of the state that took place during the neo-liberal decade. Some members of the team co-ordinating São Paulo's housing and sanitation policy were given responsibility by the new ministry, and are promising substantial transformations. According to Ermínia Maricato, current Executive Secretary of the Ministry for Cities, the main aims of the new office are to reinstate urban policy as a federal government responsibility and to establish nationwide housing, sanitation and transport systems for the common good. Active support for popular participation schemes through the Cities Conference leads one to ask whether this could be a time when the production of habitat by means of self-administration might be extended to the whole of Brazil, as a major alternative to traditional housing programmes and to the power of the capitalist contractors. Have we finally arrived at a transitional point in Brazilian society, at which, as Lefèvre imagined, one giant *mutirão*, bringing together technical experts and the people, would be realized as the expression of a new country under construction?

In Weimar Germany, artists such as Brecht and Murnau would often finish their works by offering the public two possible endings, a happy one or its exact opposite. They believed that the moment required their audience to learn the competence to distinguish between the two fables.

In some respects, the outcome of the present

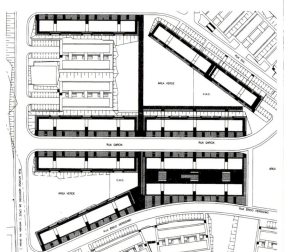

Passo, Mutirão Sanko, for Associação de Luta por Moradia Unidos da Leste, Diadema, São Paulo, 1996. This project has set a high standard in an area particularly affected by illegal settlements (above right). The triangular spaces, shown on the site plan between the blocks (above left), are reserved for sports facilities. Future inhabitants decided to invest in the colourful window frames, of a much better quality than those used by developers in other housing developments (opposite left). Construction was carried out using reinforced ceramic masonry and steel staircases (opposite right).

narrative also remains unresolved. However, a year after Lula's election, a different and dramatic outcome is looking increasingly plausible. Beyond the actual policy-making and strategic choices – if any – of Lula's government, the hopes for any alternative course for the country are severely undermined by hurdles of unprecedented proportions.

The Brazil we have to face now is another country: it is a nation with an economic system that adds almost no value to the world's production cycles, with rising unemployment, decreasing social mobility, and masses of poor people who still live concentrated in large ungovernable cities, and who have no means of alternative survival within the current system. It is a society that produces fear and violence, and whose citizens have never before experienced such a level of inequality or conflicting interests.

The social composition of Brazil at the moment is, in a word, monstrous. The sociologist Francisco de Oliveira, one of the last remaining representatives of the Brazilian critical tradition, compared Brazil to a duckbilled platypus, an incongruous beast, stranded at the crossroads of an evolution that has moved on.[23] The zoomorphic analogy suggests a society that has lost the ability to choose, and has come to embody a 'truncated evolution'. In Oliveira's paradoxical vision – expressed without complacency at the very moment of the Left's great victory in the 2002 elections – the country's state of underdevelopment still contained the promise of a future redemption. However, the latest technological revolution put an

end to any remaining hopes of transforming Brazil into a modern wage-based capitalist society. Its informal labour-reserve army continues to expand as redundancy, flexibilization and outsourcing seem now to accomplish 'the extraction of surplus with no resistance'. With this in mind, we may reflect on the cynical view expressed by German sociologist Ulrich Beck, who regards Brazil as the epitome of things to come on a world scale: 'the brave new world of work' can be found in Brazil.[24]

The creation of building sites run by their workers occurred at the same time as the country revealed its continuing inability to grow. The *mutirões* became oases of social innovation in the midst of neighbourhoods full of violence, at the mercy of the drug trafficker's curfew and of the evangelical Pentecostal Churches' trumpets of salvation. In July 2003, in the biggest complex of *mutirões* in São Paulo, the Fazenda da Juta, the traffickers, laid down their 'law', in the process 'accepting or vetoing the presence of visitors, establishing where and when residents can move around, even making decisions on the creation of new neighbourhoods'.[25] In the *mutirão* of União da Juta, 'an armed man single-handedly shut the baker's, but allowed it to stay open until all the bread that had been made had been sold'. The association's community centres lives under the threat of closure – 'we work with the traffickers' kids and we live among them'.[26]

At this time it makes sense to affirm that the passage from Brasília to the *mutirões* is riddled with impasses and contradictions, a fifty-year history during which rare chinks of light have been sealed up one after another. The have-nots organized into *mutirões* (or on settlements resulting from the recent agrarian land reform) are certainly potential candidates for a different future. But while this horizon of emancipation remains there is no possible respite from the current destructive phase of capitalism. In this context, the passage from Brasília to the *mutirões* cannot be interpreted in evolutionary terms of advance or regression but only as the representation of a defeated society.

It remains to be said that probably the most dynamic and transforming initiatives in the production of the built environment during this period were not those originating in the hands of great architects and their designs, but those which came about through the co-ordination of the social movements and the *assessorias técnicas* supporting them. In particularly unequal societies like Brazil, the democratization of architecture requires not only distributing its benefits more widely, but also, above all, concentrating upon social equality in the relationships through which people come together to produce buildings.

CHAPTER SIX
RECENT WORK: CASE STUDIES
BY ADRIAN FORTY & ELISABETTA ANDREOLI

RECENT WORK: CASE STUDIES

A survey of Brazilian architecture over the last fifteen years shows some important continuities with the work of the mid-century, but a striking change in the kind of projects undertaken by architects. In common with countries in other parts of the world, there has been a decline in major state building programmes, and most of the work carried out by architects in Brazil, as elsewhere, consists no longer of infrastructural projects, but has been for private or institutional clients, or social co-operatives. In the Brazilian context, where modern architecture was initially sponsored by the state, and very largely identified with the state, this change in patronage represents a shift more striking than the shift that has occurred elsewhere apart from former Communist countries. Whereas in the 1950s and 1960s, the very largest projects were treated as opportunities for innovative and experimental architecture, now experiments are confined to smaller-scale buildings. It is these projects that this survey concentrates upon, with examples of housing, welfare buildings, and arts and community buildings. The exception to this general diminution of the scale of innovative architecture are the infrastructure projects of João Filgueiras Lima, or 'Lelé' as he is widely known, whose system-built schools and hospitals are a direct continuation of the tradition of the 'heroic' period of Brazilian architecture, such as the Disabled Support Centre in Brasília, completed in 2001.

The last fifteen years have seen the development of tendencies that are certainly not unique to Brazil, but common throughout the world, though in the examples reproduced here, they carry a distinctive Brazilian inflection. The renovation and conversion of old buildings to arts and community use has been a feature of all cities, and São Paulo has a fine example in the State Art Gallery (1993-9), where Paulo Mendes da Rocha took the uncompleted original building, gave it new environmental systems and partially lined the interiors with exquisite Brazilian hardwoods, but left the raw unfinished brickwork of the original untouched. Another renovation, illustrated here, is the KKKK Cultural Complex (1996-2001) by Brasil Arquitetura, an arts and community building for the local community in the former rice warehouse built by a Japanese company in the 1920s in the Ribeira Valley. This project follows in the tradition of the conversions of old industrial buildings to community use, such as the Bahia Museum of Popular Art at Salvador (1959-63) and the SESC-Pompéia Factory (1977-82) in São Paulo by Lina Bo Bardi, with whom Marcelo Ferraz, founding member of Brasil Arquitetura, had previously worked. In this project, we see some of the same features as at SESC-Pompéia, spaces for undefined collective use and a relaxed informality about the whole enterprise.

What above all is noticeable in all these projects since the 1990s is the way that many traces of the previous, 'heroic' period of Brazilian architecture reappear, but unselfconsciously absorbed into current practice. Earlier features, such as its capacity to be accommodating, to be ambiguous and to avoid all definitive positions appear again in these works, but they are not flaunted in the way that the architects of the mid-century found necessary. An exceptional example of the way contemporary buildings incorporate these traditions is in the 2001 Carambó Pavilion of Una Arquitetos. This modest outdoor room, an extension to an existing house, is set in stunning landscape, and made entirely of materials that would have been familiar in the eighteenth century - rough stone, *muxarabis* screens, timber and tile. At first sight, it hardly seems a modern building at all, but for the long cantilever of the room from the terrace, though closer inspection reveals that its archaic components are put together in a thoroughly modern way. This is a work that, in all its simplicity, is entirely consistent with the idea promoted by both Lucio Costa and Lina Bo Bardi, that in Brazil, it was the business of the architect to translate the country's cultural heritage into a modern architectural language.

The Dental Surgery (2000) and the Aldeia da Serra House (2002), by MMBB Arquitetos are both demonstratively twenty-first century buildings, but at the same time refer to and reinterpret the traditions of Brazilian modern architecture. The use of timber screens in the Dental Surgery – here to give privacy as well as to protect from sunlight – the relative openness of the interiors, and the extensive fair-faced in-situ concrete combined with large areas of glass all connect these buildings to the architecture of the 'heroic' period of Brazilian Modernism. In the Aldeia da Serra House, the unconventional entry, from above, or from below, via a staircase in an open core, again, without actually reproducing this feature from any Brazilian building of the 1950s or 1960s, gives the house a recognisable affinity with São Paulo private houses of those years.

And finally, we might notice in recent schemes that are for public or social use, a liberal, not to say extravagant, provision of covered but unenclosed public space, dedicated to no particular purpose. This is a clear echo of the 1950s and 1960s, of works like Niemeyer's covered promenades at Ibirapuera (1951) in São Paulo, or Bo Bardi's São Paulo Museum of Art (1957–68). Paulo Mendes da Rocha's archway in the Plaza of the Patriarch (1994–2002) in São Paulo belongs entirely in this tradition. A great steel canopy shades part of the square, and defines it as a public area. In a country where so many places are now surrounded by security fences and gates, this generosity, this hope that everyone might share in the benefits of architecture, is distinctive of the optimism that still pervades Brazil's architecture.

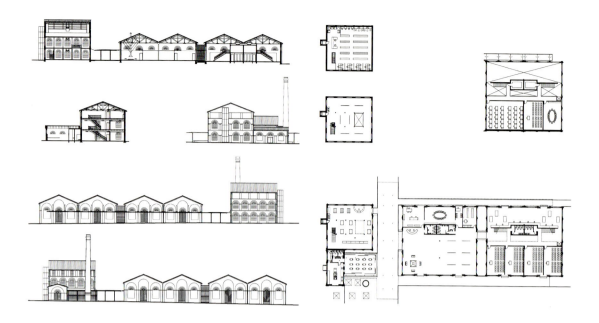

KKKK CULTURAL COMPLEX

Architect Brasil Arquitetura (Francisco de Paiva Fanucci, Marcelo Carvalho Ferraz)
Design Team Anderson Freitas, Pedro Barros
Structural Engineer Jayme Bechara
Client Government of the State of São Paulo, Government of the City of Registro
Area 2,900 m² / 31, 204 sq ft
Location Registro
Completion Date 2001

The colonization of the Ribeira Valley by Japanese immigrants in the early twentieth century had its focal point in the Port of Registro. The Japanese company Kaigai Kogyo Kabushiki Kaisha established a rice-processing plant on the banks of the Ribeira river in 1920, to serve the Japanese pioneers who had settled in the area. Their produce would be processed and stored there, and then shipped out on the river, the only access to Registro at the time. Four warehouses for storage and offices as well as a block for the processing plant were built, using load-bearing brick walls, iron supports, timber trusses and tiled roofs, many of which had been imported from England.

After forty years of neglect, in 1996, the authorities decided to transform the abandoned site into a cultural complex that would include a teacher-training centre, a social centre for the people of Registro and, finally, the Museum for Japanese Immigration.

Brasil Arquitetura reorganized the existing facilities in order to accommodate this varied programme of uses. The buildings needed restoration, and much care was taken researching the appropriate materials. The architects also introduced new elements, carefully distinguishing them from the existing constructions. Pathways were sheltered with a concrete canopy, replacing the original tiled canopy, already demolished that had linked the different parts of the complex. In this way, circulation routes around the site were rearranged according to the new functions performed by each building. Small gardens were created in the leftover spaces between the warehouses, protected by wooden trellises. Interiors were adapted, with the use of mezzanines and freestanding volumes, to be used as exhibition galleries and classrooms. A new building, on the eastern edge of the site, was designed to house a theatre. Also built in concrete, its white facades make it the most eye-catching addition to the complex.

The KKKK Complex is at the heart of a new green area by the banks of the Ribeirao river that was planned to reactivate the original – and later abandoned – connection between the city of Registro and the river, providing not only the opportunity to reclaim the historical memories associated with it but also the opportunity to recuperate a long-forgotten site for effective use by the people of Registro.

Aerial view showing the original brick buildings in the foreground and the white box of the theatre on the edge of the site (above). The new concrete canopy covers the circulation routes around the site (opposite above). The spaces between warehouses have been converted into gardens with the use of wooden trellises (opposite below left). The factory was strategically located on a bend of the Ribeirao River, with views both up and down stream. The two-storey rice-processing plant now houses the Museum of Japanese Immigration while the warehouses are multi-funtion rooms (opposite below right).

The theatre's stage is reversible and can be used for events inside the auditorium as well as outside on the lawn (below). Both its marginal position on the site and its distinctive white concrete facades mark it from the original buildings (right). Wooden trellises were used throughout as a device for controlling interior temperature and lighting (opposite below right and opposite above). With the introduction of mezzanines, ramps and canopies the existing space was adapted for its new uses, as in the K3-K4 warehouse seen here (opposite below left).

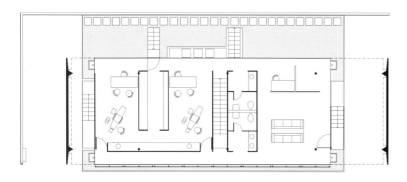

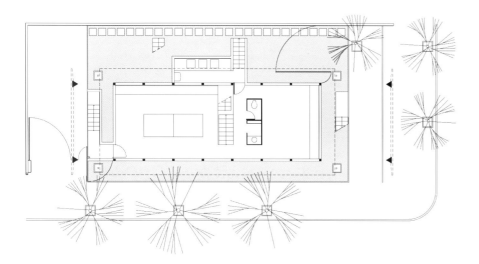

DENTAL SURGERY

Architect MMBB Arquitetos (Angelo Bucci, Fernando de Mello Franco, Marta Moreira, Milton Braga)
Design Team Keila Costa, Sandra Llovet Vilà
Structural Engineer Ibsen Puleo Uvo
Client João Gomes Pereira Filho, Mariana M Rodrigues Pereira
Area 182 m² / 1,958 sq ft
Location Orlândia, São Paulo
Completion Date 2000

This dental surgery and laboratory building in Orlândia, a small town in the state of São Paulo, is the combined setting for two complementary professional activities: a clinic and a laboratory. Designed to take into account the regular grid pattern of surrounding streets, the building sits on a corner site, aligned with the perimeters and setbacks of its more conventional neighbours. However, it is not enclosed like them by boundary walls, and consequently remains open to the outside. The entrance at street level is positioned halfway between the two floors that make up the design. The public areas of the clinic are contained on the upper level by a glass and concrete box supported on a clever structural system that makes it look as if it were hovering above the ground. The laboratory is on the level below, partially underground and connected by an internal staircase. Two parallel corridors running along the main axis connect all the spaces, the one on the street side is for public access, the one facing the back is for staff use only. Much care has been taken to protect the building from excessive solar exposure. A detachable wooden sun-breaker screens the glass wall on the north facade both from light and street view. Separate from the box, a concrete wall forms a portico, framing the building and also sheltering the external entrance area.

The appearance from the street of this lightweight box of wood and glass evokes the memory of the town's earliest buildings, which were supported on *pilotis*. It borrows from São Paulo's modern tradition that emphasizes the symbolic and expressive character of the single structural element. In the entrance area, under the portico, a conspicuous lightweight concrete stair leads to the public area, introducing a factor of diagonal tension. At the back, all the building's activities are visible behind glass.

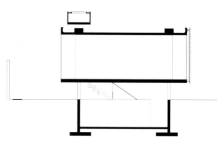

The layout in two levels is displaced in relation to the street level (see section, above), with the upper floor (top left) raised on *pilotis* and the lower floor (middle left) partially underground, giving the appearance of a light box gently hovering over the ground (opposite).

The glass box housing the main activities is protected by a wooden sun-breaker (below left) and a concrete portico (above), which also provides shelter for the entrance stairs (below right and opposite top right). The lower level accomodates the laboratory and servicing area and receives natural lighting from the gap left by the raised upper level (opposite above left). The south facade facing the back of the plot is left unscreened and provides an independent entrance for the lower level (opposite below).

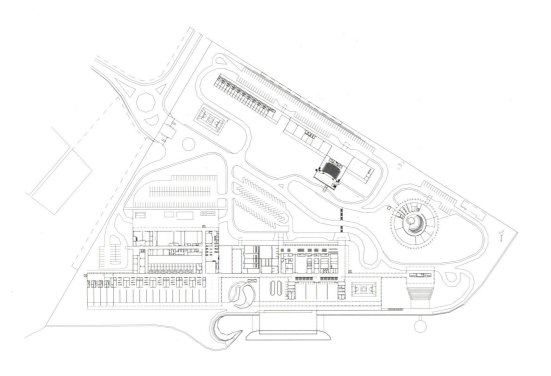

DISABLED SUPPORT CENTRE OF LAGO NORTE

Architect João Filgueiras Lima
Design Team Franciso A N Filho, Ana Amélia Monteiro
Structural Engineer Roberto Vitorino
Client Sarah Network of Rehabilitation Hospitals
Area 25,241 m² / 271,593 sq ft
Location Brasília
Completion Date 2001

Sarah Lago Norte is one of the Sarah Network of Hospitals built in different parts of Brazil by the engineer João Filgueiras Lima, or 'Lelé', using the system of concrete prefabrication developed by him. Like the other hospitals, this one is for the physiotherapeutic treatment of patients suffering from locomotor and neurophysiological disorders. Located on the shore of the placid Lake Paranoá, the hospital has facilities for 160 inpatients, a care and diagnostic centre, a rehabilitation centre with gymnasium and hydrotherapy units, a children's rehabilitation service, a convention centre for 400 people, and general support services.

The site, on a gentle slope towards the lake, is landscaped into a series of terraces, connected by ramps. The long building facing the lake contains the gymnasium and hydrotherapy units, and the curve of its roof is designed to draw cool air from the lake in at the bottom of the building and discharge warm air out through the louvred rooflights. Here, as in all Lima's hospital buildings, there is careful attention to lighting and ventilation wholly by natural means.

The building is produced with standardized components designed by Lima and manufactured in plants under his direct control. The fittings and much of the basic equipment are also designed by Lima, and manufactured at the Technology Centre of the Sarah Network in Salvador. This control over the entire building process, from the serialization of building components to the management of construction and of maintenance, has successfully reduced construction times and led to cheaper and better maintained buildings. Serialization has not, however, been at the cost of repetition or monotony in the architecture: the interiors of the Sarah hospitals are remarkable for their lively, varied and playfully invigorating environments.

The design adapted the building to the slope of the terrain (see elevation, above left) through a series of landscaped terraces accommodating the different areas of the hospital (above and see plan, top left). Fully accessible circulation routes around the site are provided, and with the use of specially designed mobile stretchers patients can be taken right up to the sheltered waterfront (opposite).

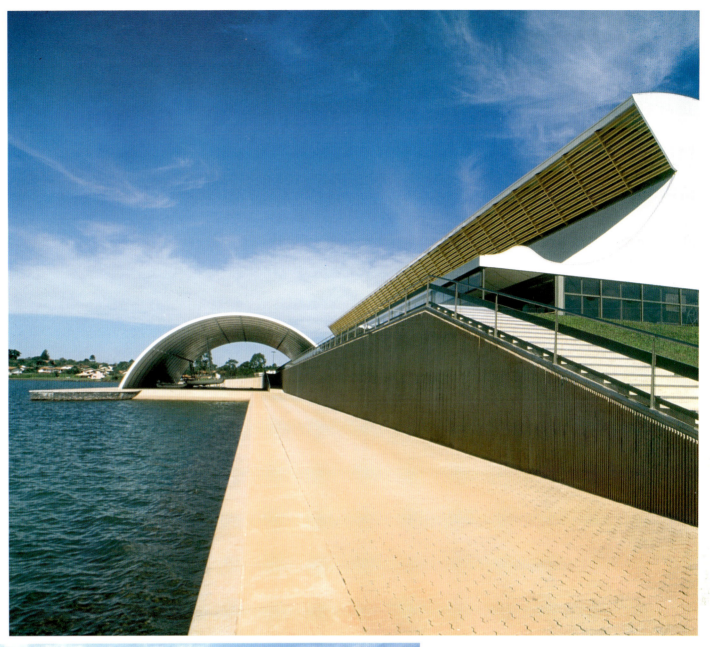

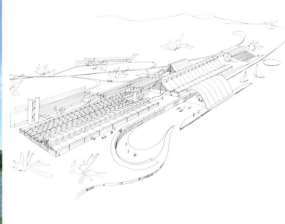

The children's rehabilitation gymnasium is 50 m wide and includes an internal garden linked to the rehabilitation area. A central skylight made of transparent polycarbonate provides natural lighting and ventilation, with an extractor on the apex (opposite). The main gymnasium also receives natural lighting through a continuous skylight both in the sports court (above left) and in the pool area (above right). An auditorium with 400 seats, part of a research centre, is located on the highest level of the site (below right)

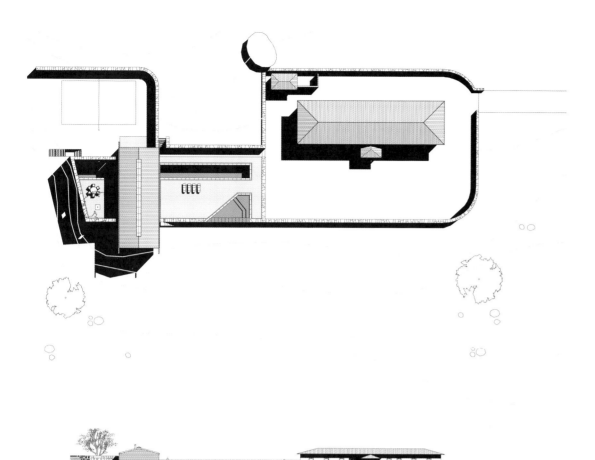

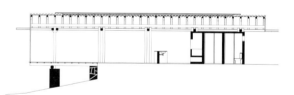

CARAMBÓ PAVILION

Architect Una Arquitetos (Cristiane Muniz, Fábio Valentim, Fernanda Barbara, Fernando Viégas),
Marcus Vinícius Barreto Lima
Design Team Camila Lisboa, Guilherme Petrella, Mariana Alves de Souza
Structural Engineer Marcus Vinícius Barreto Lima
Client Sylvio Iasi Jr.
Area 150 m² / 1,614 sq ft
Location Joanópolis
Completion Date 2002

An addition to a restored nineteenth-century ranch house, this pavilion provides an outdoor room for leisure and relaxation. The very beautiful natural setting is high up in the Serra da Mantiqueira, near Joanópolis, in the state of São Paulo. The buildings are in a wide valley where cattle graze, and are surrounded by vegetation-covered mountains.

The new pavilion is on an axis perpendicular to the existing house, and following the custom of rural buildings in São Paulo of locating each use in a separate structure, is detached from the main house. Between the two is a broad, tiled terrace, partly bounded by a rubble-stone wall, but completely open to the landscape on one side. A long swimming pool connects the new building to the old. The effect of the pavilion and terrace is to reconfigure and give scale to the landscape, enhancing its beauty. Openings in the rubble walls frame views of the surrounding scenery and parts of the existing house, while the screens of the pavilion slide back to open the interior to the landscape.

In the tradition of Lucio Costa, this project has a strong feel of an old colonial building, and is at the same time unmistakably modern. The most obvious sign that this is not a vernacular building is the long cantilever carrying the pavilion beyond the terrace, but the same message is given more subtly by the construction. The frame is of locally-grown eucalyptus, but the timbers are not joined by conventional carpentry methods. Instead, each member only touches the next, and is attached by steel wire, in a manner that seems crude and archaic, and yet at the same time is reminiscent of the simplified joints of European modernist designers like Mies van der Rohe and Gerrit Rietveld. The separation of elements is a recurring theme: walls do not touch the roof, and the enclosing screens, open gratings of *ipê*, a rain forest hardwood, are independent of the main structure. The pavilion's ambiguity as to whether it is an old or a new structure is one of its most poetic themes.

The Pavilion is detached from the main house, following local architectural traditions, as shown in the site plan (top left) and elevation (above left). The gentle slope of the terrain is emphasized by cantilevering part of the volume over the edge of the rubble wall (opposite below right and left, also see section, above). Clay-rich soil from the site was used to cast and fire the floor tiles while the timber for the structural system was taken from trees grown locally (opposite above right).

Through the use of sliding sun-breakers, the Pavilion can be both completely open, framing views of the landscape (above and opposite below left), or closed and protected from the elements (below left and opposite above).

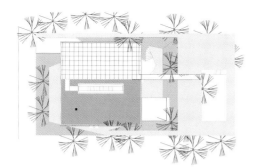

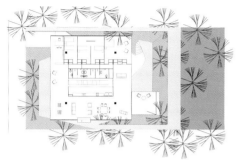

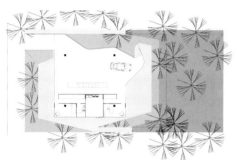

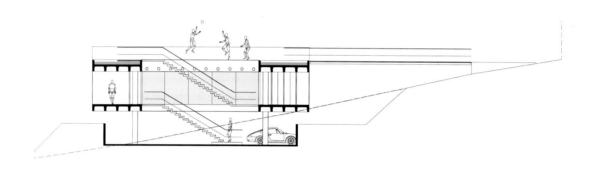

ALDEIA DA SERRA HOUSE

Architect MMBB Arquitetos (Angelo Bucci, Fernando de Mello Franco, Marta Moreira, Milton Braga)
Design Team Anna Helena Vilella, Eduardo Ferroni, Maria Júlia Herklotz, André Drummond
Structural Engineer Ibsen Puleo Uvo
Client José Henrique Mariante, Beatriz Arruda Mariante
Area 256 m² / 2,754 sq ft
Location Aldeia da Serra, São Paulo
Completion Date 2002

This concrete and glass house in the suburbs of São Paulo is a contemporary reinterpretation of the Paulista Modernism of the 1960s. Situated on a long, steeply-sloping site with an 8 m fall, each of the three levels connects to the ground, the upper two by means of bridges.

Entrance to the house is either from below, or more spectacularly from above, over the bridge, across the roof and down through the central staircase. The roof is a pond, which maintains the water-tightness of the concrete. The living area is on the first-floor *piano nobile*, and is wrapped around the open staircase core, and the bedrooms set to one side.

In the tradition of Paulista Modernism, the house is supported on four columns, here set inside, and the floor and roof slabs cantilevered from them. The deep coffering of the soffits emphasizes the weight and depth of the cantilever. The interior is enclosed on all four sides by floor-to-ceiling glass attached without any frame being visible from inside, again emphasizing the apparent weight of the cantilevers.

Apart from the steel staircase and bridges, all the visible structural surfaces are either concrete or glass. The internal floors are finished with a mix of concrete and marble, and the external floors are polished concrete. Screens at the sides of the house protecting the interior from sunlight are made of composite wood and cement panels.

The layout of the house follows a geometrical composition based on a 90 cm square module, which forms the two identical concrete slabs. These, in turn, mirror each other, and combined with the slope of the terrain generate the space of the house's three levels. In this composition the house is superficially symmetrical, arranged around the floor columns and the central spine of the staircase. However, the absolute symmetry is interrupted repeatedly – by, for example, the single column that rises above the roof to carry the oblong water tank; the staircase, which is slightly displaced in relation to the plan; or the cutting short of the grass bank on the lower side of the house.

Two concrete slabs raised on *pilotis* create three levels (see above left from top: roof, upper and lower level plans). The sloping terrain interacts with each of these floors (see section, above right), to which it is connected by ramps (opposite above and below left) on the back facade. The front and back facades remain exposed to the exterior with the use of sliding glass panes set in the concrete slabs. Side facades are sheltered by cement and wood panels over movable windows (opposite below right).

Recent Works: Case Studies

The composition of the house is organized around the staircase which cuts through the slabs connecting the lower level with the rooftop solarium (opposite), providing natural lighting to bathrooms and the kitchen (below right). Space division is achieved by a combination of concrete partitions and sliding doors (above left and right). The lower level accommodates the parking space, entrance and servicing areas (top right).

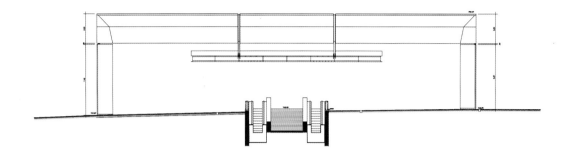

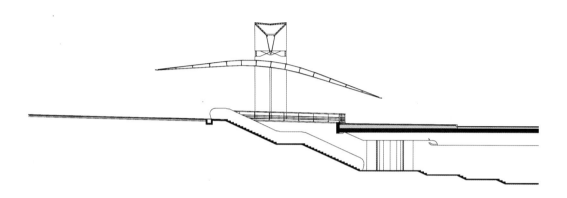

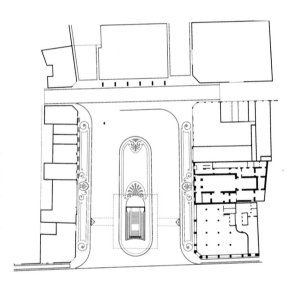

PLAZA OF THE PATRIARCH

Architect Paulo Mendes da Rocha
Design Team Eduardo Argenton Colonelli, Silvio Oksman, Katia Bomfim Pestana,
Giancarlo Latorraca, Marcelo Laurino
Structural Engineer Julio Fruchtengarten, Paulo Mattos Pimenta, Fernando Stucchi,
Maubertec Engenharia e Projeto Ltda
Client Associação Viva O Centro, UNIBANCO, Empresa Municipal De Urbanização
Area 120 m² / 1,291 sq ft (portico)
Location São Paulo
Completion Date 2002

The Plaza of the Patriarch is a square in the old central business district of São Paulo, now suffering from the removal of many businesses to the periphery of the city. Several buildings in the old centre are now unoccupied except for their street frontages. The question of how to reverse this decline has been a pressing issue for São Paulo architects and planners.

The Plaza had for many years been used as a bus terminus. Paulo Mendes da Rocha's scheme involved moving the bus stop elsewhere, freeing up the space for pedestrians; restoring the old Portuguese mosaic tiled paving of the square; renovating the existing underground passage; introducing new lighting in order to enhance the existing buildings; and creating the steel canopy above the steps down to the shopping arcade. As Mendes da Rocha explains, rather than a simple restoration of old buildings, the aim was to utilize architecture's symbolic force, putting into the city a new element that would be expressive of current uses and habits of city living.

The steel canopy and its supporting frame

appear large in relation to the scale of the square. However, the canopy acts as an open shelter, in the manner of the tradition of Brazilian Modernism, and the supporting frame provides a gateway to this part of the city. Critics have complained that the frame blocks the view of buildings in the square, like the seventeenth-century Church of Saint Anthony. In defence though, others have insisted that the frame makes a necessary transition between the much larger scale of the adjacent Anhangabaú Valley and the viaduct across it, and in this way draws these two parts of the city together, while framing views in both directions.

The first step in this urban project was to pedestrianize the plaza restoring the Portuguese mosaic floor (opposite bottom right and plan, above left). The steel canopy over the entrance to the underground passage is the main architectural element (opposite and cross and long section, above left).

Recent Works: Case Studies

The portico links the old and new town, framing the views of the surrounding buildings and the cityscape beyond.

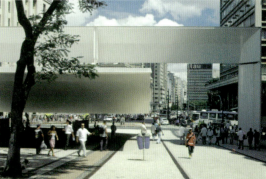

NOTES

INTRODUCTION

1. Zilah Quezado Deckker, *Brazil Built: The Architecture of the Modern Movement in Brazil* (London, Spon, 2001).
2. Reyner Banham, *Guide to Modern Architecture* (London, Architectural Press, 1962), p.36.
3. Claude Lévi-Strauss, *Tristes Tropiques* (1955) transl. J. & D. Weightman (London, Penguin, 1976), pp.118-9.
4. Lévi-Strauss, op. cit., p.118
5. David Underwood, *Oscar Niemeyer and the Architecture of Brazil* (New York, Rizzoli, 1994).
6. Carlos Eduardo Dias Comas, 'Niemeyer's Casino and the Misdeeds of Brazilian Architecture', *Journal of Romance Studies*, 2:3 (Winter 2002), pp.73-87; and 'Rapport du Brésil' in J.-F. Lejeune (ed.), *Cruauté et utopie, villes et paysages d'Amerique latine* (Brussels, CIVA, 2003), pp.173-180.
7. Homi K. Bhabha, *The Location of Culture* (London and New York, Routledge, 1994), p.112.
8. See Felipe Hernández, 'On the notion of architectural hybridisation in Latin America', *Journal of Architecture*, 7:1 (Spring 2002), pp.77-86; and Felipe Hernández, 'Éspaces d'Hybridation: Les Maisons des Architectes', in J.-F. Lejeune (ed.), *op.cit.*, pp.109-117.
9. Felipe Hernández, 'The transcultural phenomenon, and the transculturation of architecture', *Journal of Romance Studies*, 2:3 (Winter 2002), pp.1-15, p.1.
10. Susan Bassnett and Harish Trivedi, 'Introduction. Of colonies, cannibals and vernaculars' in Susan Bassnett and Harish Trivedi (eds.), *Postcolonial Translation: Theory and Practice* (London and New York, Routledge, 1999), pp. 1-18. Also Else Vieira, 'Liberating Calibans: Readings of Antropofagia and Haroldo de Campos' Poetics of Transcreation'in in Susan Bassnett and Harish Trivedi (eds.), op. cit., pp.95-113.
11. See for example Stanislaus von Moos, 'Urbanism and Transcultural Exchanges, 1910-1935: a Survey', in H. Allen Brooks (ed.), *Le Corbusier: The Garland Essays* (New York and London, Garland Publishing, 1987), pp.225-6.
12. Otto Neurath, 'Städtbau und Proletariat "Der Kampf"', *Sozialdemokratische Monatsschrift* (Vienna, 1926), pp.236-242 (quoted in Günther Uhlig, 'Town Planning in the Weimar Republic', *Architectural Association Quarterly*, 11:1 (1979), p.24.
13. See Deckker, *Brazil Built*, pp.200-1.
14. For an interesting discussion of Bo Bardi's Museums, and her strategies for merging popular Brazilian art with European modern art and architecture, see Zeuler Lima and Sandra Vivanco, 'Culture translated and devoured: two Brazilian museums by Lina Bo Bardi', *Journal of Romance Studies*, 2:3 (Winter 2002), pp.45-60.

CHAPTER ONE

1. Siegfried Giedion, 'Architecture in the 1960's: hopes and fear', in *Zodiac*, 11 (1963). Preface to the Italian second edition of *Space, Time and Architecture*. Giedion begins the essay by referring to the symposium 'Modern Architecture, Death or Metamorphosis?', which took place in 1961 at the Metropolitan Museum of New York.
2. See 'Nine Points on Monumentality', manifesto written by Giedion, Fernand Léger and Josep Lluis Sert in 1943.
3. Giedion, 'Le Brésil et l'Architecture Contemporaine' in *L'Architecture d'Aujourd'hui*, 42-43 (1952). Also published as the preface for Henrique Mindlin, *Modern Architecture in Brazil* (New York, Reinhold Publishing, 1956).
4. Nikolaus Pevsner, 'Modern Architecture and the Historian, or The Return of Historicism' in *Journal of the Royal Institute of British Architects*, 68 (1961), pp. 230–240.
5. Pevsner, art.cit., p.230.
6. Pevsner, art.cit., p.236
7. Pevsner, *An Outline of European Architecture*, 6th edn (London, John Murray, 1957), p. 429.
8. Pevsner, *An Outline of European Architecture*, loc.cit.
9. Reyner Banham, *Guide to Modern Architecture* (London, The Architectural Press, 1962).
10. Banham, op.cit., p.140.
11. Banham, op.cit., p.36.
12. Philip L. Goodwin, *Brazil Builds: architecture new and old, 1652-1942* (New York, MoMA, 1943).
13. The relocation of the Portuguese Court to Brazil in 1808 brought about significant cultural and economical changes. In 1816, the Emperor Dom João VI commissioned a delegation of French artists known as the 'French Artistic Mission' to help him Europeanize the country. The architect Grandjean de Montigny introduced the Neoclassical style, which successfully spread throughout Brazil

during the nineteenth century, and against which the Neocolonial Movement in the first quarter of the twentieth century, and the Modern Movement in the second quarter, reacted.
14. See Henry-Russell Hitchcock, *Latin American Architecture since 1945* (New York, MoMA, 1955); Mindlin, op.cit.; Stamo Papadaki, *The Work of Oscar Niemeyer* and *Oscar Niemeyer: Work in Progress* (New York, Reinhold Publishing, 1950 and 1956); Klaus Franck, *Affonso Eduardo Reidy, Works and Projects* (New York, Reinhold, 1956); Yves Bruand, *Arquitetura Contemporânea no Brasil* (São Paulo, Perspectiva, 1981). The main periodicals that published special issues on Brazil are: *L'architecture d'aujourd'hui*, 13–14 (1947), and 42-43 (1952); *The Architectural Review*, 567 (1944), and 679 (1953); *Casabella-Continuità*, 200 (1954); and *The Architectural Forum, 5:87* (1947). For an overview of these publications see: Nelci Tinem, *O alvo do olhar estrangeiro: o Brasil na historiografia da arquitetura moderna* (João Pessoa, Manufatura, 2002).
15. See Lúcio Costa, *Registro de uma vivência* (São Paulo, Empresa das Artes, 1995).
16. See Carlos A. F. Martins, 'Construir una arquitectura, construir un país' in Jorge Schwartz (ed.), *Brasil 1920-1950: de la Antropofagia a Brasília* (Valéncia, IVAM, 2000).
17. Timber lattice-work used as protection from excessive light and heat. They were originally used in balconies in Islamic architecture, and then Portuguese colonial architecture where they also gave privacy to interiors, especially allowing women to participate of street life without being seen. See James Steven Curl, *Oxford Dictionary of Architecture*, (Oxford University Press, 1999) under 'mushrabeyeh'.
18. Kenneth Frampton, 'Homenagem a Niemeyer', *AU*, 15 (1987), p. 58.
19 Giedion, *L'architecture d'aujourd'hui*, 42–43 (1952). According to Giedion, even with 'a low level iron and cement production', in the main Brazilian cities 'skyscrapers grow everywhere'. And such a voluptuous property scene is accompanied by an unprecedented architectural sophistication that appears to burst out from the native soil almost inexplicably, particularly if compared to the North American example, 'with its chain of great predecessors since 1880' such as H. H. Richardson, Louis Sullivan and Frank Lloyd Wright. For further examination on this subject see: Carlos A. F. Martins, 'Hay algo de irracional...' in *Block. Revista de Cultura de la Arquitectura, la Ciudad y el Territorio*, 4 (Buenos Aires, Universidad Torcuato di Tella, 1999).
20. See 'Report on Brazil' in *The Architectural Review*, 694 (October 1954), pp. 238–9. Published in the same issue are statements by other important architects who visited the country at that time, such as Walter Gropius and Ernesto Nathan Rogers. For an overview of this debate see: Ana María Rigotti, 'Brazil Deceives' in *Block*, 4, (1999).
21. See Bruno Zevi, 'La moda lecorbuseriana in Brasile: Max Bill apostrofa Oscar Niemeyer', *Cronache di Architettura I 1954-55* (Bari, Laterza, 1971). Zevi was also Brasília's most passionate critic on the occasion of the International Critics Congress (AICA), which took place in Brazil in 1959. See 'Inchiesta su Brasília' in *L'architettura – Cronache e Storia*, 49:7, (1959).
22 Giulio Carlo Argan, 'La Architettura Moderna in Brasile', *Comunità*, 24 (1954).
23. The legimitization of the Baroque style as the expression of a 'native genius', in which 'characteristically Brazilian traces' were shown for the first time, appears in the book by Mindlin (op. cit., 1956), echoing Costa's interpretative shift in favour of the legitimization of the 'aesthetic intention'. See Costa, 'Depoimento' (1948), and 'Considerações sobre arte contemporânea' (1952) in op. cit. (1995).
24. *Cobogó, combogó, combogê* are names – generally used in the north of Brazil – to describe a perforated brick or a hollow element made of cement. They are thought to be associated with the perforated bricks of North African origin. See Corona & Lemos, *Dicionário de Arquitetura Brasileira* (São Paulo, Edart, 1972), quoted by Telles, "Lucio Costa: monumentalidade e intimismo" in *Novos Estudos*, 25 (São Paulo, Cebrap, 1989), p. 85.
25. Telles, 'O desenho: forma e imagem' in *AU*, 55 (1994), p. 91.
26. Telles, art. cit. (1994), p. 94.
27. Tiles in this case refer to both *azulejos* (normal tiles) and *pastilhas* (smaller tiles approximately 2 sq cm in size).
28. Lorenzo Mammì, 'João Gilberto e o projeto utópico da bossa nova', *Novos Estudos*, 34 (São Paulo, Cebrap, 1992, p. 69).
29. See David Underwood, *Oscar Niemeyer and Brazilian free-form modernism* (New York, Georg Braziller, 1994); and Anna Rosa Cotta and Attilio Marcolli, 'Considerazioni su Brasília', *Casabella-Continuità*, 218 (1958).
30. This is the case of Leonardo Benevolo, *Storia dell'Architettura Moderna* (Bari, Laterza, 1960); and Frampton, *Modern Architecture: a Critical History* (London, Thames & Hudson, 1980). In William Curtis' book, Brazilian architecture is grouped together with Latin American production and placed beside that of Japan and Australia. See: Curtis, *Modern Architecture since 1900* (London, Phaidon Press, 1982).
31. According to Zilah Quezado Deckker, 'the rupture with Modernism that occurred during the 1970s brought about a new appreciation of regional specificity distinct from the universal and technological imperatives of pre-war European Modernism. For [William] Curtis and [Kenneth] Frampton, Brazilian architecture seemed to be a continuation of the International Style rather than forming a specifically post-war programme.' Quezado Deckker, *Brazil Built: The Architecture of the Modern Movement in Brazil* (London, Spon Press, 2001), p. 169.
32. See Otília B. F. Arantes and Paulo Eduardo Arantes, *Um ponto cego no projeto moderno de Jürgen Habermas: arquitetura e dimensão estética depois das vanguardas* (São Paulo, Brasiliense, 1992); and Otília B. F. Arantes, *O lugar da arquitetura depois dos modernos* (São Paulo, EDUSP, 1993) and *Urbanismo em fim de linha* (São Paulo, EDUSP, 1998).
33. In the case of fine art, this recognition occurred through the works of Hélio Oiticica and Lygia Clark, taking place extemporarily only at the end of the 1980s and via routes that are outside those of the original context in which they were conceived. See Rodrigo Naves, 'Um azar histórico – desencontros entre moderno e contemporâneo na arte brasileira', *Novos Estudos*, 64 (São Paulo, Cebrap, 2002).
34. Modernist here refers to artists associated with Brazilian *Modernismo*. *Modernismo* is somewhat distinct from Modernism as it refers to those artists that took the modern European aesthetic 'translating' it into the national context. *Modernismo* generally refers to production from the 1922 Modern Art Week in São Paulo (although exceptions such as Anita Malfati and Lasar Segall exist) to the work of artists such as Portinari in the 1930s.
35. *Cerrado* is the Portuguese name for a low form of vegetation typical of central Brazil.
36. Written between 1933 and 1980, his texts were compiled in the following publications: Aracy Amaral (ed.), *Mundo, homem, arte em crise* (São Paulo, Perspectiva, 1975); Aracy Amaral (ed.), *Dos murais de Portinari aos espaços de Brasília* (São Paulo, Perspectiva, 1981); and the four volumes of selected texts: Otília B. F. Arantes (ed.), *Mário Pedrosa: Política das artes* (1), *Acadêmicos e modernos* (2), *Forma e percepção estética* (3), and *Modernidade cá e lá* (4), (São Paulo, EDUSP, 1995).
37. See Mário Pedrosa, 'A cidade nova, síntese das artes' in Amaral (ed.), op. cit., 1981.
38. Developmentalism in the Latin American context refers to the political economic policies developed in response to the Depression of the 1930s and continued up until the 1970s. The collapse of world trade in the 1930s left Latin American countries without a market for their primary products, while still being heavily dependent upon imports from the developed world for many manufactured products (such as, in the construction industry, steel and cement). The basic features of developmentalism were import substitution, fostering investment in the domestic production of previously imported goods, and tariffs, to protect these new industries against more cheaply produced foreign products. The result was a planned capitalist economy, implemented by a partnership between the state and those big industries that were given favoured status. The aim was to force investment, even if this created dependency on foreign loans, or encouraged direct foreign investment, in the expectation that the stimulus within the sheltered economy would accelerate the rate of economic growth in the country and enable it eventually to achieve parity with the most fully developed countries. The policy rested upon the assumption that developing countries needed different strategies from fully developed countries, until they reached a comparable economic level. The policy started to be abandoned in the 1970s, when it became clear that less developed countries were not 'catching up' with the most advanced countries, and finally collapsed in the debt crisis of the 1980s, when the extent of indebtedness of Latin American countries to the first world revealed the fallacy of the whole strategy. The political economist and social theorist most associated with the doctrine of developmentalism was Raúl Prebisch.
39. Brasília fell on the side of universalism in the 'dialectics of localism and cosmopolitanism' through which Antonio Candido defined Brazilian 'spiritual life'. See Candido, 'Literatura e cultura de 1900 a 1945 (panorama para estrangeiros)' in T. A. Queiróz (ed.), *Literatura e sociedade – estudos de teoria e história literária*, 8th edn (São Paulo, 2000). Candido is a social scientist and author of seminal books and essays on Brazilian literary theory and criticism. Among them is *Formação da Literatura Brasileira*, where the author elaborates an important interpretative system for the whole national literary production. See Candido, *Formação da literatura brasileira: momentos decisivos* (São Paulo, Martins, 1959).
40. See note 34.
41. *Carioca* is the generic term for someone, or something, from Rio de Janeiro.
42. Referring to that which comes from São Paulo.
43. Brasília is situated in a region of plateaus called *chapadões*. These geological formations were described by João Guimarães Rosa in the following manner: 'They are formed of bad quality soil of various types over infertile sandstone. (Brasília is a typical *chapada*...) They are so porous that when it rains no mud is formed neither is there any torrents. The water infiltrates quickly leaving no traces, and neither is it noticeable shortly after it has rained.' Edoardo Bizarri, *João Guimarães Rosa: Correspondência com seu tradutor italiano* (Rio de Janeiro Nova Fronteira/UFMG, 2003), p. 40.
44. The culture *of the sertão* is typified by the *jagunço* – the name that, according to Antonio Candido's definition, is given 'as much to the salaried burly foreman and to the comrade in arms as to the actual boss that uses them in order to put in place his conscious transgressions or to establish a private order that sometimes becomes itself public law.' Candido, 'Jagunços mineiros de Cláudio a Guimarães Rosa' in *Vários Escritos* (São Paulo, Livraria Duas Cidades, 1970), pp. 140–41.
45. Guimarães Rosa, *Grande Sertão:Veredas* (Rio de Janeiro, José Olympio, 1956).
46. See Guimarães Rosa, 'As margens da alegria' and 'Os cimos' in *Primeiras estórias* (Rio de Janeiro, José Olympio, 1962).
47. Guimarães Rosa, 'As margens da alegria', *Primeiras estórias*, p.7.
48. José Miguel Wisnik, 'O Famigerado' in *Literatura Scripta* 10:5 (Belo Horizonte, PUC-MG, 2002) p. 178.
49. Pedrosa, 'Reflexões em torno da nova capital' in Amaral (ed.), op. cit. (1981).
50. Traditional large estates are known as *latifúndios*, a term derived from Classical Rome. In Latin America the phenomenon of land accumulation is closely related to that of the *minifúndios,* or small farmsteads, and is a pattern inherited from colonial land-ownership schemes known in Brazil as *Capitanias Hereditarias*. The sharp increase of the rural population together with the growth of large estates has underlined the process of land concentration in the hands of few landowners, at the same time encouraging the dismemberment of smaller estates with the consequent rise of the *minifúndios.* This tendency has been somewhat reinforced by the modernization of agriculture which privileges intensive farming in large estates, thereby giving rise to a mass of land-less agricultural workers ie a rural proletariat.
51. See Pedrosa, 'Lições do Congresso Internacional de Críticos' in Amaral (ed.), op. cit. (1981). The essay includes a summary of statements by André Chastel, William Holford, Bruno Zevi, Richard Neutra, Eero Saarinen, M. F. J. Kiesler, Douglas Haskell, André Wogenscky, Hain Gamzu, Alberto Sartoris, Meyer Shapiro and Charlotte Perriand at the AICA Congress in 1959. Additionally, it is worth seeing: Françoise Choay, 'Brasília: une capitale préfabriqué', *L'oeil*, 59 (1959); and Pier Luigi Nervi, 'Critica delle strutture', *Casabella-Continuità*, 223 (1959).
52. Frampton, *Modern Architecture: a Critical History*, 3rd ed., (London, Thames and Hudson, 1992), pp. 183, 256–57 and Manfredo Tafuri and Francesco Dal Co, *Modern Architecture* (Abrams, New York, 1979), pp. 378–79.
53. 'This might be a quite important consideration,

because the Baroque town was generated from a point and the discipline of the geometry governed all its parts, but in this plan there is no such simple principle; it is generated by a series of principles of which not one completely dominates'. 'Capital Cities', discussion with Lucio Costa, Arthur Korn, Denys Lasdun and Peter Smithson, *Architectural Design*, 28 (1958), p. 440.
54. William Holford in Pedrosa, op. cit. (1981) p. 369.
55. See Matheus Gorovitz, *Brasília, uma questão de escala* (São Paulo, Projeto, 1985).
56. See Telles, 'Arquitetura moderna no Brasil: o desenho da superfície' (Master's Dissertation, São Paulo, FFLCH-USP, 1988). This view is posited by Telles as early as the essay 'A arquitetura modernista: um espaço sem lugar' in Sérgio Tolipan (ed.), *Sete ensaios sobre o modernismo* (Rio de Janeiro, Funarte, 1983) and is reconsidered in 'Lucio Costa: monumentalidade e intimismo' in *Novos Estudos*, 25 (São Paulo, Cebrap, 1989).
57. Telles, op. cit., 1989, quoting Costa from Alberto Xavier (ed.), *Lucio Costa: obra escrita* (Brasília, Universidade de Brasília, 1968).
58. In this sense Paulo Mendes da Rocha's comments are pertinent: 'For Brazilians during those years, the construction of Brasília was a very important event. It acted as a stimulus in that it inaugurated the somewhat diffused notion of constructing a city in an exemplary manner. Let us create a city! Because we want to! Place it in the interior of the continent, so that it actually contradicts our apparent destiny, that which has been imposed upon us by colonization and its policy of inhabiting the coast. In fact, this interiorization or internalization of the Brazilian reflection about the possibilities of the wealth of these remote territories, about the immensity of the continent, necessarily brought with it a reflection about Latin America.' Paulo Mendes da Rocha, 'Cultura e natureza' in Hélio Piñon, *Paulo Mendes da Rocha* (São Paulo, Romano Guerra Editora, 2002), p. 17.
59. See Telles, op. cit. (1989), p. 94.
60. Telles, 'A casa no Atlântico', *AU*, 60 (documento Paulo Mendes da
Rocha, 1995), p. 81.
61. See Sérgio Ferro, 'Reflexões sobre o brutalismo caboclo', interview with Marlene Millan Acayaba in *Projeto*, 86 (1986).
62. *Desenho* (drawing), for Artigas, is defined as a projective intention, a design that, as it is traced on paper, carries with it an emancipatory and pre-emptive finality. See Vilanova Artigas, 'O desenho' in *Caminhos da arquitetura* (São Paulo, Fundação Vilanova Artigas/Pini, 1986).
63. Yves Bruand, *Arquitetura contemporânea no Brasil* (São Paulo, Perspectiva, 1981), p. 299. On another level, the identification of the structural truth of the constructed form undertaken by Artigas was forewarned by Niemeyer's notorious self-criticism published in 1958. In his essay, the *Carioca* architect announces his objective of abandoning the 'excessive tendency towards originality' in favour of a compact geometrism that would accentuate the character and the hierarchical meaning of the building, expressed as such no longer through its secondary elements 'but by its own structure, accordingly integrated within the original aesthetic concept.' This statement, according to Artigas, marked 'the starting point for a new phase of development for national architecture'. See Niemeyer, 'Depoimento'; and Vilanova Artigas, 'Revisão crítica de Niemeyer' in Alberto Xavier (ed.), *Depoimento de uma geração* (São Paulo, Cosac & Naify, 2003).
64. See Pedro Fiori Arantes, *Arquitetura nova: Sérgio Ferro, Flávio Império e Rodrigo Lefèvre, de Artigas aos mutirões* (São Paulo, Editora 34, 2002).
65. Ferro (1986), op.cit., p. 68.
66. As Ferro demonstrated, the 'backwardness' of Brazilian civil construction is not conjunctural but structural. Since 'the possible value-added within civil construction (as in other archaic areas of production) is so high, its excess produces an "over-pouring" capable of providing for the rest of the economy, including its most modern sectors, homogenizing in this way the levels of profit. Therefore its "backward" character is functional rather than "anomalous" and because of this there is interest in preserving the status quo.' Pedro Fiori Arantes, op. cit. (2002), p. 105.
67. See Hélio Piñon, 'Quando o projeto revela a geografia oculta' in Piñon, *Paulo Mendes da Rocha* (São Paulo, Romano Guerra Editora, 2002); and Sophia Telles, 'Museu da escultura", *AU*, 32 (1990).

CHAPTER TWO

1. Warchavchik, 'Acerca da arquitetura moderna' (1925) in Alberto Xavier (ed.), *Depoimento de uma Geração* (São Paulo, Cosac & Naify, 2003), pp. 35-38.
2. Santos, *Quatro Séculos de Arquitetura* (Rio de Janeiro, IAB, 1981), p. 108.
3. See ch. 1, note 17.
4. On this tendency see Jorge Czajkowski, 'Mestre da justa medida' in *AU*, 48 (1993), pp. 69-80.
5. The fibres and leaves of the *carnaúba (Copernicia prunifera)*, *babaçu (Orrbygnya speciosa)* and *buriti (mauritia flexuosa L)* are traditionally used in the Amazon region as building materials. These three species belong to the *Palmae* family. They are relatively tall palm trees (between 10 and 35 metres) whose different parts are put to various uses by the local population and therefore figure prominently in popular culture as well as in literature (Mário de Andrade, Guimarães Rosa) and explorers' writings (Humboldt called *carnaúba* the 'tree of life'). See *Biblioteca Virtual do Estudante Brasileiro.*
6. On this tendency see Hugo Segawa, 'Os materiais da natureza e a natureza dos materiais' in Segawa (ed.), *Arquiteturas no Brasil/Anos 80* (São Paulo, Projeto, 1998), pp. 34–46.
7. Oscar Niemeyer, 'Pampulha: Arquitetura' in *Pampulha* (Rio de Janeiro, Imprensa Nacional, 1944) Reprinted in Xavier (ed.), op. cit., pp. 244-245.
8. Niemeyer, 'Depoimento' (1958) in Xavier (ed.), op. cit., p.244-245.
9. João Vilanova Artigas, "O desenho" in Rosa Camargo Artigas et al. (eds), *Vilanova Artigas* (São Paulo, Fundação Vilanova Artigas, Instituto Lina Bo e P. M. Bardi; Lisboa, Editorial Blau, 1997), p. 136.
10. Vilanova Artigas, 'Anhembi Tênis Clube' in Rosa Camargo Artigas, et al. (eds), op.cit., p. 95.
11. Vilanova Artigas, 'Casa Elza Berquó' in Rosa Camargo Artigas et al. (eds), op.cit., p. 138.
12. On the use of the term 'structure' in modern architecture see Adrian Forty, *Words and Buildings*, (London, Thames & Hudson, 2000), pp. 276–85.
13. Alan Colquhoun, *Modern Architecture*, (Oxford University Press, 2002) p. 222.
14. The distinction between analytical and synthetical Brutalism was made by Jorge Czajkowski. See 'Perspectiva Histórica da Arte e da Arquitetura no Modernismo' in *Módulo - Arte e Arquitetura*, 76 (Rio de Janeiro, Avenir Editora, 1983), pp. ii-iii.
15. Sergio Ferro, 'Arquitetura Nova' in *Teoria e Prática* 1 (São Paulo, 1967).
16. Ferro, *O Canteiro e o Desenho* (São Paulo, Projeto, 1979).
17. Paulo Mendes da Rocha, 'Genealogia da Imaginação', in Rosa Camargo Artigas (ed.), *Paulo Mendes da Rocha* (São Paulo, Cosac & Naify, 2000), pp. 71–72.
18. Mendes da Rocha, 'Cultura e Natureza', in Hélio Piñón, *Paulo Mendes da Rocha* (São Paulo, Romano Guerra Editora, 2002), p. 33.
19. '*Engenho'* is the faculty of invention but also shares with the English 'wit' the meaning of 'practical talent or cleverness; skill, ingenuity' See *Shorter Oxford English Dictionary* (Oxford University Press, 1967) and *Grande Dicionario da Língua Portuguesa*, (Lisbon, Texto Editora, 2004).
20. Lina Bo Bardi, 'SESC–Fábrica da Pompéia' in Marcelo Ferraz (ed.), *Lina Bo Bardi* (São Paulo, Empresa das Artes, 1993), p. 220.
21. Bo Bardi, art. cit., p. 282.
22. Bo Bardi, *Tempos de Grossura*, (São Paulo, Instituto Lina Bo e P. M. Bardi), 1994.
23. Bo Bardi, 'Tempos de Grossura' in Marcelo Ferraz (ed.), op. cit., p. 214.
24. Mendes da Rocha, 'Cultura e natureza'in Piñón, op. cit., p. 38.
25. Joaquim Guedes, 'Atenção e sensibilidade na escolha dos produtos', *AU*, 70, (1997), p. 75.
26. João Filgueiras Lima, "RENURB – pré-fabricação em argamassa armada. Saneamento básico de Salvador, 1980-1982" in Giancarlo Latorraca (ed.), *João Filgueiras Lima, Lelé* (São Paulo: Instituto Lina Bo e P. M. Bardi; Lisboa, Editorial Blau, 1999), p. 105.
27. Filgueiras Lima, op. cit., p. 30.

CHAPTER THREE

1. Sérgio Buarque de Holanda, *Raízes do Brasil* (Rio de Janeiro, José Olympio, 1936).
2. The Estado Novo was the authoritarian regime established by Getúlio Vargas's coup in 1937, who had been President of Brazil since 1930. It was characterized by the concentration of power in the hands of the President and of the central government with subsequent loss of autonomy by the states of the nation; large infra-structural investments which allow for the industrial development in the following decades (1950s); the introduction of labour legislation; the creation of unions linked to the state apparatus. Conservative, modernizer and populist, the estado Novo played a fundamental role for the economic and cultural modernization of Brazil in the 20th century.
3. For a description of developmentism see ch. 1, n. 38. For a discussion on Modernism's agenda see also Otília Arantes and P. Arantes, *Um Ponto Cego no Projeto Moderno de Jürgen Habermas* (São Paulo, Brasiliense, 1991)
4. The literature on this building considers four different versions:
1) a study developed by the Brazilian team for the Castelo site (within the zoning defined by Alfred Agache for the city centre) before Le Corbusier's arrival;
2) a study developed under Le Corbusier's supervision for the site of his choice, next to the beach;
3) a study developed for the Castelo site against Le Corbusier's will, on the eve of his departure;
4) a definite study for the Castelo site by the Brazilian team, following Le Corbusier's return to Europe.
See Elizabeth Davis, *Le Corbusier : riscos brasileiros* (São Paulo, Nobel, 1987) Yves Bruand, *Arquitetura contemporânea no Brasil* (São Paulo, Editora Perspectiva, 1981)
5. This refers to the notion proposed by Roberto Schwarz in describing certain cultural characteristics of Brazilian literature as representing 'misplaced ideas'. See: Schwarz, R. *Misplaced Ideas: Essays on Brazilian Culture*. Edited and introduced by John Gledson. (Verso. London and New York, 1992).
6. See also, Otília B. F. Arantes, *Urbanismo em fim de linha* (São Paulo, EDUSP, 1998)
7. See Otília B. F. Arantes, *Sentido da formação: três estudos sobre Antonio Candido, Gilda de Mello e Souza e Lúcio Costa* (Rio de Janeiro, Paz e Terra, 1997).
8. Francisco de Oliveira, *A economia brasileira: crítica à razão dualista* (São Paulo, Cebrap/Vozes, 1981).
9. Lucio Costa, *Registro de uma Vivência* (Empresa das Artes, São Paulo), p. 212.
10. There were various large-scale complexes built, primarily in São Paulo by COHAB (Companhia Metropolitana de Habitação de São Paulo) from the 1970s onwards: Carapicuíba (1978–82), Itaquera I (1977–82), Teotônio Vilela (1981–83), Adventista (1986–90), etc.
11. Nabil Bonduki (ed.), *Affonso Eduardo Reidy* (São Paulo, Instituto Lina e P. M. Bardi; Lisbon, Editorial Blau, 2000), p.22.
12. See the Municipality of São Paulo's website for this and other figures, at www.prefeitura.sp.gov.br.
13. "Brasil ganha 717 favelas em nove anos", *Folha de São Paulo* (January 7, 2001).
14 Milton Santos, A Urbanização Brasileira (São Paulo, Hucitec, 1996).
15 Aldaíza Sposati (ed.), *Mapa da Exclusão Social* (PUC-São Paulo, 2000).

CHAPTER FOUR

1. See Colin Rowe, *The Architecture of good intentions: towards a possible retrospect* (London, Academy Editions, 1994).
2. Flexibilization and resort to tradition are not antagonical terms, nor are they strategies exclusive to Brazilian architecture. It is worth noticing the case of both Finland and Japan, where in the works of Alvar Aalto and Kenzo Tange these two alternatives often merge.
3. Ricardo Benzaquen, *Guerra e Paz – Casa-Grande e Senzala e a obra de Gilberto Freyre nos anos 30* (Rio de Janeiro, 34 Letras, 1994).
4. The *'sobrados'* were two-storey houses that generally contained a commercial outlet on the ground floor and the home of the owner above. A staircase at the back of the building connected the two storeys.
5. '*Sala-mirante'* in the original. The expression is by Carlos E. D. Comas, *Revista De Cultura Brasileña*, 2 (September 1998), p. 105.
6. The idea unfolds from Ronaldo Brito's remark about the peculiar way in which Brazilian neo-concrete artists push the limits and eventually break the 'ideal closure of geometrical forms' in the effort to make them derive less from mathematical deductions and more from interactive experiences. See Ronaldo Brito, *Richard Serra* (Rio de Janeiro, Centro de Arte Hélio Oiticica, 1997), p. 25.
7. See Sophia S. Telles, 'Arquitetura moderna no Brasil: o desenho da superfície' (Master's Dissertation, São Paulo, FFLCH-USP, 1988), p. 72.
8. See Oscar Niemeyer, *A*

forma na arquitetura (Rio de Janeiro, Avenir, 1978).

9. See for example Niemeyer's Grand Hotel of 1940 in Ouro Preto.

10 The expression 'Carioca school' has often been employed and yet it has not been properly conceptualized. Generally, it refers to projects by architects based in Rio de Janeiro dating from 1930s up to the construction of Brasília – a period when Rio de Janeiro had the hegaemony of the architectural avant guard – but is not restricted to a geographical identification. There is a regionalist aspect to such a label since it is used to differentiate this kind of architecture from the one produced by the *Paulista* school' of Sao Paulo-based architects such as Artigas. The 'lighness and sensuality' of *Carioca* architecture and the 'weight and density' of *Paulista* architecture are the usual descriptions used to distinguish the two schools, but they are obviously too generical and insufficient. In anycase, the important thing is not to give the idea that by 'school' one means an organized group sharing defined ideas, writing manifestos and promoting shared activities, as it was the case with the artistic avant-guard.

11. Private interview given to Eduardo de Jesus Rodrigues (September, 1978).

12. As defined by Flávio Motta who describes the space of Mendes da Rocha's house as the room where everybody accepts familiarity with the others. The analogy refers to the treatment of a private space as if it were a space for collective use, as in a *favela*, where a small room is occupied by many dwellers. See Flávio Motta, 'Paulo Mendes da Rocha', *Acrópole*, 343 (September 1967).

13. Sophia Telles, *AU,* 60, (June/July 1995), p. 81.

CHAPTER FIVE

1. A number of different authors employ the concept of underdevelopment. I am using the definition of the great Brazilian economist Celso Furtado, according to whom 'underdevelopment has it roots in a precise relationship, created in a particular historical context, between the internal process of exploitation and the external process of dependence (…) Underdevelopment needs to be seen as a process, that is, as a group of elements which interact and reproduce themselves in time, allowing capitalism to spread over large areas of the world without jeopardizing pre-existing social structures.' Amongst the translations of Furtado's works into English, see: *Underdevelopment and dependence: the fundamental connections* (Centre of Latin American Studies, University of Cambridge, 1974) and *Economic development of Latin America: historical background and contemporary problems* (Cambridge University Press, 2003).

2. The architects of this generation who 'learned' with Brasília and who were responsible for alternative and critical practices are by no means restricted to those who feature in this text. Outside São Paulo, at least three figures stand out: Carlos Nelson Ferreira dos Santos, with his work alongside the popular movements in Rio de Janeiro and in the Brás de Pina *favela*; Acácio Gil Borsói, in Pernambuco, the first to exploit alternative technology for housing production combined with popular participation; and João Filgueira Lima, or Lelé, with his factories of prefabricated reinforced concrete for the construction of hospitals in the Sarah Network, the drainage system of gullies, and various other public buildings (see pp. 104–104 and 214–217).

3. On the working conditions in Brasília, see Nair Bicalho de Souza, *Os construtores de Brasília* (Petrópolis, Vozes, 1983) and Vladimir Carvalho's video-documentary *Conterrâneos velhos de guerra,* (Riofilme/Sagres, 1992).

4. About Vilanova Artigas, see Rosa Camargo Artigas et al. (eds), *Vilanova Artigas* (São Paulo, Fundação Vilanova Artigas, Instituto Lina Bo e P. M. Bardi; Lisboa, Editorial Blau, 1997) and Vilanova Artigas, *A função social do arquiteto* (São Paulo, Nobel/Fundação Artigas, 1989); João Massao Kamita, *Vilanova Artigas* (São Paulo, Cosac & Naify, 2000).

5. About the work of the three architects, see Ana Paula Koury, *Grupo Arquitetura Nova* (São Paulo, EDUSP/Fapesp, 2003) and Pedro Fiori Arantes. *Arquitetura Nova: Sérgio Ferro, Flávio Império e Rodrigo Lefèvre, de Artigas aos mutirões,* (São Paulo, Editora34, 2002).

6. Sérgio Ferro, 'Depoimento' in Maria Cecília dos Santos, *Maria Antonia: uma rua na contramão* (São Paulo, Nobel/EDUSP/FAPESP, 1995).

7. Opinion given in a famous interview to a Brazilian magazine of wide circulation, *Manchete*, in 1953, reproduced in *Arte em Revista*, 4 (São Paulo, Kairós, 1980). Max Bill's testimony gave rise to an emphatic defense of Brazilian architects, especially on the part of Lucio Costa.

8 *Cinema Novo* was the main vanguard movement of Brazilian cinema, which tried to avoid the reproduction of typical Hollywood patterns. Its works were close, as far as visual solutions and social questions were concerned, to Italian neo-realism. See Ismail Xavier. *Allegories of underdevelopment: aesthetics and politics in modern Brazilian cinema* (Minneapolis, University of Minnesota Press, 1997).

9. It was the historian Sérgio Buarque de Holanda, one of the founding fathers of the modern interpretation of Brazilian society, who wrote about the 'anti-ethics of work' that engendered both the Brazilian ideal-type, the 'cordial man', and the disordered cities of Portuguese colonization. See: *Raízes do Brasil* (São Paulo, Companhia das Letras, 1995).

10. Vilanova Artigas, op.cit. (1989).

11. When building the famous dome of Santa Maria del Fiore in Florence, the Italian Renaissance architect famously confronted the corporations and guilds and established a new logic of production, governed by the architect's design. His intention was to show that the Florentine artisans could be replaced by any others, as their work was now subject to external authority. See: Manfredo Tafuri, *L'architettura dell'umanesimo* (Rome, Laterza, 1980).

12. The vault is a self-supporting structure used to cover any construction – an age-old technique usually employing clay bricks. Vaults are created by translocating an arch, and may have various outlines. Their designation depends on their profile, sides and elements of construction. *Arquitetura Nova* vaults were born as circular arches, and progressively reached the optimum shape of a catenary (a curve similar to a second degree parabola), in which the bending moment is zero.

13. In Brazil, as in the rest of Latin America, there is a huge debate about self-help housing which has produced a number of academic research projects, books and texts. It was in England, however, that the best international debate on the topic can be found, especially after the 1960s and 1970s, in the works by Charles Abrams and John Turner and the critiques they received. Two collections of essays offer a summary of the debate: Peter Ward (ed.), *Self-Help Housing: a critique* (London, H. W. Wilson Co, 1982); Kosta Mathéy (ed.), *Beyond self-help housing* (London, Mansell,1992).

14. Artigas' quotation

15. Artigas actually worked a number of times for the State during the dictatorship, building dozens of hospitals, train stations, schools, sports stadiums, seven residential areas and even a barracks. As he stated later: 'I lived the 1970s surrounded by fear', and yet, 'it is undeniable that I took a little advantage of the economic miracle'. Artigas, 'Depoimento' in Alberto Xavier (ed.), *Depoimento de uma geração* (São Paulo, Cosac & Naify, 1987).

16. About the BNH and the housing production during the dictartoship, see Ermínia Maricato, *Política habitacional no regime militar* (Petrópolis, Vozes, 1987).

17. Henri Lefebvre, *Le droit à la ville* (Paris, Anthropos, 1968).

18. In the 1970s, multi-lateral institutions began to defend housing policies for the Third World based on self-help as well as on the policy known as 'site and services'. Such proposals endorsed the fact that peripheral countries were unable to reproduce the housing models of the welfare state. The Habitat meeting in 1976 and current World Bank policies directly or indirectly employ Turner's theories in order to defend the reduction of public production and subsidies, the use of residents as unpaid labour-force as well as a progressive, piecemeal building process.

19. About the PT government in São Paulo, see Paul Singer, *Um governo de esquerda para todos: Erundina na prefeitura de São Paulo 1989-1992* (São Paulo, Brasiliense, 1996). About the housing policies developed by this administration, see: Ermínia Maricato, 'Enfrentando desafios – a política desenvolvida pela Secretaria de Habitação e Desenvolvimento Urbano da Prefeitura de São Paulo' (Master's Dissertation, University of São Paulo); Nabil Bonduki. *Arquitetura & habitação social em São Paulo, 1989-1992* (São Paulo, EESC-USP, 1993); Reginaldo Ronconi, *Habitações construídas com o gerenciamento dos usuários, com organização da força de trabalho em regime de mutirão* (Master's Dissertation, University of São Paulo, 1995); and Ângela Amaral, *Habitação: avaliação da política municipal* (São Paulo, Polis/PUC-SP, 2001).

20. In Brazil this technology has been greatly developed, mainly through the effort of the architect João Filgueiras Lima, also known as 'Lelé'. See Marcelo Ferraz (ed.), *João Filgueiras Lima,* (São Paulo, Instituto Lina Bo Bardi, 1998).

21. This argument is reproduced by various different authors (amongst them, Rod Burgess in his accurate critique of John Turner's view) based on the text *Economia brasileira* by Francisco de Oliveira (1973). Oliveira refers specifically to self-help housing, and his critique is at least ten years ahead of the first *mutirões*. It is worth remembering that the original criticism, made by Engels in *The Housing Question*, makes no distinction between different forms of housing production. On the contrary, Engels believed that any form of housing provision for the working classes (whether by the state, capitalism, or workers' associations), by the means of suppressing rent, reduces the cost of work-force reproduction, leading to a fall in salaries.

22. Cooperativism has been a fierce topic of debate in Brazil for some ten years. The economist Paul Singer, the main proponent of the theory of 'economy of solidarity' in Brazil, analyses cooperatives as socialist implants in the capitalist order and reopens the discussion on the theory of 'social revolution' (as opposed to the Leninist idea of revolution as a rupture of the political order) in his book *A Utopia Militante* (Petrópolis, Vozes, 1998).

23. Francisco de Oliveira, *Crítica à Razão Dualista – O Ornitorrinco* (São Paulo, Boitempo, 2003). An indispensable text to understand contemporary Brazil.

24. Ulrich Beck, *The brave new world of work* (London: Polity, 2000).

25.'A lei do tráfico', *Folha de São Paulo*, July 8, 2003.

26.'Tráfico impõe regras e fronteiras em São Paulo' *Folha de São Paulo*, July 6, 2003.

FURTHER INTEREST

PUBLICATIONS

Despite the notable body of works published in Brazil on the subject of Brazilian architecture, there are still relatively few books available to English-speaking readers. In addition to the publications detailed in each chapter's endnotes, below is a list of further readings on the subject. For a broader approach to Brazil's architecture we also include some works on other aspects of Modern Brazil.

Architecture

Adam, William Howard, *Roberto Burle Marx: The Unnatural Art of the Garden* (New York, MoMA, 1991).
Anelli, Renato *Rino Levi - arquitetura e cidade* (São Paulo, Romano Guerra Editora, 2001).
Bo Bardi, Lina and Aldo Van Eyck. *São Paulo Art Museum* (São Paulo, Instituto Lina Bo e P.M. Bardi; Lisboa, Editorial Blau, 1997).
Cavalcanti, Lauro, *When Brazil was Modern, Guide to Architecture, 1928-1960* (Princeton Architectural Press, 2003).
Conduru, Roberto, *Vital Brazil* (São Paulo, Cosac & Naify Edições, 2000).
Emanuel, Muriel (ed.), *Contemporary Architects* (London, St. James Press,1994).
Holston, John, *The Modernist City: An Anthropological Critique of Brasilia* (University of Chicago Press, 1989).
Junqueira de Camargo, Mônica, *Joaquim Guedes*, (São Paulo, Cosac & Naify Edições, 2000).
Lejeune, Jean-Francois (ed.), *Cruelty And Utopia: Cities And Landscapes Of Latin America* (Princeton Architectural Press, 2005)
Montero, Marta Iris et al. (eds), *Roberto Burle Marx: The Lyrical Landscape* (University of California Press, 2001).
Montezuma, Roberto (ed.), *Architecture Brazil 500 years: a reciprocal invention* (Recife, UFPE, 2002).
Niemeyer, Oscar, *Curves of Time* (London, Phaidon Press, 2002).
Niemeyer, Oscar, *Oscar Niemeyer: Serpentine Gallery Pavilion 2003* (London, Serpentine Gallery and Trolley, 2003).
Oliveira, Olivia de (ed), *Lina Bo Bardi, Obra construida*, 2G, 23-24 (Barcelona, Editorial Gustavo Gili, 2003).
Segre, Roberto, *Comtemporary Brazilian Architecture* (Petrópolis, Viana & Mosley, 2003).
Siqueira, Vera Beatriz, *Burle Marx* (São Paulo, Cosac & Naify Edições, 2001).
Spiro, Annette, *Paulo Mendes da Rocha: Works and Projects* (Zürich, Niggli, 2002).
Vaccarino, Rossana et al., *Roberto Burle Marx: landscape reflected* (Princeton Art Press, 2000).
Wisnik, Guilherme, *Lucio Costa* (São Paulo, Cosac & Naify, 2001).

Other Fields

Bardi, Pietro Maria, *Profile of the New Brazilian Art* (São Paulo, Kosmos, 1970).
Darcy, Ribeiro, *The Brazilian people : the Formation and Meaning of Brazil* (University Press of Florida, 2000).
Labaki, Amir (ed.), *The films from Brazil: from The Given Word to Central Station* (São Paulo, Publifolha, 1998).
Levine, Robert M. and Crocitti, John (eds), *The Brazil Reader: History, Culture, Politics* (Durham, Duke University Press, 1999).
Neistein, Jose, *Art in Brazil from its beginnings to modern times: a selected, annotated bibliography* (São Paulo, Livraria Kosmos Editora; Washington, BACI, 1997).
Pires do Rio Caldeira, Tereza, *City of Walls: crime, segregation and citizenship in São Paulo* (University of California Press, 2000).
Sullivan, Edward J. (ed.), *Body & Soul* (New York, Guggenheim Museum, 2002).
Veloso, Caetano, *Tropical Truth: A Story of Music and Revolution in Brazil* (Alfred.A Knopf, New York, 2002).
Xavier, Ismail, *Aesthetics and Politics in Modern Brazilian Cinema* (University of Minnesota Press,1997).

PLACES TO VISIT

For those interested in gaining first-hand knowledge of Brazil's modern architecture, the two main obstacles will be firstly, the extraordinary scale of the country, and secondly, the private ownership of the majority of the modern buildings. The following will give you an indication of which important architectural works to prioritize in the main cities – however, trips to secondary locations can also be very rewarding.

São Paulo

Among the 'must see' buildings, open to the public and easy to locate, are: MASP (São Paulo Museum of Art); SESC-Pompéia; Pinacoteca do Estado (National Art Library); Universidade de São Paulo (campus of the University of São Paulo); Parque Ibirapuera (Ibirapuera Park); FIESP Cultural Centre; MuBE (Brazilian Museum of Sculpture); Terminal Rodoviario de Jaú (Jaú Bus Terminal). Unfortunately, the large majority of private houses are not open to the public.

Oswaldo Bratke
Casa Oscar Americano (1952)
Av. Morumbi, 3700
Morumbi
Private building open to
the public.

Oscar Niemeyer
Edificio Copan (1951-53)
Av. Ipiranga, 200
Santa Efigênia
Private building with
restricted access.

ÁlvaroVital Brazil
Edificio Esther (1935-38)
Av. Ipiranga, 480
Santa Efigênia
Private building with
restricted access

Lina Bo Bardi
Casa de Vidro (1949-51)
Rua General Almério de
Moura 200
Morumbi
Tel. +55.11.37449902
Private building, open to the
public by appointment.

Rino Levi
Instituto Sedes Sapientiae
(Sedes Sapientiae Institute
1940-42)
Rua Marques de
Paranaguá, 111
Consolação
Private building with
restricted access.

Paulo Mendes da Rocha
Loja Forma (Forma Shop,
1987-94)
Av. Cidade Jardim, 924
Cidade Jardim
Private building open to the
public.

Eurico Prado Lopes and Luis
Telles
Centro Cultural São Paulo
(São Paulo Cultural Centre,
1982)
Rua Vergueiro, 1000
Paraíso
Public building.

**Mutirões (Public Housing
Projects)**

Usina
Mutirão Copromo (199–97)
Av Getulio Vargas s/n
Jardim Piratininga, Osasco
Private buildings with
restricted acces.

Mutirão Uniao da Juta
(1992–98)
Rua Augustin Luberdi, 1053
Fazenda da Juta
Private buildings with
restricted acces.

Passo Assessoria
Mutirão Sanko (1997–2000)
Av Monteiro da Cruz, 1552
Jardim dos Eucaliptos
Diadema
Private buildings open to the
public.

Cooperaativa e Ação Direta
Mutirão Sao Francisco VIII,
(1990–93)
Av dos Sertanistas, 26
Jardim São Francisco

Private buildings open
to the public.

EMURB e Peabiru
MutirãoVila Nova
Cachoeirinha (1991–92 and
1998-2000)
Rua Engenheiro Paulo
Sérgio, s/n
Vila Nova Cachoeirinha
Public borough.

Institutions

Instituto Lina Bo and P.M.
Bardi
Rua General Almério de
Moura, 200
Tel. +55.11 37449902
www.institutobardi.com.br

Instituto Moreira Salles
Rua Piauí, 844, 1º andar
Higienópolis
Tel. +55.11.38252560
www.ims.com.br

Fundação Artigas
Rua Bento Freitas 306, 5º
andar
Centro
Tel. +55.11.32596944

Rio de Janeiro

In addition to those public
buildings, which are open to
the public and easy to locate,
such as MESP (Ministry of
Education and Health, now
Palacio Capanema), MAM
(Museum of Modern Art),
Universidade do Brasil
(campus of the Federal
University of Rio de Janeiro),
MAC (Museum of
Contemporary Art), it is worth
trying to visit some of the
following:

Affonso Eduardo Reidy
Conjunto Habitacional
Pedregulho (1950-52)
Rua Capitão Félix, 50
São Cristóvão
Private building with
restricted access.

Oscar Niemeyer
Casa das Canoas (1953)
Estrada das Canoas, 2310
São Conrado
Tel +55.21.25091844
Private building open to the
public by appointment.

Banco Boavista (Boavista
Bank, 1946)
Praça Pio X, 118
Centro
Tel. +55.21.25340311
Private building open to the
public by appointment.

Lucio Costa
Conjunto Residencial Parque
Guinle (1948-54)
Rua Gago Coutinho, 66
Laranjeiras
Private building with
restricted access.

M M M Roberto
Associação Brasileira de
Imprensa (Brazilian Press
Association, 1936-1838)
Rua Araújo Porto Alegre, 71
Centro

Tel. +55.21.22821292
Private building open to
the public by appointment.

João Filgueiras Lima
Sarah Rio de Janeiro,
Av. Salvador Allende, s/n
Ilha da Pombeba
Jacarepaguá
Private building open to the
public.

Institutions

Fundação Oscar Niemeyer
Rua Conde Lages, 25
Gloria
Tel. +55.21.25091844
www.niemeyer.org.br

Burle Marx e Cia, Ltda
Rua Alice, 29
Laranjeiras
Tel. +55.21.25583235
www.burlemarx.com.br

Casa de Lucio Costa
Av. Delfim Moreira
1212/cobertura
Leblon
Tel. +55.21.259-0284
Centro de Arquitetura e
Urbanismo
Rua São Clemente, 117
Botafogo
Tel. +55.21.2286.8606
www.rio.rj.gov.br

Sítio Roberto Burle Marx
Estrada da Barra de
Guaratiba, 2190
Barra de Guaratiba
Tel. +55.21.2558-3235
Open to the public by
appointment.

Instituto Moreira Salles
Rua Marquês de São
Vicente, 476
Gávea
Tel. +55.11.32847400

Salvador

Lina Bo Bardi, Marcelo
Carvalho Ferraz, Marcelo
Suzuki
Casa do Benin (Benin House,
1987)
Rua do Passo
Pelourinho
Private building open to the
public.

Casa de Oludum (Oludum
House, 1988)
Rua Gregório de Matos
Pelourinho
Private building open to the
public.

Lina Bo Bardi
Museu de Arte Popular (Folk
Art Museum, renovation,1959)
Solar do Unhão
Av. Do Contorno
Public building open to the
public.

João Filgueiras Lima
Secretarias Administativas da
Bahia (Administrative Centre
Secretariat, 1973-1974) and
Tribunal Regional Eleitoral da
Bahia (Regional Electoral
Tribunal, 1997)
Av. Luis Viano Filho s/n
Paralela

Public buildings open to the
public.

Sarah Salvador (Salvador
Sarah Hospital, 1994)
Av. Tancredo Neves, 2782
Caminho das Árvores
Private building, open to the
public

Brasília

In addition to going to the
famous governmental
buildings (some with
restricted access) and Oscar
Niemeyer's Cathedral along
the Monumental Axis, the
following are also worth a
visit:

João Filgueiras Lima
Sarah Brasília (Braísilia Sarah
Hospital, 1980)
SMHS Quadra 501 Conj. A
Private building open to the
public.

Sarah Lago Norte (Lago
Norte Sarah Hospital, 2001)
SHIN QL 13 Lote C
Private building open to the
public.

Oscar Niemeyer
Ordem dos Advogados do
Brasil (Association of
Brazilian Lawyers, 1997)
Setor de Autarquias Sul,
Quadra 5. Lote 2, Bloco N
Private building with
restricted access.

Procuradoria Geral da
República (Office of the
Attorney General, 2002)
Setor de Administração
Federal Sul, Quadra 04,
Conjunto C
Public building with
restricted access.

Superior Tribunal da Justiça
(High Court of Justice,
1989-95)
SAFS - Quadra 6, Lote 1,
Trecho III
Tel. +55.61.3198000
Public building open to the
public by appointment.

Institutions

Museu da Memoria Candanga
Via EPIA sul, it.D, Conj.HJKO
Nucleo Bandeirante
Tel. +55.61.3013590
www.depha.df.gov.br/musviv
m.htm

Museu da Cidade
Centro Cultural Tres Poderes
Praça dos Tres Poderes
Plano Piloto
Tel. +55.61.3256244

Belo Horizonte

Belo Horizonte is an industrial
city where the style of
architecture typical of the
1980s has been particularly
influential and successful. It is
also the place from where to
visit Niemeyer's Pampulha
buildings and the colonial
towns like Diamantina,
Congonhas and Ouro Preto,

former capital of the Minas
Gerais region. Ouro Preto is
scattered with the splendid
Baroque churches of
Aleijadinho, whom Lucio
Costa considered to be the
first truly Brazilian artist.
Niemeyer's Grand Hotel is
situated in Ouro Preto.
Other buildings of interest
are:

Oscar Niemeyer
Edificio Niemeyer (Niemeyer
Building, 1954)
Praça da Liberdade
Private building with
restricted access.

Gustavo Penna
Escola de Arte Guignard,
(Guinard Art School, 1995)
Rua Ascanio Bulamarque,
540
Mangabeiras
Private building open to the
public.

Eolo Maia and Sílvio Podesta
Centro de Apoio Turístico
(Tourist Information Centre,
1991)
Praça da Liberdade
Funcionários
Public building open to the
public.

Eolo Maia and Jô Vasconcelos
Centro Empresarial Raja
Gabaglia (Raja Gabaglia
Business Centre,1989)
Av. Raja Gabaglia
Santa Lucia
Private building open to the
public.

João Filgueiras Lima
Sarah Belo Horizonte
(Belo Horizonte Sarah
Hospital, 1997)
Av. Amazonas, 5953
Gameleira
Private building open to the
public.

INDEX